IT'S A JOKE

GYLES BRANDRETH

TREASURE PRESS

First published in Great Britain as
four separate titles by Carousel Books.

1000 Jokes : The Greatest Book of Jokes Ever Known
Text copyright © 1980 Gyles Brandreth
Illustrations copyright © Transworld Publishers Ltd.

1000 Laughs: The Silliest Book of Laughs Ever Known
Text copyright © 1985 Gyles Brandreth
Illustrations copyright © 1985 Transworld Publishers Ltd.

1000 Riddles: The Greatest Book of Riddles Ever Known
Text copyright © 1980 Gyles Brandreth
Illustrations copyright © 1980 Transworld Publishers Ltd.

1000 Twisters: The Greatest Book of Tongue-Twisters Ever Known
Text copyright © 1982 Gyles Brandreth
Illustrations copyright © 1982 Transworld Publishers Ltd.

This omnibus edition first published in Great Britain in 1989 by

Treasure Press
Michelin House
81 Fulham Road
London SW3 6RB

Reprinted 1990, 1991

ISBN 1 85051 479 8

Printed in Czechoslovakia
50 674/02

CONTENTS

CONTENTS

1000 JOKES

Barney: I've owned this car for fifteen years and never had a wreck.
Prospective Buyer: You mean you've owned this wreck for fifteen years and never had a car.

Tony: Father, will you help me find the lowest common denominator in this problem?
Father: Gosh, haven't they found that yet – they were looking for it when I was a lad.

Mr Brown: I haven't seen your dog lately.
Mr Green: No, I had it put down.
Mr Brown: Was it mad?
Mr Green: Well, it wasn't exactly pleased.

What's on telly tonight Jimmy?
'Same as usual – the goldfish bowl and lamp.'

While visiting his friends in County Mayo, Paddy was dismayed when a torrential storm developed. His friend Rory said 'You must stay the night with us – you can't go home in this storm.' 'Thanks very much,' said Paddy, 'I'll just pop home and get me pyjamas.'

Judge: I've decided to give you a suspended sentence.
Prisoner: Thank you, your honour.
Judge: What for? You're going to be hanged.

'Mummy, does God use our bathroom?'
'No darling, why do you ask?'
'Well, every morning Daddy bangs on the door and shouts, 'Oh God, are you still in there?'

Susan: Did Margaret inherit her beauty.
Jean: Yes, her father left her a chemist's shop.

Mother: Why are you keeping this box of earth, Willy?
Willy: It's instant mud-pie mix.

Boy: (Howling) A crab just bit my toe.
Father: Which one?
Boy: How do I know? All crabs look alike to me.

Boss (to department head): How many people work in your office?
Dept. Head: About half of them, sir.

'Why are you scratching yourself, Mary?'
'Nobody else knows where I itch.'

Doctor: Good morning, Mrs Potter, I haven't seen you for a long time.
Mrs P: I know Doctor, I've been ill.

Reggie: We've got a new dog – would you like to come round and play with him?
Ron: Well he sounds very fierce – does he bite?
Reggie: That's what I want to find out.

Waiter: How did you find your chop sir?
Diner: I looked under a chip, and there it was.

Insurance agent: This is a particularly good policy, madam. Under it, we pay up to a thousand pounds for broken arms and legs.
Woman: Good heavens – what do you do with them all?

Mother: Bobby's teacher says he ought to have an encyclopedia.
Father: Let him walk to school like I had to.

Teacher: In what part of the world are people the most ignorant?
Sammy: Tokyo.
Teacher: Why do you say that?
Sammy: Well, my geography book says that's where the population is the densest.

'How long will the next bus be?'
'About eighteen feet.'

Englishman to Paddy: Have you any idea how many sheep there are in this field?

Paddy: Sure – there's three hundred and eighty-six.

Englishman: Good heavens – you're quite right. How did you know?

Paddy: Well, I just counted the legs and divided them by four.

'Doctor, I keep thinking I'm a goat.'
'How long have you had this feeling?'
'Ever since I was a kid.'

Mother: There were two doughnuts in the larder this afternoon, Tommy, now there's only one. How's that?

Tommy: I suppose because it's dark in there – I didn't see the other one.

Safebreaker: I think I need glasses.
Mate: How's that?
Safebreaker: Well, I was twirling the knobs of a safe and an orchestra began to play.

Once the night watchman received a pound too much in his pay-packet, but didn't mention it to his boss. But his boss found out and deducted it the following payday.

'Hey,' said the watchman, 'I'm a pound short this week.'

'You didn't say anything last week when you were paid a pound too much, I noticed.'

'No', replied the watchman. 'I can overlook one mistake, but when it happens twice, it's time to speak up !'

A Martian landed at a fun-fair, just as somebody hit the jack-pot and the coins came flooding out. Turning to the machine, the Martian said, 'You shouldn't be out with a cold like that.'

> *Tommy:* Dad, what are four grapes and three grapes ?
> *Dad:* Don't you know a simple sum like that – haven't you done a problem like that before ?
> *Tommy:* No, dad, we always use bananas at school.

'Doctor – I can't get to sleep at night.'
'Don't worry – lie on the edge of the bed and you'll soon drop off.'

Teacher: Jimmy, give me a sentence with the word 'centimetre' in it.
Jimmy: Er ... My sister was coming home by bus and I was centimetre.

Mother: Bobby, have you given the goldfish fresh water today?
Bobby: No, they haven't finished what I gave them yesterday.

Dad: How were your exam questions Ben?
Ben: Fine – but I had difficulty with the answers.

'That's a dreadful bump on your head, Patrick, how did it happen?'
'Somebody threw tomatoes at me.'
'Heavens, how could tomatoes cause a bump like that?
'They were in a tin.'

Frankie: Which month has twenty-eight days?
Peggy: All of them.

Mike: I saw all your chickens out in your front garden yesterday.
Patrick: Yes, they heard that men were coming to lay a pavement, and they wanted to see how it was done.

Teacher: Why do we sometimes call the Middle Ages the Dark Ages? *Betty:* Because they had so many knights.

A little boy saw a grass snake for the first time.
'Mother,' he cried, 'here's a tail without a body.'

Teacher: Polly, how can you prove the world is round? *Polly:* I never said it was, miss.

A boy and an old man were standing in the aisle of a crowded bus. 'Pass farther down the bus,' called the conductor.
'He's not my father,' said the boy, 'he's my grandfather.'

In St James's Park a man holding a
penguin went up to a policeman.
'I've found this penguin,' he said.
'What shall I do with him?'

'You'd better take him to the zoo,'
said the policeman. The next day,
the policeman again saw the same
man with the penguin. 'I thought I
told you to take him to the zoo,' he
said.

'I did that yesterday,' said the
man. 'And today I'm taking him to
the pictures.'

Captain: Why didn't you stop the
ball?
Goalie: I thought that's what the
nets were for.

Pupil (indignantly): I don't think I
deserve a nought on this test.
Teacher: Neither do I, but it's the
lowest mark I can give you.

Joe: I fell over twenty feet last night.
Max: Good heavens – weren't you hurt?
Joe: No – I was just trying to get to my seat in the cinema.

Two flies were on Robinson Crusoe's head.
'Goodbye for now,' said one. 'I'll see you on Friday.'

Sign in a police station:
'Thirty days hath September, April, June and the Speed Offender.'

Big man (in a theatre, to a small boy sitting behind him) Can you see, sonny?
Boy: No, sir, not at all.
Big man: Then just watch me and laugh when I do.

Vicar: Now, Georgie, you shouldn't fight, you should learn to give and take.
Georgie: I did, I gave him a black eye and I took his apple.

'My uncle has 500 men under him.'
'He must be very important.'
'Not really – he's a maintenance man in a cemetery.'

Richard: Would you punish a boy for something he didn't do?
Teacher: Of course not.
Richard: That's good. I haven't done my homework.

The new workman opened his lunch-packet and took out two sandwiches. He opened one and his face fell. 'Fish-paste,' he said. He looked again, and the same thing happened, 'More fish-paste,' he grumbled. When he was disappointed for the third time, his mate said, 'Why don't you get your wife to make you something else.' 'I'm not married,' said the man, 'I make these sandwiches myself.'

'Waiter, there's a dead fly in my soup'
'Yes, sir, I know – it's the heat that kills them.'

The aeroplane was so old, it even had an outside lavatory.

Two boys were paddling in the sea at
Brighton.
'Gosh, ain't your feet dirty, ' said
one.
'Yes,' replied the other, 'we didn't
come last year.'

Little Bernie was taking
his new dog for a walk when a
policeman stopped him.
'Has your dog got a licence?' the
policeman asked.
'Oh no.' answered Bernie. 'He's not
old enough to drive.'

Teacher: Sidney, can you tell me
how fast light travels?
Sidney: I don't know, but it always
gets here too early in the morning.

Teacher: Why were you absent
yesterday, Tommy?
Tommy: The doctor said I had acid
indigestion.
Teacher: Then you'd better stop
drinking acid.

18

Two fleas were leaving the cinema,
and one said to the other: 'Shall we
walk or take a dog?'

Mrs Jones: Will you join me in a cup
of tea?
Mrs Smith: I don't think there'd be
room for both of us.

The visitor from London was
boasting in a Manchester pub about
all the famous people who had been
born in London. 'Have many big
men been born in Manchester?' he
asked the landlord. 'None', said the
landlord, 'only babies.'

Betty: That man next door has got
carrots growing out of his ears.
Harold: How terrible!
Betty: It certainly is. He planted
parsnips.

'Did you know that deep breathing
kills germs?'
'Yes, but how do you get them to
breathe deeply?'

Do you know the one about the
cornflakes and the rice krispies who
had a fight?
– I can only tell you a little at a time
as it's a serial.

What is red and stupid?
A blood-clot.

Big brother (to shop assistant): My
mother would like a dozen nappies
for the new baby.
Assistant: Here we are. That will be
three pounds for the nappies, and
75 pence for the tax.
Big brother: Don't bother about the
tacks. My mother uses safety pins.

Did you hear about the vegetarian
cannibal?
– He would only eat Swedes.

Nurse: Well, Mr Smith, you seem to
be coughing much more easily this
morning.
Mr Smith: That's because I've been
practising all night.

Traffic policeman: When I saw you
driving down the high-street, lady, I
said to myself, 'Sixty at least.'
Lady Driver: Oh no, officer – it's just
this hat makes me look older.

Should you stir your tea with your
left hand or your right hand?
Neither – you should use your spoon.

Dentist: Please stop howling. I haven't even touched your tooth yet.
Patient: I know, but you're treading on my foot.

Teacher: Can you name four animals of the cat family?
Mary: Mother cat, father cat, and two kittens.

Advertisement in local paper:
LOST – WRIST WATCH BY A LADY WITH A CRACKED FACE.

Nobby: Dad, I'm too tired to do my homework.
Dad: Now, my lad, hard work never killed anyone yet.
Nobby: Well, I don't want to run the risk of being the first.

Customer: I'd like some poison for mice please.
Chemist: Have you tried Boots?
Customer: I want to poison them, not kick them to death.

Teacher: Jimmy, how do you spell elephant?
Jimmy: E-l-e-f-a-n-t.
Teacher: The dictionary spells it 'e-l-e-p-h-a-n-t'.
Jimmy: You didn't ask me how the dictionary spelt it.

Passenger: Is this my train?
Inspector: No, it belongs to British Rail?
Passenger: Don't be funny – I mean can I take this train to London?
Inspector: No, sir, it's much too heavy.

Monty: Is it really bad luck to have a black cat follow you?
Mike: Well, it depends on whether you're a man or a mouse.

An American visiting London saw a restaurant which claimed they could supply any dish requested.
So he asked the waiter for kangaroo on toast.
After a while the waiter came back and said, 'I'm so sorry, sir, but we've run out of bread.'

Don: Why did Ron sleep under the oil tank last night?
John: Because he wanted to get up oily this morning.

Sammy: Mummy, how much am I worth to you?
Mother: Why, you're worth more than a million to me, dear.
Sammy: Well, could you advance me twenty-five pence?

Teacher: Brown, stop showing off. Do you think you're the teacher of this class?
Brown: No sir.
Teacher: Right, then stop behaving like a fool.

Customer: Waiter, I've only got one piece of meat.
Waiter: Just a moment, sir, and I'll cut it in two.

Customer: I'd like to try that dress in the window.
Assistant: I'm sorry, madam, I'm afraid you'll have to use the fitting room, like everybody else.

There was an Arab who was so fat, his camel had its hump underneath.

How do you keep flies out of the kitchen?
– Put all the rubbish in the lounge.

Customer to Bank Manager: How do I stand for a £3,000 loan?
B. Manager: You don't – you grovel.

Would you like to buy a pocket calculator, sir?'
'No thanks, I know how many pockets I've got.'

Customer in butcher's shop: Have you got a sheep's head?
Butcher: No, it's just the way I part my hair.

Hotel receptionist in France, to Englishman: Are you a foreigner?
Englishman: Certainly not. I'm British!

Mother Lion: Son, what are you doing?
Baby Lion: I'm chasing a man round a tree.
Mother Lion: How often must I tell you not to play with your food.

Father: Freddie, you're a pig. Do you know what a pig is?
Freddie: Sure, dad. A pig is a hog's little boy.

Nurse: Can I take your pulse?
Patient: Why? Haven't you got one of your own?

What did the gas-meter say to the tenpence piece?
- Glad you dropped in, I was just going out.

Barber: Were you wearing a red scarf when you came in?
Customer: No.
Barber: Oh, then I must have cut your throat.

A man came back to the car dealer from whom he had bought a new car. 'I believe you gave me a guarantee with my car,' he said.
'That's right, sir,' the dealer answered. 'We will replace anything that breaks.'
'Fine. I need a new garage door.'

Visitor: Is this a healthy place to live?
Local yokel: Yessir. When I arrived here I couldn't walk or eat solid food.
Visitor: What was the matter with you?
Local yokel: Nothing – I was born here.

Doctor: Mrs Smith, you have acute angina.
Patient: I came to be examined, not admired.

Estate agent to young couple: First you tell me what you can afford, then we'll have a good laugh about it, and go on from there.

Angry boss to office boy: You are late again this morning.
Office boy: I overslept.
Angry boss: You mean you sleep at home *as well?*

'Will the band play anything I request?'
'Certainly, sir.'
'Well, ask them to play chess.'

Harry: This lamb is very tough.
Polly: I'm sorry – the butcher said it was a spring lamb.
Harry: Well, I must be eating one of the springs.

Proud Mother: My baby is a year old now, and he's been walking since he was eight months old.
Bored visitor: Really? He must be awfully tired.

Rich customer on phone to fishmonger: Please send me a dozen oysters, not too large, not too small, not very old, not tough and not sandy.
Fishmonger: Yes, madam. With pearls or without?

Judge: Have you been up before me before?
Prisoner: I don't know, what time do you get up?

Father was showing Tommy the family album, and came across a picture of himself and his wife on their wedding day.
'Was that the day Mummy came to work for us?' Tommy asked.

Disgusted diner: What do you call this stuff, coffee or tea?
Waiter: What do you mean, sir?
Diner: It tastes like paraffin.
Waiter: Well, if it tastes like paraffin, it must be coffee; our tea tastes like turpentine.

1st Soldier: Our C.O. rose from the ranks.
2nd Soldier: Is that so?
1st Soldier Yes – he used to be a taxi-driver.

Wife: Do you have a good memory for faces?
Husband: Yes – why?
Wife: I've just broken your shaving mirror.

Motorist: When I bought this car you said it was rust free. The underneath's covered with it.
Dealer: Yes, sir. The car's rust free. We didn't charge for it.

Have you heard the one about the man who always wore sunglasses?
– He took a dim view of things.

'I wonder why these seaside boarding house keepers are called land-ladies?'
'Because they charge the earth'

Cinema attendant: That's the sixth ticket you've bought.
Customer: I know – there's a girl in there that keeps tearing them up.

Susie: Mother, what was the name of the last station our train stopped at?
Mother: I don't know – can't you see I'm reading?
Susie: Well, it's too bad, because little Benny got off there.

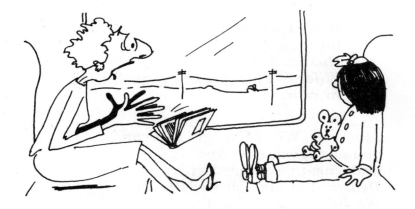

Teacher: Bobby, can you name the four seasons?
Bobby: Salt, pepper, vinegar and mustard.

Sergeant (to new recruit): And what were you then, before you joined the army?
New Recruit: Happy, sergeant.

Doctor: I am sorry to have to tell you that you may have rabies, and it could prove fatal.
Patient: Well, doctor, please give me pencil and paper.
Doctor: To make your Will?
Patient: No – I want to make a list of people I want to bite.

Teacher: If you found five pence in one pocket and ten pence in the other, what would you have?
Willy: Somebody else's trousers.

Peter: My teacher was cross because I didn't know where the pyramids were.
Mother: (absently) Well, dear, next time remember where you put things.

Betty: What do you think of Red China?
Mary: Well, it would look nice with a white tablecloth.

Jack: What did the bald man say when he received a comb for his birthday?
Tom: I don't know, what did he say?
Jack: Thanks very much, I'll never part with it.

Sally: Did you see the guards change when you were in London?
Lulu: No, they always pulled the blinds down.

The cannibal came home to find his wife chopping up snakes and a very small man. 'Oh no,' he groaned. 'Not snake and pygmy pie again!'

'Why are you jumping up and down?'
'I've just taken some medicine and I forgot to shake the bottle.'

Writer: I took up writing full-time a year ago.
Friend: Have you sold anything?
Writer: Yes – my t.v., all the furniture, the house ...

It's easy to make time fly. Just throw an alarm clock over your shoulder.

'My husband is so ugly when he goes to the zoo he has to buy two tickets: one to get in and one to get out.'

Army colonel: I'd like some pepper, my good man.
Shop assistant: Certainly, sir. What sort would you like – white pepper or black pepper?'
Army colonel: Neither – I want writing pepper.

Teacher: Which is farther away – Canada or the moon?
Bobby: Canada.
Teacher: Why do you say that?
Bobby: We can see the moon, and we can't see Canada.

Customer: You said this simple gadget was foolproof. I can't see how to use it.
Shopkeeper: Then it's what it says it is. It proves you're a fool.

A guide was showing a man from Texas Niagara Falls.
Guide: I'll bet you don't have anything like this in Texas.
Texan: Nope, but we got plumbers who can fix it.

How can you decide whether to use a screw or a nail when doing carpentry? Drive in a nail – if the wood splits, you should have used a screw.

Sign in a Volkswagen factory:
THINK BIG – and you're fired.

A man was driving down a one-way street the wrong way and was stopped by a policeman. 'This is a one-way street,' said the officer. 'I know,' said the motorist, 'I'm only going one way.'

Greengrocer: Yes, madam, they're beautiful tomatoes – they come from the Canaries.
Customer: Fancy, I always thought they were grown, not laid.

'I've never been troubled with back-seat drivers.'
'Why, what car do you drive?'
'A hearse.'

A woman dashed into a hardware shops and asked to be served at once. 'Give me a mouse-trap please.' she gasped. 'I've got to catch a train.' 'I'm sorry,' said the assistant. 'We haven't got any as big as that.'

Teacher: What is the difference between the death rate in Victorian England and the present day?
Pupil: It's the same, miss. One per person.

'Do you write with your left hand or your right hand?'
– Neither – I write with a ball-point pen.

'My brother bought a baby car – but it won't go anywhere without a rattle.'

Customer: Those strawberries look as if they were picked weeks ago, yet your notice says Fresh Today.
Greengrocer: That's right. This notice *is* fresh today. I've just written it out.

Mr Johnson: Are you using your mower this afternoon?
Mr Smith: Yes.
Mr Johnson: Fine. Then can I borrow your tennis racket, as you won't be needing it.

Salesman: Little boy, is your mother at home?
Willy: Yes, sir.
Salesman (after knocking for some time and getting no reply): I thought you said she was at home.
Willy: She is, but we don't live here.

Judge: Tell me, why did you park
your car here?
Motorist: Well there was a sign
which said FINE FOR PARKING.

'I've just lost my dog.'
'Well, why don't you put an
advertisement in the paper?'
'What's the good of that – my dog
can't read.'

Mother: Freddie, why is your face so
red?
Freddie: I was running up the street
to stop a fight.
Mother: That's a very nice thing to
do. Who was fighting?
Freddie: Me and Jackie Smith.

Dolphins are so intelligent that
within a few weeks of captivity they
can train a man to stand on the edge
of their pool and throw them fish
three times a day.

Mother: Did you behave well in
church today, Marjie?
Marjie: I certainly did. A nice man
offered me a plate full of money, and
I said, 'No thank you."

Pamela: I've added these figures ten times, miss.
Teacher: Good girl.
Pamela: And here are the ten answers.

'I went to the dentist this morning.'
'Does your tooth still hurt?'
'I don't know – the dentist kept it.'

A beautiful young lady kissed a Prince last night – and he turned into a toad.

Bill: Do you have holes in your trousers?
Jim: Certainly not.
Bill: Then how do you get your legs through?

Sol: I say, that's a hundred-pound cheque you're writing.
Gus: Yes, I'm sending it to my sister for her birthday.
Sol: But you haven't signed it.
Gus: No, I don't want her to know who sent it.

Due to a strike at the meteorological office, there will be no weather tomorrow.

A grammar school boy took out of
the library a book whose cover read
How to Hug, but discovered to his
disappointment that it was Volume 7
of the Encyclopedia.

A man walked into a baker's shop
and asked for a bath bun.
'Certainly, sir,' replied the assistant.
'Anything else?'
'Yes,' said the man, 'I'll have a
sponge to go with it.'

Percy: How do fishermen make
their nets, Dad?
Dad: Easily. They just take a lot of
holes and sew them together.

Customer: Ironmonger, have you
got one inch nails?
Ironmonger: Yes, sir.
Customer: Then will you scratch my
back please – it's itching something
awful.

Two Red Indians were watching
some distant smoke-signals. When
they were finished, one Indian
turned to the other and said, 'We
shall have to do something about
Little Big Horse, his spelling is
something awful.'

Do you know how to make a slow
horse fast?
No – do you?
Yes – just don't give him anything to
eat.

Last week a man fell into a keg of
beer and came to a bitter end.

Dentist: I'm afraid your teeth will
have to come out.
Patient: Oh dear, that will be an
awful wrench.

'My dog has no nose.'
'How does it smell?'
'Terrible.'

Wholesome – the only thing from which you can take the whole and still have some left.

'Every day my dog and I go for a tramp in the woods.'
'Does the dog enjoy it?'
'O yes – but the tramp is a bit fed up.'

'I hear you've fallen in love with Dracula.'
'Yes, it was love at first bite.'

Doorman: Your car is at the door, sir.
Car owner: Yes, I can hear it knocking.

Young man: Er, excuse me – but would you come out with me tonight.
Dolly: Oh, I don't go out with perfect strangers.
Young man: Who said I was perfect?

Barry: How many balls of string would it take to reach the moon?
Garry: Only one – if it were long enough.

Mother: Now, Monty, you know you're not supposed to eat with your knife.
Monty: I know, ma, but my fork leaks.

A drunk raced after a fire engine, but collapsed exhausted after a hundred yards, 'Alright,' he shouted, 'keep your rotten ice-cream.'

One egg boiling in a pan said to
another egg in the pan: 'Gosh, it's
hot in here.'
Said the other egg: 'Wait till you get
out, you'll have your head bashed in.'

Patient: Will my measles be better
next week, doctor?
Doctor: I don't like to make rash
promises.

Customer (to Bank Manager): Will
you help me out, please?
B.M. Certainly – go through that
door there.

Old man (to his wife): What on earth
are you doing?
Wife: Knitting up some barbed-wire
fence.
Old man: How can you do that?
Wife: I'm using steel wool.

1st Ghost: I see 'Psycho' is on telly
again tonight.
2nd Ghost: Yes – last time I saw it, it
nearly frightened the life into me.

After the dance, the young man
asked the young lady if he could see
her home – so she showed him a
photograph of it.

Bert: Mum, there's a man with a bill
at the door.
Mummy: Don't be silly, dear, it
must be a duck with a hat on.

Bright Billy: Dad, is your watch
going?
Dad: Yes, of course it is.
B. Billy: Then when's it coming
back?

Pedestrian – a person who can be
easily reached by car.

'Will you kiss me?'
'But I have scruples.'
'That's alright – I've been
vaccinated.'

Man on telephone to Weather Bureau: What are the chances of a shower today?
Weatherman: It's okay with me, sir. If you want one, take one.

Patient: And when my right arm is better, doctor, will I be able to play the trumpet?
Doctor: Of course you will.
Patient: How marvellous – I never could before.

Winnie: I must say Norman is very full of himself, isn't he?
Babs: Yes – especially when he bites his nails.

Lady on phone: Doctor, what can I do – my little boy has swallowed my pen?
Doctor: Use a pencil.

Teacher: Now, Jackie, what is the highest form of animal life?
Jackie: I think it's the giraffe, miss.

'Why were you driving so fast?' said the policeman to the speeding motorist.
'Well, my brakes are faulty and I wanted to get home before I had an accident.'

The absent-minded professor was going round and round in a swing door. 'What's the matter?' asked a friend.
'I can't remember whether I'm on my way in or on my way out,' replied the Prof.

Harry: Have you read the Bible?
Sally: No, I'm waiting for the film.

Friend: Your dog's got a funny bark.
Dog-owner: Yes, he's a dachshund, and speaks with a German accent.

Teacher: Now, Brian, what is the formula for water?
Brian: H,I,J,K,L,M,N,O.
Teacher: Now then, you're not in the nursery you know.
Brian: Well, you did say it was H to O.

The cantankerous old lady who lived alone had not been invited to her neighbour's picnic. On realizing their oversight the neighbours sent round to ask her to come along.
'It's too late now,' she snapped. 'I've already prayed for rain.'

Patient: What can you give me for flat feet, Doctor?
Doctor: Have you tried a bicycle-pump?

He: Why were the Red Indians the first people in North America? *She:* Because they had reservations.

Teacher: In some countries they use fish as a means of exchange.
Willy: Gee, it must be messy getting chocolate out of a machine.

What did the hamburger say to the tomato?
– That's enough of your sauce.

Guide (on safari): Quick, sir, shoot that leopard right on the spot.
Lord Clarence: Be specific, man, which spot?

The more we study, the more we
know.
The more we know, the more we
forget.
The more we forget, the less we
know.
So, why study?

Notice in a pet shop: IN THE
INTEREST OF DOGS, HYGIENE IS
NOT PERMITTED IN THIS SHOP.

Woodwork master: What are you
making there, Jimmy?
Jimmy: A portable, sir.
W. master: A portable what?
Jimmy: I don't know yet, sir. I've
only made the handle.

The life-long Socialist dying on his
bed, decided to become a Tory.
When asked why he was doing this,
he told his puzzled family: 'I'd
rather it was a Tory that died than a
Socialist.'

The fat lady walked into the dress
shop. 'I'd like to see a dress that
would fit me.' she told the assistant.
'So would I,' said the tactless
assistant.

Teacher: What family does the
rhinoceros belong to?
David: I don't know, miss, nobody
in our street has one.

'Waiter, have you got frogs' legs?'
'No, sir, I always walk this way.'

A woman took her dog back to the
pet shop and complained 'This dog
makes a shocking mess all over the
house, and you told me he was
house-trained.'
'That's right, he is,' said the shop
owner. 'He won't go anywhere else!'

Lady: Waiter, please bring me coffee
without cream.
Waiter: I'm afraid we've run out of
cream. Would you like it without
milk instead?

Penicillin – the present for the man
who has everything.

Visitor: Does your dog like
children?
Dog-owner: Yes, but he prefers
biscuits and gravy.

Waiter: What can I get you sir?
Diner: Steak and chips.
Waiter: Would you like anything
with it sir?
Diner: If it's anything like the last I
ate here, you'd better bring me a
hammer and chisel.

One day a worried-looking man
knocked at a lady's door. 'I'm very
sorry, lady,' he said, 'I've just run
over your cat and I'd like to
replace it.'
'Well,' said the lady doubtfully, 'can
you catch mice?'

The Scotsman was asked for a
donation to the orphanage, so he sent
them two orphans.

Willy came home from Sunday
School and asked his mother:
'Do people really come from dust'.
'In a way', said his mother.
'And do they go back to dust?
'Yes, in a way.'
'Well, mother, I've just looked under
my bed, and there's somebody either
coming or going.'

Customer: Why is this chop so very
tough?
Waiter: Well, sir, it's a karate chop.

Patient: I still feel very tired, doctor.
Doctor: Didn't you take those
sleeping pills I gave you?
Patient: Well, they looked so
peaceful in the little bottle that I
didn't like to wake them up.

A farmer had a large hay field. His
son didn't want to stay on the farm
so he moved to town, but the only job
he could get was shining shoes, so
now the farmer makes hay while the
son shines.

What were Tarzan's last words?
– Who greased the vine?

Teacher: How many feet are there in a yard?
Joe: It depends how many people are standing in it.

Cecil: Do you know how many days belong to the year?
Claud: All of them, I suppose.
Cecil: Nope, just 325. The rest are Lent.

1st Cannibal: I feel sick every time I eat a missionary.
2nd Cannibal: That's because you can't keep a good man down.

How do you get down from a camel?
– You don't. You get down from a duck.

'My mother gave Dad some
soapflakes instead of cornflakes for
his breakfast, by mistake.'
'Was he cross?'
'He certainly was. He foamed at the
mouth.'

'My husband is very religious – he
won't work if there's a Sunday in the
week.'

A boy took his dog with him to the
cinema to see 'Gone With The Wind'.
The usherette was about to make the
dog leave when she saw it seemed to
be enjoying the film, so she let it stay.
After it was over, she spoke to the
boy. 'I was surprised to see your dog
enjoying the film,' she said.
'So was I,' said the boy. 'He didn't
like the book one bit.'

Have you heard the one about
quicksand? It takes a long time to
sink in.

Customer (to Barber): That's a lot
to pay for a haircut – after all I'm
nearly bald.
Barber: Yes, that's the trouble. It
was the time taken to find it to cut
which cost the money.

Footballer: I've a good idea to improve the team.
Manager: Good. When are you leaving?

Sid: My father can play the piano by ear.
Don: That's nothing – my father fiddles with his whiskers.

Father: Don't go into the water right after lunch.
It's dangerous to swim on a full stomach.
Son: That's alright, I'll swim on my back.

Bus conductor: This coin you've just given me has a hole in it.
Young passenger: So has this ticket you've just given me.

'I was an unwanted child – my mother wanted puppies.'

Mr Pigeon to Mrs Pigeon: Look, dear, there's a railway station – let's fly over it and do some train-spotting.

The old lady was being interviewed by the local press after she had reached the age of 110. 'What do you think is the reason for your long life?' they asked her.
She thought for a while. 'Well,' she said, 'I suppose it's because I was born such a long time ago.

Tim: Mother, you'd better come out. I've just knocked over the ladder at the side of the house.
Mother: I'm busy – run and tell your father.
Tim: He already knows. He's hanging from the roof.

Mr Brown: I've noticed Mr Johnson's manners have improved lately.
Mrs Brown: Yes, he got a job in a refinery.

My wife reads the obituary columns every morning, and can't understand how people keep dying in alphabetical order.

Barber (to boy customer): Who cut your hair last time – your Mum?
Boy: Yes, she did it with a pudding basin.
Barber: I thought so. Next time, tell her to use scissors.

Blenkinsop: One of my ancestors died at Waterloo.
Bloggs: Really, which platform?

Two children were watching a motor-boat pulling a man on skis across a lake. 'What makes that boat go so fast?' asked little Lucy.
'It's because that man on the string is chasing it,' said her brother.

Mother: Didn't I tell you to let me know when the soup began to boil?
Joe: Yes, and I'm telling you. It was half past one.

Did you hear about the ex-
policeman who became a barber?
He kept nicking his customers.

Teacher: When do the leaves begin
to turn?
Student: The night before an
examination.

Gormless Gus went into a shop with
a mince pie stuck in each ear.
'Excuse me,' said the shop assistant,
'but you've got mince pies in your
ears.'
'You'll have to speak up,' said
Gormless Gus.'I've got mince
pies in my ears.'

'Come in number 9 – your time is
up.'
'But we've only got eight boats.'
'Are you in trouble Number 6?'

Postman: I have a parcel here but the name on it is obliterated.
Jackson: Can't be for me then, my name's Jackson.

The poet had been droning on at the party about his various sources of inspiration. 'Yes,' he told the young girl, 'I'm at present collecting some of my better poems to be published posthumously.'
'Lovely,' said the girl. 'I shall look forward to it.'

Which pantomime is about a cat in a chemist's shop?
– Puss in Boots.

Harry and Larry were given a toboggan for Christmas. After they had been out playing in the snow Larry was in tears.
'Now, Harry,' said father, 'I told you to let Larry use the toboggan half the time.'
'So I did,' said Harry, 'I had it going down, and he had it going up.'

Why do cows in Switzerland have bells round their necks?
– Because their horns don't work.

In Dodge City the Sheriff arrested
Lulu Belle for wearing a taffeta
dress.
'What's the charge, sheriff?' she
asked.
'Rustlin' of course,' he replied.

Dan: When I grow up I'm going to be
a policeman and follow my father's
footsteps.
Stan: I didn't know your father was a
policeman.
Dan: He's not, he's a burglar.

Tommy: Are worms good to eat?
Dad: I shouldn't think so. Why?
Tommy: There was one in your pie.

'Could you see me across the road,
constable?'
'I could see you a mile away,
madam.'

Mother: How was the choir's Christmas visit to the Old Folk's Home?
Olive: Oh, we gave them a couple of Carols.
Mother: 'Away in a Manger?'
Olive: No, Carol Jones and Carol Taylor.

Teacher: What is pop-art?
Freddie: It's what Dad says to Mum when he's just going to pop-art for a quick one.

Diner: Where's the rum in this rum-pie?
Waiter: Well, would you expect to find a dog in a dog biscuit?

'Is your new horse well-behaved?'
'Oh yes. When we come to a fence, he stops and lets me go over first.'

Husband: What would you like for your birthday?
Wife: Oh ... let it be a surprise.
Husband: Right .. BOO!

Jill: Daddy, Jack's broken my new doll.
Daddy: How did he do that?
Jill: I hit him on the head with it.

Lady, visiting artist in his studio; Do you like painting people in the nude?
Artist: No, personally I prefer painting with my clothes on.

Mother: Willy, it's rude to keep stretching across the table for the cake. Haven't you got a tongue?
Willy: Yes, but my arm's longer.

A woman was driving the wrong way down a one-way street and was stopped by a policeman.
'Didn't you see the arrows?' he asked.
'Arrows? I didn't even see the Indians.'

Little Caroline was drawing a Nativity picture – there was Mary and Joseph, shepherds and wise men.
'What's that in the corner?' asked her teacher.
'That's their telly, of course,' replied Caroline.

Percy: I've just got a bottle of vodka for my mother-in-law.
Bertie: Sounds like a good swap.

Teacher: Now, Brenda, how many fingers have you?
Brenda: Ten.
Teacher: Right. Now if you lost four of them in an accident, what would you have?
Brenda: No more piano lessons.

Old Lady (to Baker): What's that loaf up there?
Assistant: That's a tin loaf, madam.
Old Lady: Oh I think I'd better have something a bit softer. My teeth aren't what they used to be.

Charlie had eaten too many jam tarts, and clutched his stomach and groaned.
'Are you in pain?' asked his mother.
'No,' moaned Charlie, 'the pain's in me.'

Friend: And what are you going to give your baby brother for his birthday, Janet?
Janet: I don't know – last year I gave him measles.

Cousin Ted: How's your father getting on with his new dairy farm?
Cousin Ned: He makes all the cows sleep on their backs, so the cream will be on top in the morning.

Shop owner: Yes, madam, these are the same pork pies we've had for years.
Customer: Could you show me some you've had more recently please?

Our family was so poor, my sister was made in Hong Kong.

Anybody who boasts about his ancestors is admitting that his family is better dead than alive.

Mr Mouse discovered Mrs Mouse drowning in a bowl of water, so he dragged her out and gave her mouse to mouse resuscitation.

Lucy was finishing her prayers. 'God bless my mother and my father and make Rotterdam the capital of Holland.'
'Why, Lucy' asked her mother. 'Why did you say that?'
'Because,' explained Lucy, 'that's what I wrote on my exam-paper.'

Rose found her sister Mary wearing her fur-lined rubber shoes, and demanded to know the reason why.
'Well,' said Mary, 'you wouldn't like me to get your new silver dancing pumps wet, would you?'

Our neighbour believes in free speech. Particularly long distance phone calls from our house.

The visitor stared in amazement at the child knocking nails into the posh Scandinavian furniture.
He turned to his host. 'Don't you find it expensive to let your son play games like that?' he asked.
'Not really,' replied the host. 'I get the nails wholesale.'

Policeman: I'm sorry sonny, but you need a permit to fish here.
Sonny: That's alright, thanks. I'm doing okay with a worm.

Young Tim was raking leaves with his father who was telling him about how the fairies turned the leaves brown. He looked up pityingly at his father. 'Haven't you ever heard of photosynthesis?' he asked him.

Dora: Listen, I can hear the band playing The Men of Harlech?
Mona: Really – who's winning?

Music Teacher: What is the meaning of 'allegro'?
Susie: It's what a line of chorus girls make with their legs.

Gordon: How's your sister getting on with her reducing diet?
Charlie: Fine – she disappeared last week.

Morris: Can you spell blind pig?
Norman: B-l-i-n-d p-i-g.
Morris: No. It's b-l-n-d p-g. With two i's he wouldn't be blind.

Ramon from Madrid was on holiday
in Killarney and talking to Patrick.
'We have a word in Spanish,' he said,
Mañana. It means tomorrow –
always tomorrow.
Do you have a word for it in your
country?'
After a pause Patrick said, 'No, I
don't think we have any word with
such a sense of urgency.'

Brown: I cured my son of biting his
nails.
Green: Oh, how did you manage
that?
Brown: I knocked all his teeth out.

What does 36 inches make in
Glasgow?
–One Scotland yard.

The lazy man tried to get a job at the
Bakers because he thought life
would be one long loaf.

Motorist: Can you tell me the way to
Bath?
Policeman: I always use soap and
water myself.

'Susan I think your husband dresses
nattily!'
'Natalie who?'

Visiting the Modern Art Museum, a lady turned to an attendant standing nearby. 'This,' she said, 'I suppose is one of those hideous representations you call modern art?'

'No, madam,' replied the attendant. 'That one's called a mirror.'

The Irishman wanted to go surf-riding, but he couldn't persuade the horse to go into the water.

English Teacher: Simon, I'd like you to make up a sentence with a direct object.
Simon: (after a pause): 'Miss, everybody thinks you are beautiful and clever.'
English Teacher: Well thank you, but what is the direct object?
Simon: A good report, Miss.

Eve: That's a nice coat you're wearing – what fur is it?
Amy: I don't know, but everytime I pass a dog, the fur goes up at the back.

'I say, what a lovely colour that cow over there is.'
'It's a jersey.'
'Oh – I thought it was her skin.'

A very fat lady sitting on the bus, noticed three elderly ladies standing. Turning to the man next to her, she said: 'If you were a gentleman you'd get up and let one of those ladies sit down.'
'If you were a lady,' he replied, 'you get up and let all three of them sit down.'

'The only thing my husband ever achieved on his own is his moustache.'

Mother: Why is your little brother crying?
Billy: Because I won't give him my piece of cake.
Mother: Is his piece gone?
Billy: Yes – he cried when I ate that, too.

Sign in a Police Station: IT TAKES ABOUT 3500 BOLTS TO PUT A MOTOR CAR TOGETHER BUT ONLY ONE NUT TO SCATTER IT ALL OVER THE ROAD.

Molly: Why does your brother spend so much time playing football?
Polly: Oh, he just does it for kicks.

New Husband: Just think darling – we've now been married for twenty-four hours!
New Wife: Yes, darling, and it seems like only yesterday.

'My wife and I don't argue – she goes her way, and I go hers.'

A chap was spreading powder in the middle of the road. 'What do you think you're doing?' asked a policeman.
'Spreading crocodile powder,' said the man.
'There's no crocodiles around here.' said the policeman.
'Well, it just shows how effective it is, doesn't it.'

Gormless Gus took a friend driving on a narrow mountain road. After a while the friend said, 'I feel very scared whenever you go round one of those sharp bends.'
'Then do what I do,' said Gus, 'close your eyes.'

Inscription on the tombstone of a hypochondriac:
'I *told* you I was ill.'

One day Mr Jones came home to find
his wife wringing her hands and
weeping. 'Oh dear,' she said, 'the
cat's eaten your dinner.'
'Never mind,' he said.'We can get a
new cat tomorrow.'

Doctor, after listening to his
patient's numerous complaints: 'I'll
write something out for you.'
Patient: Is it a prescription?
Doctor: 'No, it's a letter
of introduction to the undertaker.'

The pub beer wasn't very good. 'If
this beer had a head on it,' said a
customer, 'it would hang it in
shame.'.

Simple Simon went to buy a pillow
case. 'What size?' said the assistant.
'I don't know,' said Simon. 'But I
wear a seven-and-a-half hat.'

'Our next comedian is so bad that
when he took part in an open-air
show in the park, twenty-six trees
got up and walked out.'

Passenger: How can I make sure the
trains are running on time?
Porter: Just before one comes in, put
your watch on the line.

Jinks: I notice your neighbour doesn't let his chickens run loose any more. Why is that?
Binks: Well I hid six eggs under a bush the other night. Next day I made sure he saw me collect the eggs.

A young lady went into a bank to withdraw some money.
'Can you identify yourself?' asked the clerk.
The young lady opened her handbag, took out a mirror, looked into it and said, 'Yes, it's me all right.'

Piano Tuner: I've come to tune your piano.
Lady: But we didn't send for you.
P. Tuner: No, but your neighbours did.

Young man: I've come to ask for your daughter's hand.
Father: You'll have to take all of her, or it's no deal.

Father (at breakfast): My, son, that was some thunderstorm we had last night.
Son: It certainly was.
Mother: Oh dear, why didn't you wake me up? You know I can't sleep in a thunderstorm.

Customer: Those sausages you sent me were meat at one end and bread at the other.
Butcher: Yes, madam, in these times it's difficult to make both ends meat.

Lady: I found a fly in one of those currant buns you sold me yesterday.
Shop owner: Well bring it back and I'll exchange it for a currant.

Man to psychiatrist: 'I'm worried – I keep thinking I'm a pair of curtains:
'Stop worrying, and pull yourself together.'

Father: When I was your age, I had lovely wavy hair.
Son (looking at father's bald head): Well, since then it's certainly waved you goodbye.

'If my parents knew I was here tonight as compère they'd be ashamed – they think I'm in prison.'

Bobby had been warned to be on his best behaviour when his wealthy aunt visited. After tea, Bobby asked, 'Auntie, when are you going to do your trick?'
'What trick is that, dear?' she enquired.
'Well,' said Bobby, 'Daddy says you drink like a fish.'

Bertie: I had a trip by the seaside yesterday.
Gertie: I'm sorry to hear that – did you hurt yourself?

An Irish woman expecting her sixth child was horrified to read in her newspaper that every sixth person born in the world is Chinese.

The medical lecturer turned to one of his students and said: 'Now Merryweather, it is clear from this X-ray that one of this patient's legs is much shorter than the other. This accounts for the patient's limp. But what would *you* do in a case like this?'

Merryweather thought for a moment, then said brightly, 'Well, sir, I should imagine that I would limp too.'

Father: Well, my boy, do you think the new teacher likes you?
Jock: Oh yes, dad, she puts a wee kiss on all my sums.

Lady: What's the best way to keep fish from smelling?
Fishmonger: Just cut off their noses, lady.

Johnny: Mother, you promised to take me to see the monkeys today.
Mother: Johnny, how could you want to go and see monkeys when Grandma is here?

'Now I'd like to introduce somebody who, ten years ago, was an unknown failure. Now he's a famous failure.'

Jock: Am I your closest friend?
Duncan: I think you must be – you never give me anything.

Sammy had been on an outing with his father.
'Well,' said his mother on their return, 'did you like the zoo?'
'Oh it was fine,' replied Sammy.
'And Dad liked it too – especially when one of the animals came romping home at twenty to one.'

News broadcast: Two prisoners escaped today from Wakefield prison. One is seven feet tall and the other is four feet six. The Police are hunting high and low for them.

Overheard in Post Office.
'I want a dog licence please.'
'Yes, madam. What name?'
'Rover.'

Patient (to Psychiatrist): The trouble is, I can't help pulling funny faces.
Psychiatrist: That doesn't sound very serious.
Patient: But it's not *my* face I want to pull ... it's other people's.

Brown: The police are looking for a man with one eye called Bloggs.
White: What's his other eye called?

Cloakroom attendant: Please leave your hat here, sir.
Club customer: I haven't got a hat.
Attendant: Then I'm afraid you can't come into the Club. My orders are that people cannot enter unless they leave their hat in the cloakroom.

Teacher: Order, children.
Willy: I'll have ice cream and dough-nuts.

A lady decided to breed chickens but she didn't have much luck. At last she wrote to the Ministry of Agriculture for some advice. She wrote: 'Dear Sir, Every morning I find one or two of my prize chickens lying stiff and cold on the ground with their legs in the air. Would you kindly tell me what is the matter?' A few days later she got this reply: 'Dear Madam, Your chickens are dead.'

Flora: Either the boss takes back what he said, or I walk out.
Dora: What did he say?
Flora: He told me to take a week's notice.

Office Manager: Look at all the dust on this desk. It looks as if it hasn't been cleaned for a fortnight.
Cleaning lady: Don't blame me, sir, I've only been here a week.

Father(on Jubilee Day): Where's your mother, Rosie?
Rosie: Upstairs, waving her hair.
Father: Good heavens, can't we afford a flag?

One bird to his friend: Look, there's Concorde. I wish I could go as fast as that.'
Friend bird: You could, if your bottom was on fire.

The pilot felt a gun sticking in his back, and a voice hissed in his ear:
'Take me to London.'
'But we're going to London,' said the pilot.
'I know. But I've been hi-jacked to Cuba twice before, so this time I'm taking no chances.'

Greedy Boy: I got through a jar of jam today.
Friend: From your size it must have been a tight squeeze.

'Are you trying to make a fool out of me?'
'Certainly not – why should I try to change Nature?'

'Hard lines,' said the egg in the monastery, 'Out of the frying pan into the friar.'

It was a very fancy high-class greengrocers, but the customer gasped when he was charged 75 pence for a pound of apples. He gave the girl a pound and staggered out of the shop.
'You've forgotten your change, sir,' said the girl.
'Keep it,' he said weakly. 'On my way out I trod on a grape.'

Reggie: My brother thinks he's a chicken.
Freddie: Well, why don't you take him to the doctor.
Reggie: We would, but we need the eggs.

A young man went into a pet-shop and asked for 300 beetles, 6 rats and five mice.
'I'm sorry sir,' said the petshop manager, 'but we can only supply the mice. Why do you need all the other animals?'
'I was thrown out of my flat this morning, and the landlord said I must leave the place exactly as I found it.'

'Why are you drinking blue and white paint?'
'Because I'm an interior decorator.'

An apprentice witch-doctor was learning the tricks of the trade from an old witch-doctor.
Old W-D: Just watch what I do then voo-doo the same as I do.

Old Salt: I once had a parrot for five years and it never said a word.
Young sailor: It must have been tongue-tied.
Old Salt: No, it was stuffed.

A worm had an invitation to a picnic in a field of wheat. It went in one ear and the other.

Ned: What goes ninety-nine bump, ninety-nine bump, ninety-nine bump?
Ed: A centipede with a wooden leg.

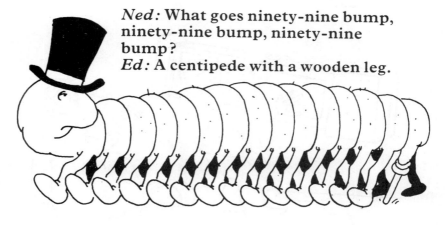

'Waiter, what soup is this?'
'It's bean soup, sir.'
'I don't want to know what it's been,
what it is now?'

Man in blood donor clinic: 'I've
come to donate a pint of blood –
where do I spit it out?'

False eyelashes are a marvellous
invention – I spent half an hour in
the bathroom trying to kill one of the
darn things.

A man bought a grandfather clock
from an antique shop. In the street
he put it over his shoulder and as he
did so knocked over an old lady.
'Idiot,' she yelled, 'who can't you
wear a wrist-watch like the rest of
us!'

Vicar: Do you say your prayers before your dinner, Pamela?
Pamela: Oh no, my mother's a good cook.

1st Businessman: My secretary has been loyal to me for years, I've seen her grow grey-headed in my service.
2nd Businessman: That's nothing; mine has been with me for three months and she's been dark brown, ash blond and now she's a red-head.

Solly: What's the weather like?
Molly: I don't know – it's so cloudy I can't see.

Grandma: I like to go to bed and get up with the chickens, don't you?
Betty: No, I like to sleep in my own bed.

Charlie: I found a horseshoe today; what do you think it means?
Dan: Perhaps the horse decided to wear socks instead.

'Why did you push her under a steamroller?'
'Because I wanted a flatmate.'

Policeman in witness box: This woman came up to me when I was in plain clothes and tried to pass off this ten pound note, m'lud.
Judge: Counterfeit?
Policeman: Yes, m'lud, she had two.

1st Pickpocket: Did you have any luck over the weekend?
2nd pickpocket: No. I spent it at a nudist camp.

Gormless Guss walked to a rocket station and asked for a ticket to the moon. 'Sorry sir,' the gateman said, 'The moon is full.'

Roger: Your overcoat is very loud.
Rodney: It's not so bad when I put on a muffler.

Judge: I shall give you a short sentence.
Prisoner: Thank you, your Honour.
Judge: Ten years.
Prisoner: Ten years – that's not a short sentence!
Judge: Yes it is – – two words.

Doctor (examining a patient): 'What's that strange growth on your head – oh, it's your head.'

Molly: Did you hear the one about the bed?
Polly: No.
Molly: It hasn't been made up yet.

'My dog plays chess with me.'
'It must be a very intelligent animal.'
'Not really. 'I've won four games out of six so far today.'

'Waiter, do you have frogs' legs?'
'Yes, sir.'
'Then leap over the counter and get me a whisky.'

A lady visiting an orchard, was amazed at the profusion of fruit, and asked the farmer: 'What do you do with all this fruit.'
'We eat what we can, and what we can't we can,' he replied.

'Waiter, there's a button in my salad.'
'Oh it must have come off when the salad was dressing.'

Stan: In his job my dad's one of the high-ups.
Dan: What does he do?
Stan: He's a steeplejack.

'Why did Lulu leave her job?'
'Illness.'
'Anything serious?'
'Yes. The boss got sick of her.'

Patient: And if I take these little blue pills as you suggested, will I get better?
Doctor: Well, put it this way; none of my patients has ever come back to ask for more.

What's the difference between an Indian elephant and an African Elephant?
– About 3,000 miles.

Waiter: We have practically everything on the menu.
Diner: So I see – would you bring me a clean one please?

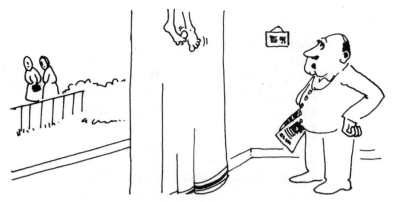

Wife: I don't think I like this bananas – only diet the doctor's put me on; it seems to be having a peculiar effect on me.
Husband: Nonsense dear. Now if you'll just stop scratching yourself and come down from the curtains ...

Barry: My dad's a big time operator.
Harry: Oh, what does he do?
Barry: He winds up Big Ben.

George: I've been hunting with my pop. We brought back four rabbits and a potfer.
Joe: What's a potfer?
George: To cook the rabbits in.

Flora: I had to give up tap dancing.
Dora: Why was that?
Flora: I kept falling in the sink.

'Doctor, I feel like a pack of cards.'
'Wait over there, I'll deal with you later.'

Hetty: My doctor put me on a diet, using more corn and vegetable oils.
Betty: Does it work?
Hetty: I don't know yet – I'm no thinner, but I don't squeak any more.

Fred: What is the noblest dog?
Ned: The hot-dog – it feeds the hand that bites it.

Judge: (to Barrister): Your client doesn't seem to take the charges very seriously.
Barrister: Well, my lord, he's a professional pick-pocket, and is apt to take things rather lightly.

Sammy: (at the Fair): Who's in charge of the Nuts?
Stall-minder: Just a minute and I'll take care of you.

Customer: I'd like two pork chops, please, and make them lean.
Butcher: Yes, madam, which way?

'This restaurant must have a very clean kitchen.'
'Thank you, sir, how did you know?'
'Everything tastes of soap.'

Minister of Defence: a man who is always ready to lay down *your* life for *his* country.

Prisoner: The judge sent me here for the rest of my life.
Governor: Have you any complaints?
Prisoner: Well, I don't call breaking rocks with a hammer *rest.*

Why did Moses have to be hidden quickly when he was a baby?
Because it was a 'rush' job to save him.

American: You English must grow awfully large.
Englishman: Why do you say that?
American: Well. I see here in the paper a woman lost five hundred pounds.

'But Cecil, it isn't our baby.'
'Shut up – it's a better pram.'

Teacher: I wish you'd pay a little attention.
Angie: I'm paying as little as I can.

After robbing the bank the thief rushed home and began to saw the legs off his bed. His wife asked him what he was doing.
'I want to lie low for a while,' he explained.

Peter: My dad makes faces all day.
Mike: Why does he do that?
Peter: He works in a clock factory.

Tommy: Jake's dad was arrested yesterday.
Timmy: Why was that?
Tommy: He went shopping after drawing twenty pounds.
Timmy: What's wrong with that?
Tommy: The drawing wasn't good enough; they spotted the forgery.

Three rather deaf old friends met
one day.
'Windy, isn't it?' said one.
'No, it's Thursday,' said the second.
'So am I,' said the third. 'Let's go and
have a cup of tea.'

'How dare you spit in front of my
wife?'
'Why, was it her turn?'

Angry man: I'll teach you to throw
stones at my greenhouse.
Little horror: I wish you would – I
keep missing it.

A visitor was being shown over a
farm, when he saw a bull in a field,
and called out: 'Is that bull safe?'
'Well,' said the farmer, 'offhand I'd
say he's a lot safer than you are.'

'I didn't come here to be insulted.'
'Why, where do you usually go?'

The German's clock would not work
properly. He prodded it, shook it,
took the back off. Finally he hissed:
'We haf vays of making you tock.'

Writer: Do you know it took me over
twenty years to find out I have no
writing ability.
Acquaintance: So what did you do –
give it up?
Writer: Oh no, by then I was so
famous I couldn't afford to.

At his execution King Charles I was
asked if he had a final request. He
said yes, he'd like to take his spaniel
for a walk around the block.

Julia: Do you like my new hair-
style?
Jack: Well, it reminds me of a
famous Italian dish.
Julia: Gina Lollobrigida?
Jack: No – spaghetti.

Mother to son: Hurry up, you'll be late for school.
Son: Don't want to go.
Mother: You must go.
Son: The teachers hate me, and the kids despise me so why should I go?
Mother: because you're forty-two years old, and you're the headmaster.

Cook: What's the best thing to put in a pie?
Maid: Your teeth.

Patient: I find it very difficult to tell the truth.
Psychiatrist: Don't worry – once you get on the couch you'll find it very hard to lie on.

'Mummy there's a man at the door with a parcel for you.
He says it's fish, and it's marked COD.'
'Well, tell him to take it back dear, I ordered haddock.'

Husband: I've just discovered oil.
Wife: Wonderful. Now we can get a new car.
Husband: We'd better get the old one fixed first – that's where the oil's coming from.

Patient: Have you got anything for my liver, Doctor?
Doctor: Have you tried onions?

Man in sea: Help, help, I can't swim.
Drunk on shore: So what? I can't play the violin but I'm not shouting about it.

Teacher: If we breathe oxygen in the daytime, what do we breathe in the nighttime?
Margie: Nitrogen?

Lady: (dials 999): Help please come to my house at once.
Policeman: What's the trouble, lady?
Lady: That dreadful new postman is sitting up in a tree in my front garden teasing my dog.

New bridegroom: Darling, do you
think you'll be able to put up with
my ugly face for the rest of your life?
Bride: I expect so, dear, you'll be out
at work all day.

Man: My dog has no tail.
Friend: Then how do you know
when he's happy?
Man: Oh, he stops biting me.

Ben: I hear the workers are striking
for shorter hours.
Len: Good thing too – I always did
think sixty minutes was too long for
an hour.

Newton discovered gravity when an
apple hit him on the head.
He was shaken to the core.

Silly Billy came home from the
railway station complaining that he
felt ill because he had ridden
backwards for three hours on the
train.
'Why didn't you ask the person
sitting opposite you to change seats?'
his mother asked.
'I couldn't, he said. 'There wasn't
anybody sitting opposite me.

A twenty-stone girl got engaged to a
twenty-seven stone man.
They planned to have a big wedding.

'Why does Dick work in the bakery?'
'I suppose he kneads the dough.'

1st patient: I see they've brought in
another case of tonsilitis.
2nd patient: Anything is better than
that lousy lemonade they've been
giving us lately.

'Would you like to come to my party
on Saturday?'
'Yes, I'd love to. What's the address?'
'Number four New Street – just ring
the bell with your elbow.'
'Why can't I ring with my finger?'
'You're not coming empty-handed,
are you?'

Customer in greengrocers: One
pound of mixed nuts, please – and
not too many coconuts.

The absent-minded professor
wished to test his class to see if they
could tell the difference between a
frog and a toad. But when he opened
the box, he took out a sandwich.
'Good heavens,' he said, 'I could have
sworn I'd just had my lunch.'

'I will now read from the Book of
Numbers,' said the Vicar – and he
opened the telephone directory.

The new hotel porter was being
instructed by the manager, who told
him always to welcome the guests by
name.
'But how will I know their name?'
asked the porter.
'Simple, it'll be on their case,' said
the manager.
The porter was later heard saying,
'Welcome to our hotel, Mr and Mrs
Simulated Leather.'

Judge: As the jury have found you Not Guilty of fraud, you are now free to go.
Prisoner: Does that mean I can keep the money?

Women are to blame for all the lying men do – they will insist on asking questions.

Pru: There are several things I can always count on.
Lou: What are they?
Pru: My fingers.

After class, the absent-minded professor asked if anybody had seen his coat.
'You have it on, sir,' he was told.
'Oh thank you very much,' he replied.
'Otherwise I might have gone off without it.'

A man bought a wristwatch and arranged to pay for it later.
He got it on tick.

A little boy noticed some green parakeets in a pet shop.
'Look mummy,' he said, 'there are some canaries that aren't ripe.'

'Gloria is the best housekeeper in the world – she's been divorced five times – and she's still got the house.'

'My wife has a slight impediment in her speech. Now and again she has to stop to take a breath.'

Mike: Does your wife cook by gas or electricity?
Jake: I don't know, I've never tried to cook her.

The creature from outer space landed in London and came upon a woman carrying a transistor. 'Earthwoman,' he said in a shocked voice, 'why do you carry your child around without clothes on?'

A policeman saw an old man pulling
a box on a lead down a busy street.
'Poor man,' he thought. 'I'd better
humour him.'
'That's a nice dog you've got there,'
he said to the old man.
'It isn't a dog, it's a box,' said the old
man.
'Oh I'm sorry,' said the policeman, 'I
thought you were a bit simple,' and
he walked on.
The old man turned and looked at
the box. 'We fooled him that time,
Rover,' he said.

Paddy asked his landlady for a full
length mirror in his room. 'You've
got a half-length mirror there now,'
she said. 'Isn't that long enough.'
'No, lady,' said Paddy. 'I've been out
three times this week without my
trousers on.'

'He's so wealthy, he bought a boy for
his dogs to play with.'

'I don't know what to buy my nephew
for his birthday.'
'Difficult – a drum takes a lot of
beating.'

Roger: My girl friend and I had a
row the other night – she wanted to
go to the ballet, and I wanted to go to
a pop concert. But we came to an
agreement.
Peter: And what was the ballet like?

Frank: Four sailors fell in the sea,
but only one of them got his hair wet.
Johnny: How was that?
Frank: Three of them were bald.

Visitor (at gate): Does your dog bite
strangers?
Man: Only when he doesn't know
them.

The professor was checking papers
in his study when his telephone rang.
His secretary answered it. 'It's a long
distance from New York,' she said.
'Yes, I know,' answered the
professor.

Customer at garage: 'I'm in a great
hurry. Don't bother with the petrol,
just give me the stamps.'

Gum Arabic: Spoken by Arabs
without teeth.

'Mummy – it's getting very hot in
here – can I come out?'
'Certainly not, do you want the fire
to spread to the rest of the house?'

Mrs Green: I see you and your
husband are taking French lessons –
why is that?
Mrs Black: We've adopted a French
baby and we want to be able to
understand him as soon as he learns
to talk.

The professor looked at one of his
students: 'Haven't you a brother who
took this course last year?' he asked.
'No, sir,' said the student. 'I'm just
taking it again.'
'My word,' said the professor,
'Amazing resemblance.'

What did the penny say when it got
stuck in the slot?
'Money's very tight these days.'

What does a Hindu? Lay eggs.

Willie: There's a black cat in the dining room, dad.
Dad: But black cats are lucky, Willie.
Willie: This one is – he's eaten your dinner.

Rory: What's in your bag?
Mike: Chickens.
Rory: Will you be giving me one of them?
Mike: No.
Rory: If I guess how many you've got then will you give me one.
Mike: Sure – if you guess correctly I'll give you both.
Rory: Six.

Two little boys were looking at an abstract painting in an art shop.
'Let's run,' said one, 'before they say we did it.'

The less people know, the more stubbornly they know it.

Sarah hadn't been paying attention when the teacher was explaining the importance of milk. When teacher asked her to name six things with milk in them she thought a moment. Then she said, 'Hot chocolate, ice-cream, rice-pudding – and three cows.'

Diner: What's the matter with this table – it's wobbling all over the place?
Waiter: The last customer spilt a bottle of wine over it, and it's still drunk.

How do we know that Moses wore a wig?
Because sometimes he was seen with Aaron and sometimes without.

Dying words of a famous Chicago gangster: 'Who put that violin in my violin case?'

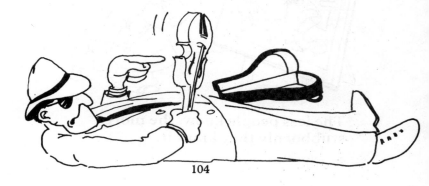

'My mother-in-law has gone to
Indonesia.'
'Jakarta?'
'No – she went by plane.'

What is the difference between
unlawful and illegal?
Unlawful is against the law. Illegal is
a sick bird.

Ben: I saw something last night that
I'll never get over.
Len: What was that?
Ben: The moon.

Ron: You dance beautifully.
Jean: I wish I could say the same for
you.
Ron: You could if you were as big a
liar as I am.

Tramp: I haven't had a square meal
for a month, lady.
Lady: Oh you poor man – here's a
dog biscuit.

Patient's brother: I'm afraid my
brother thinks he's a cat.
Psychiatrist: How long has he
thought that?
P's brother: Since he was a kitten.

Teacher (on phone): You say Tommy has a cold and can't come to school? To whom am I speaking? *Voice:* This is my father.

Adam: And I shall call that creature over there a rhinoceros. *Eve:* But why call it that? *Adam:* Because it looks like a rhinoceros, stupid.

Fifi: Did you know that not all the animals that came to Noah's Ark came in pairs? *Bibi:* Which ones didn't? *Fifi:* The worms – they came in apples.

Harry was playing the violin for his brother. 'Well how do you like it?' he asked.
His brother said, 'You should be on the radio.'
'You mean I'm good enough for that?'
'No – but then I could turn you off.'

What did Big Chief Running Water
call his two sons?
–Hot and cold.

Visitor to Zoo: Where have all the
adders gone?
Keeper: They're helping out in the
accounts department, the
computer's broken down.

Never try to drink and drive – you
might stop suddenly and spill some
of it.

The young man gave his girlfriend a
glittering necklace for her birthday.
'Ooh,' she exclaimed, 'are they real
diamonds?'
'They'd better be,' he replied, 'or I've
been swindled out of a pound.'

Teacher: Now can somebody tell me where elephants are found?
Mary: Well, elephants are so big they are hardly ever lost.

Betty: I had a fall last night which left me unconscious for eight hours.
Hetty: How dreadful! Where did you fall?
Betty: I fell asleep.

Lady on bus: Am I all right for Regents Park Zoo?
Conductor: I should think so, lady, but I'm only a conductor, not a zoologist.

The best way to make your money go further nowadays is to post it to Australia.

Frank: Am I the first man you've ever kissed?
Sue: You might be, your face looks familiar.

'What are you eating, sonny?'
'An apple.'
'Better look out for worms.'
'Let the worms look out for themselves.'

Milly: Do you have hot water at your house?
Billy: We sure do. And I'm always in it.

Holidays in Paris make you feel good enough to return to work – and so poor that you have to.

Janice: Darling, whisper something soft and sweet in my ear.
Ernest: Black forest cherry cake.

'I got a terrible fright on my wedding day.'
'Why, what happened?'
'Nothing – I married her.'

Mother: Georgie, I was hoping you would give your little brother the largest piece of cake. Even that old hen gives all the best pieces of food to her chicks, and takes only a little piece now and then for herself.
Georgie: So would I, mum, if it were worms.

Jim: I think our school must be haunted.
Tim: Why do you say that?
Jim: I'm always hearing people talk about the school spirit.

'This pair of shoes you sold me
yesterday is ridiculous.
One of them has a heel two inches
shorter than the other.
What am I supposed to do?'
'Limp.'

Waiter: And after the steak, sir,
what will you have to follow?
Diner: Indigestion, I expect.

Large Lady: I'm very annoyed with
that weighing machine.
Friend: Why's that?
Large lady: As I stepped on to it, it
said, 'One person at a time please.'

If at first you don't succeed, you're
just like 99.9 per cent of the
population.

'My uncle is a butcher, six feet tall
and wears size 12 shoes. What does
he weigh?'
'I've no idea.'
'Meat, of course.'

Visitor: And how do you like going to
school, Willie?
Willie: I like going, and I like coming
back. It's the bit in between I don't
like.

Waiter: Yes, sir, you can have
anything you see on the menu.
Diner: Well how about dirty
fingermarks, grease stains, and
gravy in that order.

Teacher: Write on one of the
following: Elizabeth the First,
Alfred the Great or John of Gaunt.
Smart Alex: I'd prefer to write on
paper.

Fat boy put a penny in the weighing
machine and stood looking at the
chart which told him how much
people of different sizes should
weigh.
After a while the chemist came out
and asked him how much he was
overweight.
'I'm not overweight,' said the Fat
boy, 'I'm just three inches too short.'

Ruby: Did you know how many sheep it takes to make one sweater? *Pearl:* I didn't even know they could knit.

Teacher: At which battle did Nelson die? *Willy:* His last one.

Chemistry teacher: What do you know about nitrates? *Student:* Well, sir, they're a lot more expensive than day rates.

Russ: I hear your uncle was drowned in a barrel of varnish. It must have been a dreadful way to go. *Gus:* Not really, he had a beautiful finish.

'You can't help admiring our boss.'
'Why is that?'
'If you don't – you're fired.'

'Do you know what C.I.D. stands for, son?'
'Yes – Coppers in Disguise.'

To avoid that run-down feeling, look both ways before crossing the road.

'Doctor, I was playing my flute and I suddenly swallowed it.'
'Never mind, look on the bright side. It could have been a grand piano.'

Gloria: Don't you feel warm doing your painting all bundled up like that?
Silly Sam: Well it says on the tin to be sure to put on three coats.

A lady was horried to see a small boy leaning against a wall smoking a cigarette, and taking swigs from a bottle of whisky. 'Why aren't you at school this time of day?' she demanded.

'School, lady,' he answered. 'Gee, I'm only four years old.'

'My friend Dopey the Dwarf has applied for a job in a circus.'
'Well, he should get on the short list.'

'Waiter, there's a twig in my soup.'
'Just a moment, sir, I'll call the branch manager.'

Frank: What would I have to give you to get a little kiss?
Za-za: Chloroform.

A man walked into the fishmongers, and pointed to a row of trout: 'I'll have five of these,' he said. 'But throw them to me.'
'Why should I do that? asked the fishmonger.
'I may be a poor fisherman,' said the man, 'but nobody is going to call me a liar, when I say I caught five trout.'

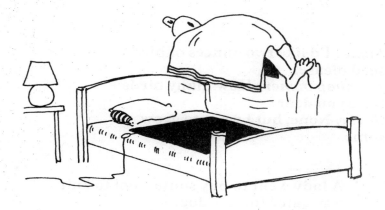

Pat: I didn't sleep well last night.
Mat: Why was that?
Pat: I plugged the electric blanket
into the toaster by mistake and I
kept popping out of bed all night.

Teacher: Can you tell me the
difference between a buffalo and a
bison?
Cockney pupil: Well you can't wash
your hands in a buffalo, miss.

Jackie: I wouldn't marry you if you
were the last person on earth.
Johnny: If I were, you wouldn't be
here.

Mrs Higgins: I'm sorry to bring you
out on such a terrible night, doctor.
Doctor: That's all right. I had to call
at a house down the road, so I
thought I'd kill two birds with one
stone.

Suzie: I'd like two ounces of bird seed please.
Pet shop owner: How many birds have you dear?
Suzie: None, but I want to grow some.

A lady went to buy some wool to knit a sweater for her dog.
'Perhaps you'd better bring him in.' said the saleslady, 'then I can tell you how much wool to buy.'
'Oh no,' said the customer, 'it's supposed to be a surprise.'

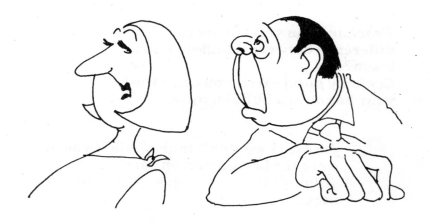

'Darling, you have the face of a saint.'
'Thank you, darling, which saint.'
'A Saint Bernard.'

The Welshman touring New York turned to his companion in the coach, a boastful American, and said: 'And where do you come from?'
'From God's own country,' replied the American.
'H'm,' said the Welshman, 'then you've got a very poor Welsh accent.'

'Your money or your life,' said the hold-up man to the miser. When there was no reply, he repeated the demand:
'Come on, man, your money or your life, which is it to be?'
'Quiet,' said the miser, 'I'm thinking about it.'

Patrick: Did you mark that place on the water where the fishing is so good?
Mike: Course I did. I put a cross on the side of the boat.
Patrick: Idiot – we might get another boat next time.

Walter: A steam-roller ran over my uncle.
Richard: What did you do?
Walter: I took him home and slipped him under the door.

Larry: It's raining cats and dogs today.
Carry: I know – I've just stepped into a poodle.

Post Office clerk: You've addressed this letter upside down.
Paddy: That's right – it's going to Australia.

Lady: Can this wool coat be worn in wet weather?
Assistant: Madam, have you ever seen a sheep carry an umbrella?

A man and his wife were looking over a house. The estate agent said to them: 'It's only a stone's throw from the bus stop.'
'We'll take it,' said the man. 'There'll always be something to do in the evening, throwing stones at buses.'

'You can't say my husband is two-
faced – or he wouldn't wear that one
all the time.'

Yesterday three Irishmen hi-jacked
a submarine, and then demanded a
million pounds – and three
parachutes.

Teacher: You missed school
yesterday, didn't you Sammy?
Sammy: Not much miss.

A man came to the police station and
complained: 'I've got three brothers
– we all live in one room. One of my
brothers has six cats, another has
five dogs, and the other has a goat.
The smell is terrible. Can you do
something about it?'
'Well, why don't you open the
windows?' asked the policeman.
'What, and lose all my pigeons,' said
the man.

Angie: How are you getting on
teaching Charlie to dance?
Rosie: Well I'm hoping soon he'll be
able to stand on his own feet instead
of mine.

Bernie: How are you getting on in your new ten-roomed house?
Barney: Not too badly. We furnished the living room by collecting cornflakes packets.
Bernie: What about the other rooms?
Barney: We can't do them yet – they're full of cornflakes.

Buster: What are you doing?
Goofy: Writing a letter to my brother.
Buster: But you can't write.
Goofy: That doesn't matter. My brother can't read.

The mother kangaroo leapt into the air with a cry of pain.
'Joey,' she said, 'how many more times do I have to tell you not to smoke in bed.'

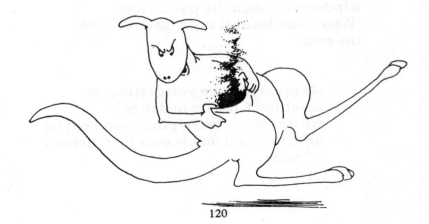

Norman: You remind me of the sea.
Gloria: Why, because I'm so wild, reckless and romantic?
Norman: No – you make me sick.

Percival was so wealthy that even the bags under his eyes had his initials on them.

'Doctor, you remember last year you told me to stay away from dampness if I wanted my rheumatism to get better?'
'Yes,' said the doctor.
'Well, it's better. Is it all right for me to take a bath now?'

Cyclist: My bike's always going wrong. I think it must have a jinx.
Friend: Yes, it's probably put a spook in your wheel.

Val (answering phone) Hello.
Voice: Hello. Is Boo there?
Val: Boo who?
Voice: Don't cry little girl. I must have the wrong number.

What are government workers called in Seville?
Seville servants.

121

The first Welsh milkman put up a
sign over his shop saying 'Idris
Evans – Dairy'. The second Welsh
milkman put up a sign saying 'Evans
– best dairy goods.' The third Welsh
milkman put up a smaller notice,
saying 'Evans the Milk – Main
Entrance.'

A novice at the stables was trying to
saddle a horse.
'Excuse me,' said the old hand, 'but
you're putting that saddle on
backwards.'
'How do you know,' snapped the
novice. 'You don't know which way
I'm going.'

Pat and Mike each kept a horse in the
same field. In order to tell which was
which they tied a green ribbon on
Pat's horse. One day the ribbon fell
off.
'How shall we tell which is which
now?' asked Pat.
'I know,' said Mike, 'you take the
brown one, and I'll have the white
one.'

Fred: I hear your wife's a poor
driver.
Ned: Yes – even the lights go white
when they see her coming.

Keep smiling – it makes everyone
wonder what you're up to.

Tourist: Whose skull is that one?
Tired guide: That, sir, is the skull of
Julius Caesar.
Tourist: Then whose is that small
one beside it?
Guide: That, sir, is the skull of Julius
Caesar when he was a small boy.

A man in an agitated state rushed
into a pub. 'Has anybody here got a
large black cat with a white collar?'
he asked.
Nobody answered. He tried again.
'Does anybody have a large black cat
with a white collar?' But still nobody
answered.
'Oh dear,' he murmured. 'I must
have run over the vicar.'

Sergeant: Let's get our bearings.
You're facing north; west is on your
left, and east is on your right.
What's at your back?
Private: My knapsack.

"I've made the chicken soup.'
'Good – I was afraid it was for us.'

Teacher: Your hands are very dirty,
Sidney. What would you say if I
came with dirty hands?
Sidney: I'd be too polite to mention
it.

'I understand you buried your
husband last week?'
'Yes – I had to; he was dead.'

Water Bailiff: Young lady, I have to
arrest you for swimming in this
river here.
Young Lady: But surely you could
have told me before I changed into
my swim suit.
Bailiff; There's no law against *that*,
my dear.

Cannibal (to his daughter): Now you
are old enough to get married, we
must look around for an edible
bachelor.

Post-office clerk: Here's your ten pence stamp.
Shopper (with arms full of shopping): Do I have to stick it on myself?
Post-office clerk: No. On the envelope.

If you sat in a bucket of glue, would you have a sticky end?

The census-taker knocked on Miss Matty's door. She answered all his questions except her age. She refused to tell him this.
'But everybody tells their age to the census-taker,' he said.
'Did Miss Maisie Hill and Miss Daisy Hill tell you their ages?'
'Certainly.'
'Well I'm the same age,' she snapped.
'As old as the Hills,' he wrote on his form.

Effie: My auntie was very embarrassed when she was asked to take off her mask at the party.
Tessie: Why was that?
Effie: She wasn't wearing one.

'Are you a mechanic?'
'No, I'm a Mactavish.'

'I can't understand how those bank robbers got away,' said the Constable. 'Were all the exits guarded?'
'Certainly, sir'.
'Well, they must have gone out by the entrance.'

'I've just bought a suit that fits me like a glove.'
'You must be very pleased.'
'Not really – four trouser legs and one sleeve.'

An ambulance man arriving at the
hospital saw two doctors searching
in the flower-beds. 'Excuse me,' he
said, 'have you lost something?' 'No,'
replied one, 'we're doing a heart
transplant for a tax inspector, and
we're looking for a suitable stone.'

Tess: They call him the wonder boy.
Bess: Why is that?
Tess: They look at him and wonder.

Think of a number between one and
twenty. Double it, subtract eighteen,
add one, subtract the number you
started with, close your eyes ....
Dark, isn't it!

Pete: My wife converted me to
religion?
Stan: How did she do that?
Pete: I didn't believe in Hell until I
married her!

127

Hold-up man: Will you give me your money or shall I shoot you?
Bert: Shoot me. I need the money for my old age.

What did the traffic lights say to the sports car?
–Don't look now, I'm changing.

Husband (to wife who is slimming) Don't you find it hard to go without sugar?
Wife: No, when I think about it a lump just comes into my throat.

Little girl: I was going to buy you some hankies for Christmas, Uncle, but I couldn't remember the size of your nose.

Dorothy: I'm not going to school any more.
Mother: Why ever not?
Dorothy: On Monday teacher said five and five makes ten. On Tuesday she said six and four makes ten. Today she said seven and three makes ten. 'I'm not going back till she makes up her mind.

Maisie: What did one tonsil say to the other tonsil?
Daisy: I don't know, what?
Maisie: Get dressed. Doctor is taking us out tonight.

Martin: Why do doctors and nurses wear masks?
Mike: So that if someone makes a mistake, no one will know who did it.

What happened to the cat who swallowed a ball of wool?
–She had mittens.

An Irishman bought a pair of water skis – now he's looking for water with a slope.

John: Why is Sunday the strongest day?
Joan: Because all the others are *week*days.

Jackson: There's one word that describes my wife – temperamental.
Jones: In what way?
Jackson: She's fifty per cent temper and fifty per cent mental!

The home team had been beaten ten nil and trooped sadly back to the dressing room. 'Cheer up, boys,' said the manager, 'at least you won something, even if it was only the toss.'

Stan: What are you taking for your cold?
Sid: What will you give me?

The cow slipped and fell on the ice. But little Audrey laughed and laughed – she knew it was no use crying over spilt milk.

'Where did I come from?' asked the baby ear of corn.
'The stalk brought you,' answered its mother.

'I wouldn't say my boss has a big mouth but he called me from London yesterday. I was in Birmingham, and we don't have a telephone.'

Husband (phoning his wife from his office): I've got two tickets for the ballet.
Wife: Oh, lovely, I'll start getting ready.
Husband: Yes, do – the tickets are for tomorrow night.

Teacher: Jimmy, can you tell me a common use for cow-hide?
Jimmy: Well, to hold the cows together.

Bert had a letter from his mother. 'Dear Bert, so much has happened since you were home. I've had all my teeth out, and a new gas-stove put in …'

131

'Why do you call your wife Camera –
that can't be her real name?'
'No – her real name's Iris, but I call
her Camera because she's always
snapping at me.'

The little girl had jelly in one ear and
custard in the other. An old lady
asked her what she was doing with
jelly in one ear and custard in the
other.
'You'll have to speak up,' said the
little girl, 'I'm a trifle deaf.'

Phil: Where did he meet her?
Bill: They met in a revolving door,
and he's been going round with her
ever since.

Teacher: Can anyone tell me what
sort of insect a slug is?
Aleck: Yes, sir – a snail with a
housing problem.

Young Larry and Barry were
watching men on high scaffolding
repairing a tall chimney.
'What would you do if you were up
there and that thing fell?' Larry
asked.
'I would wait until it got nearly to the
ground and then I would jump.'

When Buster was born they fired
twenty-one guns. Unfortunately they
all missed.

'Excuse me, can you tell me the
time?'
'I'm sorry – I'm a stranger here
myself.'

Know-all Agricultural Student:
Your methods seem very out of date
here: I'd be surprised if you could
get ten pounds of apples out of that
tree.
Farmer: So would I – it's a peach
tree.

The vacancy is for a litter-collector.
Have you any experience?
–No, but I'll pick it up as I go along.

Sunday School teacher: And what is
the Holy See of Rome?
Little Myra: It's when the Pope looks
at himself in a mirror.

Boy from City: Why are you
ploughing your field with a steam
roller?
Farmer: I'm growing mashed
potatoes this year.

Mother: How did you get Wayne to take his medicine without protest?
Father: I shot it into him with a water pistol.

Phil: Why is it dangerous to tell a secret on a farm?
Bill: I don't know. Why?
Phil: Because the potatoes have eyes, the corn have ears, and the beans talk.

Teacher: I hope I didn't see you looking at someone else's paper Jamie.
Jamie: I hope so too, teacher.

'My uncle gets a warm reception wherever he goes.'
'He must be very popular.'
'No, he's a fireman.'

134

Teacher: Do you know that Russell boy?
Principal: What about him?
Teacher: Not only is he the worst-behaved child in the school, but he has a perfect attendance record.

Ted: I have in my hand two coins – which total fifty-five pence. One is not a five-pence piece. What are the two coins?
Fred: I've no idea.
Ted: One is a fifty pence piece – the *other* is five-pence.

Teacher: What is a skeleton?
Mervyn: It's a man with his outsides off and his insides out.

It was the old missionary in Africa who gave the cannibals their first taste of Christianity.

Bud: I can find my wife anywhere I
go.
Bill: How?
Bud: I just open my wallet, and
there she is.

Vicar: (talking about the changing
fashions of the day) It's certainly
made a change to the collection.
Verger: Yes and since zips came in
we get fewer buttons on the plate.

Smith: You seem to have been
working in your garden. Mr Brown –
what are you growing?
Brown: Tired.

Algy: What kind of paper should I
use for my kite?
Reggie: What about fly-paper!

Mother: How did my best vase get
broken?
Son: I was cleaning my catapult and
it went off.

A lady dropped her umbrella over
the edge of the platform at
Paddington Station. The porters
refused to retrieve it as they
considered it beneath their station.

Percy received a letter from his
wife:
'Dear Percy, I missed you yesterday.
Please come home again and let me
have another shot.'

Mabel: You must have paid the
earth for that coat.
Jessie: No, I got it dirt cheap.

Willie: What is frozen tea?
Sammy: Iced tea.
Willy: What is frozen beer?
Sammy: Iced beer.
Willy: What is frozen ink?
Sammy: Iced ink?
Willy: Well, go and have a bath.

Dan: This match won't light.
Stan: Why, what's the matter with
it?
Dan: I don't know – it was alright a
minute ago.

Teacher: Now, Jane, your sister gave me exactly the same essay on your holiday picnic!
Jane: Well, miss, it was the same picnic.

Patient: Tell me straight, doctor, how long have I got?
Doctor: It's difficult to say, but if I were you I wouldn't start reading any serials.

Vi: Is it true you married Joe for the money his grandfather left him?
Di: Certainly not! I'd have married him whoever had left him money.

Maths teacher: If the average car is ten feet long, and if a million cars were placed end to end –
Graham: It would be August Bank Holiday on the way to Brighton.

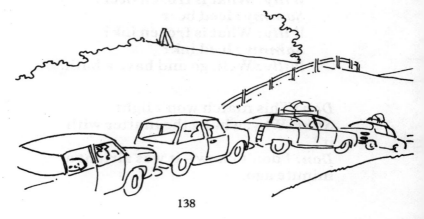

Policeman: After the way you've been driving, I shall now introduce you to Eliza.
Motorist: Who's Eliza?
Policeman: Breath-eliza.

A man was seen on a park bench today dressed only in a newspaper. He said he liked to dress with The Times.

Bob: What inventions have helped me to get up in the world?
Ben: I don't know, which?
Bob: The lift, the escalator and the alarm clock.

Salesman: Would you like to try our new oatmeal soap?
Lady: No, thank you, I never wash my oatmeal.

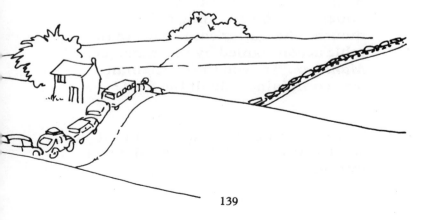

Priest (visiting Paddy in hospital):
Now, Paddy, I shall pray for you to
forgive O'Toole for hitting you on
the head with that bottle.
Paddy: Don't bother, Father, wait
till I come out of here and then you
can pray for O'Toole.

Teacher: Where was the Magna
Carta signed?
Dolly: At the bottom, miss.

Attendant at Lost Property Office:
Oh no – first you tell me what you've
lost, and then I tell you what we've
got.

Father: I'm worried about you
always being at the bottom of your
class.
Freddie: Don't worry, dad. They
teach the same thing at both ends.

A customer in a restaurant lay
under the table foaming at the
mouth. The waiter came back to the
table accompanied by the manager.
Manager: Are you the gentleman
who complained about the food?

'I've always believed in love at first
sight – ever since I first looked into a
mirror.'

Johnny: Hey, mum, the old clothes man's here.
Mum: No, Johnny, we have plenty of old clothes.

Cannibal to Missionary: Well, if God didn't intend you to be eaten, why did he make you out of meat?

Christine made her husband a millionaire.
Before she married him he was a multi-millionaire.

Morris: I hear the workers in the Mint are complaining of having too much work to do.
Harris: Yes, they're threatening to come out on strike unless they make less money.

A Frenchman jumped into a very
long river in Paris yesterday. He was
reported to be In Seine.

Teacher: Yes, Nigel, what is it?
Nigel: I don't want to alarm you,
miss, but my Dad said if I didn't get
better marks someone was going to
get a licking.

Hickory dickory dock
Three mice ran up the clock
The clock struck one
But the other two managed to get
away!

Teacher: Without oxygen, human
life would not be possible. This
important gas was discovered in
1773.
Godfrey: Miss, what did
people breathe before oxygen was
discovered?

Pretty girl at party to Best-selling author: Oh I've read all your books – the one I liked best was the one with the green leather cover and the gold lettering ...

Overheard at Magicians' Convention: 'Hi there, Terry, how's tricks?'

Paddy was stopped at the Customs. 'What's in this bottle?' asked the Customs officer.
'Sure, an' it's Holy Water from Lourdes,' said Paddy.
The Customs Officer didn't believe him and tasted it.
'It looks like whisky, it smells like whisky, and it tastes like whisky,' he said sternly.
'Glory be,' said Paddy – 'another miracle'.

Algernon Smythe-Brown: (to Bertie Billings) 'I bet my father has a higher mortgages repayment than your father.'

'I won't say my parents don't like me, but when I got home from school last week, they'd moved house.'

Upright citizen: You should pay your taxes with a smile.
Friend: Yes, I'd like to, but they insist on cash.

Doctor: How are you now, Mr Gibson, after your heart operation?
Mr Gibson: Well, doctor, I seem to have two heartbeats.
Doctor: Oh dear, I wondered where my wristwatch had gone.

Mavis: I'm thinking of divorcing Jeff, he smokes in bed.
Belle: But surely that's not sufficient reason?
Mavis: The trouble is he smokes kippers.

Ted: My dad's played at Wembley lots of times.
Ned: I didn't know he was a footballer.
Ted: He isn't. He plays in a brassband.

After being unconscious for twenty-four hours Shaun turned to see his friend Paddy just stirring at his side.
'What happened?' said Shaun.
'I don't know,' said Paddy. 'The last thing I remember thinking was how could they sell it for 75p a bottle.'

Voice on phone: Is that the Game Warden?
Game Warden: Yes, sir.
Voice: Oh, could you please suggest some games for my boy's birthday party?

The lady with the large flowery hat was stopped at the church door by the usher:
'Are you a friend of the bride?' he asked.
'Certainly not,' she snapped. 'I'm the bridegroom's mother.'

'Oh Doctor, I've swallowed the film
out of my camera.'
'Well we'll just have to hope that
nothing develops.'

Notice on Street Vendor's barrow:
CAMERAS AS ADVERTISED ON
POLICE 5.

Overheard at Nudist colony:
'Oh I didn't recognise you in glasses,
Mr Ormrod – you look
so intellectual.'

Mrs White: And where are you
living now, Mrs Green.
Mrs Green: Just by the river – drop
in some time.

Henry: This old tramp came up to
me and said he hadn't had a bite in
two weeks.
Bob: Poor chap – what did you do?
Henry: Bit him of course!

Mrs O: I bought a second hand
carpet in mint condition.
Mrs C: How could that be?
Mrs O: It had a hole in the middle.

'I think grandma needs new glasses?'
'What makes you say that, son?'
'She's been watching two pairs of
father's trousers going round in the
washing machine – and thinks she's
watching a wrestling match on telly'

Football Manager: You played a
great game there, Edwards.
Edwards: Oh sir, I thought I played
rather badly.
Manager: No, you played a great
game for the other side.

Mo: Where do you weigh whales?
Jo: I don't know.
Mo: At a whale weigh station.

Mother: Eat your cabbage dear, it
will put colour into your cheeks.
Angie: Who wants green cheeks.

'What's a girl like you doing in a nice place like this?'

Barber (to youth with slick plastered-down hair): Do you just want me to cut it or would you like an oil check too?

The man in the front row of the cinema was making loud groaning noises while tender scenes were being played on the screen. After repeated attempts to 'hush' him the manager was sent for. 'Get up!' demanded the manager. 'Oooooaaaaaggg' shouted the man. 'Where are you from?' asked the manager.
'From ... the ... balcony ...' gasped the man.

Office Manager: I'm afraid that young man I hired isn't honest.
Accounts clerk: Oh, you shouldn't judge by appearance.
Office Manager: I'm not – I'm judging by disappearance.

Roger: Do you know why Eskimos eat candles?
Reggie: No, why?
Roger: For light refreshment.

The navvies went on strike because of the new mechanical shovel. It was too dangerous to lean on.

'My wife is so fat that when I married her, to carry her over the threshold I had to make two trips.'

George: I see you're still on crutches old lad?
Desmond: Yes – that's the last time I'll try and jump over the net at table tennis.

Judge: I don't understand why you broke into the same store three nights in a row?
Prisoner: Well, your Honour, I picked out a dress for my wife, and I had to change it twice.

Auntie: Well, Gordon, suppose there were only two pieces of cake left – a large piece and a small one. Which piece would you give to your brother?
Gordon: Do you mean my big brother or my little one?

Receptionist: Doctor Chaunchadinjhi is waiting for you sir?
Patient: Which doctor?
Receptionist: Oh no, he's fully qualified.

Simon: Which side of the bed do you sleep on?
Dopey Dan: The top side, of course.

'I heard footsteps and got out of bed, and then there was a tap on my door.'
'Heavens, what a funny place for a tap.'

'Why don't you answer the
telephone?'
'It's not ringing.'
'Oh you always have to leave
everything till the last minute.'

The muddled old gentleman went up
to another man at the conference. 'I
hardly recognised you,' he said.
'You've changed so much; your hair
is different, you seem shorter, you've
done away with your glasses. What's
happened to you, Mr Frost?'
   'But I'm not Mr Frost.'
'Amazing – you've even changed
your name.'

'And how do you like the meat balls?'
'I don't know – I've never been to
any.'

Little Diana was standing in front of
her mirror with her eyes closed.
'Why are you standing there with
your eyes closed?' asked her brother.
'So I can see what I'm like when I'm
asleep,' she replied.

Man in tie store: Could you let me
have a tie that would match my eyes,
please?
Lady assistant: I'm afraid they
don't make them in bloodshot tone,
sir.

Dug: What do you think happened to the plant in our arithmetic class?
Reg: I don't know, what?
Dug: It grew square roots.

Tailor: Your suit will be ready in two months sir.
Customer: Two months. But it only took six days when God made the world.
Tailor: True, sir. But look at the state the world is in.

Maud: Samantha reminds me of a film star.
Ivy: Really – which one?
Maud: Lassie.

Voice on phone: Is Mr Miller in yet?
Secretary: No, he hasn't even been in yesterday yet.

Hoh Chang: I like velly much the flute.
English Host: And do you play it?
Hoh Chang: Play it? No, I eat it – apples, bananas – pears.

Teacher: Are you sure that's your mother's signature on this excuse-note?
Ronnie: Oh yes, miss – here's the tracing to prove it.

Patient: I always feel that I'm covered in gold paint, doctor.
Psychiatrist: Oh that's just a gilt complex.

'I think I've got measles.'
'That's a rash thing to say.'

Molly: That's a nice suit you're wearing.
Harry: Oh, do you like it?
Molly: Yes, who went for the fitting?

Student: Did you say you learned to play the violin in six easy lessons?
Master: That's right. It was the seven hundred that came afterwards that were the hard ones.

Simple Simon: I've been feeling run down doctor and I've been taking the vitamin pills, but they don't seem to do me any good.
Doctor: Perhaps it's your diet. What have you been eating?
Simple Simon: Oh, are you supposed to eat as well?

Julie: That boy's annoying me.
Wendy: Why, he's not even looking at you.
Julie: I know, that's what's annoying me.

Clare: I see you are invited to Sandra's party?
Zoë: Yes, but I can't go. The invitation says 4 to 7, and I'm eight.

Father: What's that gash on your forehead?
Silly son: I bit myself.
Father: How on earth could you do that?
Silly son: I stood on a chair.

Teacher: Wendy, say something beginning with 'I',
Wendy: 'I is ...'
Teacher: No, Wendy, you must say I'm ...'
Wendy: All right, I am the ninth letter of the alphabet.

'My sister married an Irishman.'
'Oh really?'
'No, O'Grady.'

Thief: Quick – the police are coming – jump out of the wondow!
Accomplice: But we're on the thirteenth floor.
Thief: This is no time to be superstitious.

'Waiter, this coffee tastes like mud.'
'Well, sir, it was ground only five minutes ago.

'How did you get the puncture?'
'Ran over a milk bottle.'
'But didn't you see it?'
'No – a kid had it hidden under his coat.'

Percy's mother was worried about
the health of her neighbour.
'Percy,' she said, 'run and ask how
old Mrs Jones is.'
Soon Percy was back. 'Mrs Jones was
very annoyed.' he said. 'She said it
was none of your business how old
she is.'

Girl (standing in the middle of a
busy road): Officer, can you tell me
how to get to the hospital?
Policeman: Just stay right where
you are.

Did you hear about the cross-eyed
teacher?
He couldn't control his pupils.

Man (teaching his wife to drive): I
implore you, if you can't control it,
at least run it into something cheap.

During a violent storm, an old man
fell down in the street, and was dying
when help reached him. 'Get me a
rabbi,' he pleaded, 'I'm dying'.
'What's your name?'
'Patrick O'Grady. Get me a rabbi.'
'Surely you mean a priest.'
'Not at all – I wouldn't fetch the
priest out on a night like this.'

A lady went to visit a friend and
carried a small box with holes
punched in the top.
'What's in your box?' asked the
friend.
'A cat,' said the lady. 'You see I've
been dreaming about mice at night,
and I'm so scared, this cat is to catch
the.'
'But the mice are only imaginary,'
said the friend.
'So is the cat,' whispered the lady.

Mother: Shall I put the kettle on?
Father: No, dear, I don't think it
would suit you.

Albert: Darling, when we are
married do you think you will be
able to live on my income?
Una: I think so, darling, but what
will you live on?

157

Eric: I've been asked to get married hundreds of times.
Gloria: (surprised): Who by?
Eric: My parents.

Did you hear about the man who was so mean he fired a revolver outside his house on Christmas Eve then went inside and told his children that Father Christmas had committed suicide.

A motorist driving through the Cotswolds wasn't sure he was on the right road, and stopped his car to ask a farmer in a tractor. 'Which way is it to Cheltenham?' he asked.
'Don't know,' said the farmer.
'Well which way is it to Cirencester?'
'Don't know.'
'Don't you know anything?'
'Well,' said the farmer, 'I ain't lost.'

Roger: Don't you find it sticky
travelling to town these days?
Monty: Yes – it's jam all the way.

Scientist (at Scientific congress)
Gentlemen, we have now discovered
an acid that will eat up everything.
Voice from the floor: What are we
going to keep it in?

Clever Dick (to shoe salesman): How
much are your ten pound shoes?
Salesman: Five pounds a foot, sir.

'I've got a nasty pain in my right
foot, doctor.'
'I shouldn't worry – it's just old age.'
'Well, why doesn't the other one hurt
– I've had that just as long.'

Bertie: I got 100 in biology today,
and still didn't pass.
Father: (horrified) Why ever not?
Bertie: The answer was 200.

Two ears of corn ran up a hill. What
were they when they reached the
top?
Puffed Wheat.

Man in restaurant: Excuse me, waiter, how long have you been working here? *Waiter:* About two months, sir. *Man:* Oh, then it couldn't have been you who took my order.

Sheila: I bumped into Betty today. *Frank:* Was she pleased to see you? *Sheila:* Not really – we were both in our cars at the time.

Jesse James and his faithful steed Bronco were ambushed by a band of Apache. 'Well, ol' friend,' said Jesse – 'this looks like curtains for both of us.'
Bronco looked at his master – 'What do you mean *both* of us, White man!'

'Why are you so angry?' 'Well, it's all the rage.'

Physics teacher: Is there any
difference between lightning and
electricity?
Smart Alec: Yes – you don't have to
pay for lightning.

Eric: When they take out your
appendix, it's an appendectomy;
when they take your tonsils out it is a
tonsillectomy.
What is it when they remove a growth
from your head?
Derrick: I don't know.
Eric: A hair-cut.

Penny: What do you think of the new
vicar?
Bonny: Quite good – I didn't know
much about sin until he came.

Jeff: Why are you standing in that
bowl of water?
Goofy: The tablets I'm taking say 'To
be taken in water three times a day.'

I stayed on a farm and one day a
chicken died, so we had roast
chicken. The next day a pig died and
we had pork chops. The following
day the farmer died – so I left.

'Mummy, we're pretending to be elephants at the zoo. Will you help us?'
'Of course, dear. What am I to do?'
'Well, you're the lady who feeds us buns.'

Rosie: This ointment makes my leg smart.
Rob: Well why not rub some on your head!

When I started courting my wife, she made me lay all my cards on the table – Barclaycard, Access, American Express.

Wife (to motorist husband): I could do with a nice cup of tea.
Husband: Well we'd better look for a 'T' junction.

Charlie (in the bank): Has anyone dropped a wad of notes? Several people called out, 'Yes, I did.'
Charlie: Well I've just found the rubber band.

Patient: Doctor, do you think lemons are healthy?
Doctor: Well, I've never heard one complain.

Harry's girlfriend refused to marry him because of religious differences. He was poor and she worshipped money.

Two little girls in Hollywood were talking.
Samantha: What's your new daddy like?
Christine: Oh he's okay. Have you met him?
Samantha: Yes, we had him last year.

Paula: Why are you plugging your
guitar into the lamp standard?
Peter: I like light music.

The doctor came to remove the
plaster cast from the old lady's leg.
'What a relief,' she said.'Now can I
climb stairs again?'
'Of course,' said the doctor.
'That's good,' said the old lady.
'You've no idea what a job it was
shinning up and down that
drainpipe.'

'How much is that bird?'
'Three pounds, sir.'
'I'll have it. Will you send me the
bill?'
'I'm sorry, sir, you'll have to take the
whole bird.'

'Did you hear the one about the piece
of rope?'
'No.'
'Aw, skip it.'

The show-off at the party was at it
again.
'What's he doing now?' asked Brown.
'Oh, he's doing his impression of a
river,' said Jones.
'Small at the head and big at the
mouth.'

Spike: Why is your dog running around in circles?
Mike: He's a watchdog, and he's winding himself.

Andy: What's the best thing to take when you are run down?
Sandy: The number of the car that hit you.

Steve: What kind of a dog is that?
Stan: It's a police dog.
Steve: It doesn't look like one.
Stan: Of course not. He's in the secret service.

Mayor (to Visitor): What do you think of our town band?
Visitor: I think it ought to be.
Mayor (puzzled): Ought to be what?
Visitor: Banned.

Barry: I wish I had enough money to buy an aeroplane.
Garry: What do you want an aeroplane for?
Barry: I don't. I just wish I had that much money.

Little Diana: Can you stand on your head?
Lulu: No, I can't get my feet up high enough.

Vic: I've changed my mind.
Dick: Thank goodness. Does the new one work any better?

Jackson: Why do you have two 'L' plates on your car?
Johnson: One is for my wife who's learning to drive – the other is for her mother in the back who's learning to be a back-seat driver.

Two ladies met after a long time.
Mrs Hughes: I believe your son is a
very good football player. What
position does he play?
Mrs Evans: Oh, I believe he's one of
the drawbacks.

The judge was only 4 feet 2 inches
tall.
–A little thing sent to try us.

Teacher: Hands up all those who
wish to go to Heaven. All the
children put up their hands, except
for little Barbara.
Teacher: Barbara, don't you want to
go to Heaven?
Barbara: Well, miss, me mum said I
had to go straight home after school.

Teacher: Now, Willie, if you bought
fifty apples for ten pence what would
each one be?
Willie: Rotten – at that price they'd
have to be.

Owner of rather decrepit hotel: Yes,
we have a room, but you'd have to
make your own bed.
Desperate traveller: That's okay.
Owner of Hotel: Right – there's a
hammer, and saw, and some nails.

Young angler: Is this a good river
for fish?
Old Angler: It must be – I can't get
any of them to come out.

> *Brown:* Green stole a calendar.
> What do you think the judge gave
> him?
> *White:* Twelve months.

Do twins born in Amsterdam speak
Double Dutch?

Auntie: Well, Billy, how do you like
school?
Billy: Closed.

> *Dicky:* Stan reminds me of a fence.
> *Micky:* What makes you say that?
> *Dicky:* He runs around a lot but
> never gets anywhere.

The science class had been asked to
write a five-page essay on nutrition.
When Barney handed in his essay the
teacher said, 'But I asked for five
pages – and you've only done one
page.'
'I know, said Barney. 'I was writing
about condensed milk.'

'Charlie,' called out the news editor to his cub reporter, 'did you get that story about the man who sings tenor and baritone at the same time?' 'There's no story, sir,' said the reporter. 'The man has two heads.'

'Can I buy a television licence for half-price?'
'Certainly not – why should you?'
'Well, I can only see with one eye.'

'Do you sell dog's meat?'
'Only if they come with their owners.'

Vic: She sure gave you a dirty look.
Dick: Who?
Vic: Mother Nature!

A large hole was discovered in the walls surrounding the Carefree Nudist Camp at Brownham-on-Sea. The police are looking into it.

The Income Tax inspector had been visiting the school to talk about taxes. 'I'm going to tell you now about indirect taxes. Can anybody tell me what an indirect tax is?' 'A dog licence' said Smart Alec. 'Why is that?' asked the Inspector. 'The dog doesn't pay it.'

Mrs Grabbit: Darling, the woman next door has a coat exactly like mine.
Mr Grabbit: I suppose that's a hint that you want a new coat?
Mrs Grabbit: Well, it would be cheaper than moving house.

Father (going through his morning mail): I see Mrs Simpkins has notified us of her change of address.
Mother: She's lucky – it's years since I've had a change of a dress.

'My brother's so mean – he promised me a food mixer for a wedding present, and when it came I opened the parcel and there it was – a wooden spoon.'

Bossy lady: I throw myself into everything I undertake.
Fed-up neighbour: Well, why not go and dig a deep well.

Mr Ward: Doctor says I must get rid of twenty pounds.
Mr Ward: I'll help you dear. I'll go out and buy a new dress and you'll get rid of twenty pounds in no time.

Benjie was sent to the greengrocers
for three pounds of bananas. After
he came home his mother phoned
the shop and complained, 'I sent my
son for three pounds of bananas
and you've only given him two.'
'Madam,' said the shopkeeper, 'my
scales are correct. Have you weighed
your son?'

'My wife is so thin when she goes to
the park, the ducks throw her bread.'

Goofy's mother told him to get out of
the house – and suggested he go
window-shopping.
He did, and came back with five
windows.

Leslie: Did your mother go in for
weight-lifting?
Wesley: No,why?
Leslie: Well, how did she ever raise a
dumb–bell like you?

Tony: Where do you have the longest
view in the world?
Tim; I've no idea. Where?
Tony: By a roadside where there are
telephone poles, because then you
can see from pole to pole.

Teacher: What did James Watt do when he saw steam coming from the kettle?
Bright boy: He decided to make a nice cup of tea.

'Waiter, there's a fly in my soup.'
'If you throw it a pea it will play water polo.'

Mother: Where are you off to, Hubert?
Hubert: I'm going to watch a solar eclipse.
Mother: Alright, dear, but don't get too close.

Vera: Is your electric toaster a pop-up?
Val: No, it's a Red Indian model.
Vera: What's that?
Val: It sends up smoke signals.

Phil: My girlfriend's like the back of a watch.
Bill: What do you mean?
Phil: She's always behind time.

'Why does George work as a baker?'
'To earn an honest crust.'

A little boy at the seaside saw a beautiful new Rolls Royce parked on the promenade, and with his metal-ended spade he scratched several lines across its side. His father, who was following him, clouted him. 'What have I told you,' he said. 'If you break that spade, you won't get another one.'

A baby mouse saw a bat for the first time. He ran home yelling, 'Mummy, mummy, I've just seen an angel.'

Effie and George had been going steady for thirty-five years. One day after reading a love-story, Effie said, 'Let's get married, George.'
'Don't be silly,' said George. 'Who'd marry us at our time of life?'

Steve: I think dentists must be very unhappy at their work.
Dave: Why do you think so?
Steve: Well, they always look down in the mouth.

Mother: When that horrid boy threw stones at you, you should have come to me instead of throwing them back at him.
Jimmy: What good would that do? You can't hit the side of a house.

Teacher: If you washed cars for twenty people and they each gave you twenty pence, what would you get?
Gilbert: A new bicycle.

Policeman (apprehending a burglar): Anything you say may be held against you.
Burglar: Miss World.

Artist: You're the first model I've ever kissed.
Model: I bet you say that to all your models. How many have you had?
Artist: Well, there was a vase of flowers, the duckpond, the loaf of bread . . .

The time and motion study expert stopped to speak to the glamorous typist. 'I'm bound to tell you that I shall put in my report that you waste too much time on your appearance.' 'Go ahead,' she said, 'but I've only been here two months and I'm engaged to the boss, so it's not been entirely wasted.'

'What was Dick Turpin famous for?'
'He was one of the first road-users to cause a hold-up.'

'Beneath my husband's cold hard exterior – there's a cold, hard interior.'

Molly: What's the last thing you take off before going to bed?
Harold: My feet off the floor.

Bernie: Dad, would you do my arithmetic for me.
Dad: No, son, it wouldn't be right.
Bernie: Well, at least you could try.

Religious teacher: When was medicine first mentioned in the Bible?
Brian: When the Lord gave Moses two tablets.

Friend: I suppose being a dentist is very interesting.
Dentist: Not really – the drilling gets a bit boring.

Ted: What was it the hungry donkey said when he only had thistles to eat?
Ned: Thisle have to do.

Mr Briggs was making a knotty pine bookcase. His young son pointed to it and said, 'What are those holes for?'
'They're *knot* holes,' replied his father.
'Well,' said the lad, 'if they're not holes, what are they?'

Stewart: Mum, can I have five pence
for the old man who's crying
outside?
Mother: of course, dear, but what's
the old man crying about?
Stewart: He's crying 'Ice lollies,
fivepence each.'

Office Manager: How well can you
type?
Dolly: Oh not very well, but I can
rub out at sixty-five words a minute.

Physics teacher: Now on your
papers, I want you to write down
what you know about nuclear fission.
He was taken aback to read on
Jimmy Brown's paper 'Nothing.'

Ollie was looking at cars with a view
to buying one.
He pointed to a lovely streamlined
job: 'Is that a fast car?' he asked the
salesman. 'Fast,' said the salesman.
'If you got in that car now you'd be in
John o'Groats by two o'clock
tomorrow.'
Ollie went home to think about it but
came back next day. 'I've decided not
to buy it,' he said, 'I can't think of
any reason why I should be in John
o'Groats at two o'clock tomorrow.'

Tim at boarding school, sent this telegram to his father asking for money: 'No mon, no fun, your son.' Back came the reply, 'How sad, too bad, your dad.'

Smart Alec: What goes up a bell rope wrapped in greaseproof paper? *Clever Dick:* The lunchpack of Notre Dame.

The office manager looked towards his secretary who was absorbed in painting her fingernails.
'Miss Bright,' he said, 'I'd like to compliment you on your work – but when are you going to do any?'

Polly: Why are you putting starch in your whisky?
Billy: Because I want a nice stiff drink.

A man in a train leaned forward and spoke to the man sitting opposite him.

'Do you realise,' he said, 'that you are reading your newspaper upside down?'

'Of course I realise it,' snapped the other. 'Do you think it's easy?'

After the telephone had been installed in her home, the lady called the operator.

'My telephone cord is too long,' she said. 'Would you please pull it a little from your end?'

Parents spend the first part of a child's life teaching him to walk and talk, and the rest of his childhood making him sit down and keep quiet.

Prison Officer: Sir, I have to report that ten prisoners have broken out.
Governor: Blow the whistles, sound the alarms, alert the police ...
Prison Officer: Shouldn't we call the doctor first – it looks as if it might be measles.

Andy: Why were the soldiers tired on April Fool's Day?
Sandy: Because they'd just had a March of thirty-one days.

When rooting round in the attic
Gordon found the old family Bible,
and when he opened it a large
pressed leaf fell out.
'Oh,' he said, 'Adam must have left
his clothes here.'

Maisie: Does a giraffe get a sore
throat if he gets his feet wet?
Daisy: I suppose so – but not until
the next week.

Goofy Gus had a rope hanging from
a tree outside his window.
'What's that for?' asked his brother.
It's my weather forecaster,' said
Gus. 'When it moves, it's windy, and
when it's wet, it's raining.'

Pete: Why do you always part your
hair in the middle?
Steve: So that I will be evenly
balanced when I ride my bicycle.

Lady customer: I'd like a shirt for
my husband?
Assistant: Yes, madam, what size?
Lady customer: I don't know, but I
can just get both my hands round his
neck, if that's any help.

Jack: Did I ever tell you about the
time I came face to face with a lion?
Joe: No, what happened?
Jack: Well, there I was without a
gun. The lion growled menacingly,
and crept closer and closer ....
Joe: Good heavens! What did you
do?
Jack: I moved to the next cage.

Pam: You see, doctor, I'm always
dizzy for half an hour after I get up
in the morning.
Doctor: Well, try getting up half an
hour later.

Little Bobby came home from
school very fed up. 'I wish I'd lived in
the olden days,' he said.
'Oh, why?' said his mother.
'Because then I wouldn't have so
much history to learn.'

Worried lady passenger: Captain do
ships this size sink very often?
Captain: No, madam, never more
than once.

Mother was telling father what a naughty girl Debbie had been. She had had a fight with the boy opposite. 'It's all the fault of those dreadful Higgins children,' she said. 'She learned about biting and hair-pulling from them.'
'Yes,' said Debbie, 'but kicking on the shins was my own idea.'

A small boy was peering through a hole in a hedge of a Nature Camp. His friend came up to him and asked: 'Roger, what can you see? Are they men or women in there?'
'I can't tell,' replied Roger. 'None of them have any clothes on.'

Linda: Mummy, why do you have some grey hair?
Mummy: I expect it's because you are so naughty and cause me so much worry.
Linda: Oh – you must have been terrible to Grandma.

Auntie May: Well, Susan, what are you going to do when you're as big as your mother?
Susan: Go on a diet.

Clerk at Job Centre: Well they want somebody at the Eagle Laundry. Would you like to work there?
Young man: Well I've never washed any eagles, but I'm willing to give it a try.

Teacher: Sammy, what is water?
Sammy: Water is a colourless liquid that turns black when I put my hands in it.

In the snake-house at the zoo, one snake said to another:
'Are we supposed to be poisonous?'
'Why?'
'Well, I've just bitten my lip.'

Gilbert: My wife's a kleptomaniac.
Donald: Is she taking anything for
it?

Fred: What was a tortoise doing on
the M.1?
Bill: About two miles an hour.

Graham: Why is the nose in the
middle of the face?
Mike: Because it's the centre.

Teacher: Which is more important,
the sun or the moon?
Effie: The moon.
Teacher: Why do you think so?
Effie: Well the moon shines at night
when it's dark, but the sun shines in
the day when it's light anyway.

Mother: Terry did you fall down
with your good trousers on?
Terry: Yes, mum, there wasn't time
to take them off.

Brian: My wife has a marvellous
mother – she's 82 and hasn't got one
grey hair.
Bernie: Gosh, that's wonderful.
Brian: Yes – she's completely bald.

Doris: Why do they put telephone
wires so high?
Morris: To keep up the
conversation.

Father: How were your marks in the
exam, son?
Son: Under water.
Father: What do you mean?
Son: Below C level.

Reggie: I shall buy a farm two miles
long and a half inch wide.
Roger: What would you grow on a
farm that size?
Reggie: Spaghetti.

Emmy: How do you make notes of
stone?
Jamie: I don't know.
Emmy: Just rearrange the letters.

Norman: I understand your brother
had an accident when he joined the
submarine service?
Alan: Yes – he couldn't get out of the
habit of opening the windows at
night when he went to bed.

Clive: I saw you pushing your bicycle
to work this morning.
Ben: Yes, I was so late I didn't have
time to get on it.

Jed: Why did the pioneers cross to
the West in covered wagons?
Ned: I suppose they didn't want to
wait forty years for a train.

Two men sat next to each other in the
Doctor's waiting room.
'I'm aching from arthritis.' said one.
'I'm B. Bent from Birmingham,'
said the other. 'Glad to know you.'

Husband: You hadn't a rag on your
back when I married you.
Wife: Well, I've certainly got plenty
now.

Teacher: Desmond, this is the fifth
day this week you've had to stay
behind after school. What have you
to say for yourself?
Desmond: I'm certainly glad it's
Friday.

Tim: Is it legal for a man to marry his widow's sister?
Tom: Hardly – that man would be dead.

Phil: May I have a hot-dog?
Bill: With pleasure.
Phil: No – with sauce and pickles, please.

A soldier was walking along a country road with a pack on his back, and was offered a lift by a driver with an old dilapidated truck. The driver noticed the soldier was still carrying his pack on his back. 'Why don't you take that thing off your back?' said the driver. 'Well your truck seems so old, I thought I'd help by carrying this load myself.'

1st Cannibal: Am I late for lunch?
2nd Cannibal: Yes, everybody's
eaten.

Emily: Why is the sky so high?
Lou: So the birds won't bump their
heads.

Silly Billy: I eat small pieces of
metal every day.
Friend: Why do you do that?
Silly Billy: It's my staple diet.

'My husband is so mean he
complained to the doctor that he'd
got better before his medicine was
used up.'

Dickie: I think girls are too biased.
Rickie: What do you mean?
Dickie: It's bias this and bias that –
till we're broke.

Dentist: What sort of filling would
you like in your tooth?
Little Jemima: Chocolate, please.

Archie: I'm glad I'm back from
holiday – it rained all the time.
Reggie: It couldn't have been that
bad; you've got a nice tan.
Archie: That's not tan, it's rust.

'I'm afraid this food is all going to waist,' said the fat lady as she sat down to her dinner.

A Scotsman died and went to Heaven.
'Hi there,' he called. 'I'm Jock MacTavish and I've been sent to Heaven.'
'Go away,' called St Peter, 'I'm not going to make porridge just for one.'

Briggs: My uncle disappeared when he was on safari.
Bloggs: What happened to him?
Briggs: My dad says something he disagreed with ate him.

'If my husband ever had any get-up-and-go, it had got up and gone before I met him.'

Landlady (to young man who is seeking accommodation): I like to keep my house quiet – have you any children?
Young man: No.
Landlady: Any musical instruments, radio, cat or dog or other pet?
Young man: No – but my fountain pen scratches a little.

A man registered at a small hotel, and asked the manager, 'Are the sheets clean?'
'Of course they are,' said the manager. 'I washed them myself this morning – if you don't believe me you can feel them; they're still damp.'

Jack: My uncle swallowed a frog.
Jill: Goodness, did it make him sick?
Jack: Sick! He's liable to croak any minute.

A theatrical impresario was approached by a man who was bankrupt. 'I have a suggestion to put to you,' he said. 'Put £20,000 in the bank for my wife, 'he said, 'and I'll commit suicide on your stage ... all London will come to see it.'
'No thanks,' said the impresario. 'What could you do for an encore?'

191

Father: Where did your mother go?
Son: She's round at the front.
Father: I know what she looks like, I want to know where she is.

Dan: My kid brother thought a football coach had four wheels.
Stan: How many does it have?

Caller at door: Do you believe in the hereafter, madam?
Woman: Yes.
Caller: Well, I'm the landlord, and I'm hereafter the rent.

Beryl: What happened to the human cannon-ball at the circus?
Daryl: He got fired.

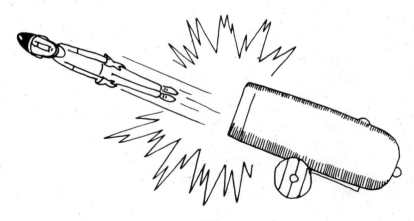

Garry: I went to see a psychiatrist
about my poor memory.
Barry: What did he do?
Garry: He made me pay in advance.

Garry: (to his bride): Would you be
very angry with me if I confess that
my upper teeth are false?
Gloria: Of course not, darling. Now I
can relax and take off my wig, my
inflatable bra and my wooden leg.

Jessica: Is it correct to say that you
water your horse?
Mother: Yes, dear.
Jessica: Then I'm going to milk my
cat.

A little chap was walking home late
at night, when he was attacked from
behind. He fought like mad, but
finally the thieves got him down and
searched his pockets. All they found
was ten pence.
'Why did you put up such a fight for
tenpence?' one asked.
'I thought you were after the two
hundred pounds in my shoe.'

Joe: When does a bed change size?
Jack: At night, when two feet are
added to it.

Two Hippies walked into a restaurant but were stopped at the door. 'You can't come in here without a tie,' the doorman said.

'Okay man,' said one Hippie and left, returning a few minutes later wearing a tie.

The doorman turned to the other Hippie. 'What about him?' he said.

'Him?' said the Hippie, 'That's my wife!'

Steve: How did you get that black eye?
Stan: I got hit by a guided muscle.

Bus conductor: Come down – you can't stand on the top of this bus.
Goofy Gus: And why not?
Bus conductor: It's a single decker.

Mandy: Where does Friday come before Thursday?
Sandy: In a dictionary.

Nellie: I'm very glad I wasn't born in
Spain.
Wallie: Why is that?
Nellie: I can't speak a word of
Spanish.

Ambulance men (to boy injured on
the road): Tell me your name, son so
that I can notify your family.
Boy: My family already know my
name.

Cecil: What is black and white and
red all over?
Algy: A newspaper?
Cecil: No, a sunburnt zebra.

Teacher: What does HNO_3 stand
for?
Smart Alec: Er .. let me see now ...
it's on the tip of my tongue.
Teacher: Well, you'd better spit it out
quick – it's nitric acid.

Pamela visited the greengrocers
with her mother, and the
greengrocer gave her an apple.
'What do you say Pamela?' said her
mother.
'Will you please peel it?' replied
Pamela.

Clive: How old is your brother?
Steve: He's a year old.
Clive: Well I've got a dog who's a year old and he can walk twice as far as your brother.
Steve: He's got twice as many legs.

Customer: Waiter, I don't like all the flies in here.
Waiter: Well, just point out the ones you don't like and I'll have them put out.

Father: Who gave you that black eye?
Jack: Nobody – I had to fight for it.

Daisy: Do you know how to make a Maltese cross?
Maisie: Stick your finger in his eye.

Auntie: Come on, Billy dear, eat up
your cabbage, it's good for growing
children.
Billy: I don't want to grow any
children.

Judge: You've been convicted six
times of this offence. Aren't you
ashamed of yourself?
Prisoner: No, your Honour. I don't
think one should be ashamed of one's
convictions.

Les: What can run across the floor
but has no legs?
Des: Water.

Eric: Why can't a bicycle stand up
by itself?
Derrick: Because it's two tyred.

Beryl: Why are contortionists
thrifty people?
Cheryl: Because they can make both
ends meets.

Briefing Officer (to new air hostess):
What would you do if you found
yourself in a shallow dive?
Air Hostess: I'd drink up quickly
and get out.

Doctor: You need glasses.
Patient: How can you tell?
Doctor: I knew as soon as you came in the window.

Teacher: (to Parent on open day: Yes, Mr Brown, I think your son will go down in History ....
Mr Brown: Oh, really ...
Teacher: Yes, and in English, Maths and Science.

Rupert: How many dead people are there in a cemetery?
Robert: All of them.

Teacher: We all know that when certain substances are heated they expand, and when they are cooled they contract. Can anyone give me an example of this?
Freddie: Well, in the winter the days are short and in the summer the days are long.

198

Tilly: Why did the germ cross the microscope?
Billy: To get to the other slide.

Wally: If you were surrounded by twenty lions, fifteen tigers, and twelve leopards, how would you get away from them.
Sally: I'd wait for the merry-go-round to stop and get off!

An American was seen putting on his bathing trunks in the middle of a desert. An Arab rode past and said to him; You know, the sea is six hundred miles from here?'
'Six hundred miles,' said the American. 'Brother – some beach!'

Sherlock Holmes was visited by his friend Doctor Watson.
'Morning, Watson,' said the great detective – 'Isn't it a bit warm to be wearing your red flannel underwear?'
'How amazing, Holmes!' How on earth could you detect that I am wearing my red flannel underwear?'
'Elementary, my dear Watson. You've forgotten to put on your trousers.'

The old man at the cinema was grubbing round under the seat to the annoyance of the lady next to him.
'I've dropped my toffee,' he explained.
'Can't you leave it until the end?' she said crossly.
'No, it's got my false teeth stuck to it.'

Teacher: Can anybody tell me something about Christopher Columbus?
Desmond: He discovered America and was very economical.
Teacher: How do you mean, economical?
Desmond: He was the only man to travel thirty thousand miles on a galleon.

Mother: I've told you a million times not to exaggerate.

Sandra: Darling, will you love me still when my hair has gone all grey? *Donald:* Of course I will. If I loved you when your hair was blonde, then brunette then black then red – why should grey make any difference?

Noah (to his son Ham who is fishing): Go easy on the bait, remember I've only got two worms.

Angie: Why do storks lift only one leg?
Georgie: If they lifted the other leg they'd fall over.

Wynn: Whenever I'm down in the dumps I buy new clothes.
Len: So that's where you get them!

Briggs: What's worse than raining
cats and dogs?
Bloggs: Hailing taxis.

Policeman: I'm afraid I'm going to
lock you up for the night.
Hooligan: Why – what's the charge?
Policeman: Oh, there's no charge –
it's all part of the service.

A spoilt child was making a nuisance
of himself laying in the aisle of the
aeroplane to the particular
annoyance of one passenger who
wanted to doze.
'I say, kid,' he said, 'why don't you go
outside and play!'

Milly: What are you writing?
Molly: I'm writing a letter to myself.
Milly: What does it say?
Molly: How do I know – I won't get it
till tomorrow.

Flora: How much money do you
have on you?
Dora: Between £68 and £70.
Flora: Isn't that rather a lot to be
carrying around?
Dora: No – Two pounds isn't very
much.

Lady patient: I seem to get fat in certain places, Doctor, what should I do?
Doctor: Stay out of those places.

Dopey Dan: What's that iron box for?
Gormless Gus: That's my pillow.
Dopey Dan: Won't it be a bit hard?
Gormless Gus: Not when I've stuffed it with feathers.

Mother: You're mopping up the spilled coffee with cake?
Brenda: Well, it's sponge cake, isn't it?

Jimmy: Mum, can I go out and play?
Mother: What, with those holes in your trousers?
Jimmy: No, with the kids next door.

Diner: Waiter, this meat isn't fit for a pig.
Waiter: I'll take it back, sir, and bring you some that is.

Gertie: (shaking her husband):
Bertie, I heard a mouse squeak.
Bertie: What do you want me to do – oil it?

Customer: Waiter, I asked for lentil soup – this tastes like soap.
Waiter: Oh, sorry sir – that must be tomato – the lentil tastes like petrol.

Freddie: I can't leave you.
Trudie: Do you love me so much?
Freddie: No, you're standing on my foot.

Cecil: How can one person make so many mistakes in a single day?
Basil: I get up early.

Hotel Manager: Well, sir did you enjoy your stay with us?
Guest: Yes, but it seems hard to leave the place so soon after buyin; it.

A woman walked into a smart dress
shop in Bond Street and said to an
assistant:
'Would you take that dress with the
red flowers, and flowing scarf out of
the window, please?'
'Certainly, madam, I'll do that right
away,'
'Thank you,' said the woman, 'it
annoys me every time I pass.'

Psychiatrists inform us that one out
of four people are mentally ill. So
check your friends – if three of them
are all right – it must be you!

Mrs Griggs: My husband beats me
up every morning.
Mrs Spriggs: How terrible!
Mrs Griggs: Yes, he gets up at seven
and I get up at eight.

Doris: Now that we're engaged, I hope you'll give me a ring.
Horace: Of course, what's your number?

Policeman: Here – why are you trying to cross the road in this dangerous place? There's a zebra crossing just a few yards up the road.
Pedestrian: Well, I hope he's having better luck than I am.

Terry: Why is the Post Office not having to have telephone poles any longer?
Gerry: Because they're long enough.

Pat: How did you manage to crash your car?
Matt: You see that ditch over there?
Pat: Yes.
Matt: Well, I didn't.

Charlie: Why does it rain, dad?
Dad: To make the grass and the
flowers grow.
Charlie: Well, why does it rain on the
pavement?

Young Joey: My mother has the
worst memory in the world?
Young Billy: Does she forget
everything?
Young Joey: No – she remembers
everything.

Tess: Jumping off Blackpool Tower
isn't dangerous.
Jess: How on earth can you say that?
Tess: The jumping isn't dangerous –
it's the sudden stop that is.

Charlie: Mum, Buster's broke a
window.
Mother: How did he do that?
Charlie: I threw a stone at him and he
ducked!

'Doctor, my hair keeps falling out.
Can you recommend anything to
keep it in?'
'How about a cardboard box!'

Husband: This coffee tastes awful.
Wife: I can't understand why. It's fresh – I made it in my dressing gown.
Husband: No wonder it tastes funny.

There was a knock on the door when a lady was taking her bath.
'Who's there?' she called.
'Blind man!'
Hearing this the lady said she'd be right there, and stepping out of the bath, she opened the door.
'Where do you want me to put these Venetian blinds, lady?' said the surprised man.

Ted: Did you say your dog's bark was worse than his bite?
Ned: Yes.
Ted: Then for heaven's sake, don't let him bark – he just bit me.

Teacher: How old were you on your last birthday?
Brian: Seven.
Teacher: And how old will you be on your next birthday?
Brian: Nine.
Teacher: That's impossible.
Brian: No it isn't, sir. I'm eight today.

Pilot: First one wing came off, then the other.
Young lady: Good heavens, what did you do?
Pilot: I grabbed a drumstick and had a second helping.

Percy: If you won't marry me, I'll hang myself in front of your house.
Marylyn: Please don't, you know father doesn't like to see you hanging around.

Father: The man who marries my daughter will get a prize.
Claud: Can I see the prize first?

Tramp: I haven't had more than one meal this week, lady.
Fat Lady: How I wish I had your willpower.

Mother: How do you like your new teacher?
Susie: Not very much.
Mother: Why is that?
Susie: She told me to sit in front for the present, but she didn't give me any present.

Teacher: Why are you late this morning, Sandra?
Sandra: Because of the sign down the road.
Teacher: What sign?
Sandra: It says 'Go Slow – School ahead'.

Wally: I'm having trouble with impetigo, miss.
Teacher: Good heavens, where do you have it?
Wally: I don't have it – I just can't spell it.

Teacher: If you had ten pence and you asked your father for another tenpence, how much would you have?
Archie: Ten pence.
Teacher: You don't know your arithmetic.
Archie: You don't know my father.

Andy: I'd like to marry a girl who could take a joke.
Sally: That's the only kind you'll get.

Keith: Don't you think I sing with feeling?
Maisie: No – if you had any feeling you wouldn't sing.

Ron: What does it mean when the barometer is falling?
Don: It means that whoever nailed it up didn't do a very good job.

Barney: Why didn't they bury the Duke of Wellington with full military honours in 1850?
Bernie: Because he didn't die until 1852.

Mickie: Why did Robinson Crusoe always have long week-ends?
Dickie: He got all his work done by Friday.

Dan: Have you ever hunted bear?
Sam: No, but I've been fishing in my shorts.

Duncan: Where does a seven foot gorilla sleep?
Duggie: Anywhere he wants to.

Commuter: What's the good of your timetable? The trains are never on time.
Porter: And how would you know they were late if it wasn't for the timetable?

Tramp: Would you give me 25 pence for a sandwich, lady?
Lady: I don't know – let me see the sandwich.

Customer: Waiter, why is this bath-bun all smashed up?
Waiter: You said you wanted a coffee and a bath-bun, and step on it, so I did.

Lindy: Can you skate?
Mandy: I don't know; I can't stand
up long enough to find out.

Teacher: But I told you all to draw a
ring, and you've drawn a square,
Willy.
Willy: It's a boxing-ring, miss.

Bertram: How did you manage to
pass the geometry test without doing
any studying?
Smart Alec: Oh, I knew all the
angles.

Tom: Will you lend me ten pounds?
Tim: I'm sorry, I can't spare ten
pounds.
Tom: All right – lend me ten pounds
and give me five pounds now. Then
I'll owe you five pounds, and you'll
owe me five pounds, and we'll call it
square.

Chrissie, the kleptomaniac, was very
grateful to her doctor for his helping
in curing her affliction. 'How can I
ever repay you, doctor?' she asked.
'Well, if you should have a remission,'
he said, 'I could do with some
binoculars.'

Clever Dick: How many peas are there in a pint?
Bozo: How many?
Clever Dick: One!

Two rich big-headed men met in a swanky hotel.
Said one: 'I'm thinking of buying all the gold-mines in the world.'
The other replied, 'I'm not sure I want to sell them.'

Visitor to Farm: Do you know how long cows should be milked?
Farmer: The same as short ones.

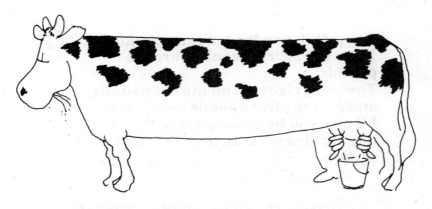

The bus was crowded and as one more man tried to get on the passengers wouldn't let him board.
'It's too crowded,' they said. 'Who do you think you are?'
'I'm the driver,' he said.

Teacher: John, give me an example
of a double negative.
John: I don't know none, miss.
Teacher: Correct.

Freda: My sister is black and blue
because she puts on cold cream, face
cream, wrinkle cream, vanishing
cream, hair cream, and skin cream
every night.
Rhoda: But why does that make her
black and blue?
Freda: She keeps on slipping out of
bed.

Gordon: What would you do if you
found £500,000.
Geoff: Well, if it was a poor person
who'd lost it, I'd return it.

Gracie: The trouble with you is
you're always wishing for something
you don't have.
Tracey: What else is there to wish
for?

'We're sending our little Willy to
camp for the summer.'
'Does he need a holiday?'
'No – we do.'

Polly: Mummy I got a hundred in
school today.
Mummy: That's splendid, dear.
What did you get a hundred for?
Polly: Two things. I got 50 in
English, and 50 in arithmetic.

'My son is a true hippy – he'd sooner
starve to death than eat a square
meal.'

Tessie: This hot weather gets me
down.
Bessie: Well, why don't you throw
the thermometer out of the window
and watch the temperature drop!

Buster: Oh, my new shoes hurt me
something awful.
Teddy: No wonder, you've got them
on the wrong feet.
Buster: But I haven't got any other
feet.

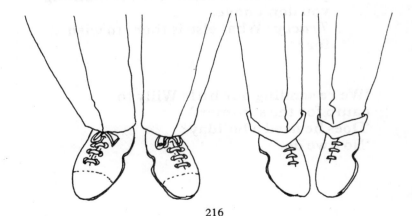

Willy: What does your mother do for
a headache?
Jimmy: She sends me out to play.

An old couple in Wales out walking
had lost their way, and darkness was
falling. They spotted a man and a
woman in a field tending their sheep,
and asked them how far it was to the
nearest town.
'Oh, five miles, isn't it,' said Ifan.
Seeing the old couple's faces fall,
Megan whispered, 'Make it two
miles, Ifan, can't you see how tired
they are.'

Sammy: There's a man at the door
with a wooden leg called Owen.
Father: What's his other leg called?

Penny: What is always coming but
never arrives?
Lenny: Tomorrow.

Newcomer: Bertie always wanted to
be a stage magician and saw
people in half.
Neighbour: Is he an only one?
Newcomer: Oh no, he has several
half-brothers and sisters.

Archie: What are you doing?
Reggie: I've just painted a picture of
a horse eating hay.
Archie: Where's the hay?
Reggie: The horse has eaten it.
Archie: Where's the horse?
Reggie: Well, it's gone – there's no
point in him hanging about when all
the hay's gone.

Chemistry teacher: Can anyone tell
me a deadly poison?
Tommy: Aviation.
Chemistry teacher: Aviation?
Tommy: Yes – one drop and you're
dead.

Learn from the mistakes of others –
you can't live long enough to make
them all by yourself.

Tina: Which members of an
orchestra can't you trust?
Tony: The fiddlers.

Patient: You were right when you said you'd have me on my feet and walking in no time.
Doctor: That's good; when did you start walking?
Patient: When I got your bill – I had to sell my car to pay it.

Judge: The next man to raise his voice in this court will be thrown out.
Prisoner: HOORAY!

Briggs: Is your house warm?
Bloggs: It should be. I gave it **three** coats last week.

Coroner (to widow): Can you remember what your husband's last words were, madam?
Widow: Yes, he said, 'I don't see how they can make a profit selling this salmon at ten pence a tin.'

The girlfriend of a hold-up man visited him in prison.
'The money,' he whispered, 'is it safe?'
'Safe as the bank of England,' she assured him. 'They've built a 25-story block of flats on top of it.'

The trumpet-player had been
blasting away all day, when there
was a knock on his door.
'I live next door to you,' he
explained. 'Do you know I work
nights?'
'No', said the trumpet-player, 'but if
you hum a few bars I'll get the
melody.'

Mavis: Does your cat have fleas?
Toots: Don't be silly, cats don't have
fleas, they have kittens.

Receptionist: Doctor, there's an
invisible man here to consult you.
Doctor: Tell him I can't see him.

Effie: I've just swallowed a bone.
Mother: Are you choking?
Effie: No, I'm serious.

The lady said a polite 'Good-
morning' to the Vicar as he passed.
'Mummy,' said Harry, 'who was that
man?'
'That's the man who married me,'
said Mother.
'In that case,' said Harry, 'who's that
man hanging around our house that
I call daddy?'

Ernie: How did you get that swelling
on your nose?
Bernie: I bent down to smell a brose.
Ernie: There's no 'b' in rose.
Bernie: There was in this one.

Mrs Hobbs to neighbour: 'My
husband always called a spade a
spade until he tripped over one in
the dark.'

The man coming round after being
involved in an accident, found
himself in hospital, and turned to
the man in the next bed:
'Was I brought here to die?' he
asked.
Cockney patient: 'No, you were
brought here yesterdie.'

Willy: What makes you think your
mother wants to get rid of you?
Wally: Why else would she pack my
lunch every day in a road map?

Sidney: Show me a tough guy and
I'll show you a coward.
Briggy: Well, I'm a tough guy.
Sidney: I'm a coward.

Neighbour: Your daughter is only
four and can spell her name
backwards? What's her name?
Proud Mother: Ada.

Molly: Have you heard the latest. It's
all over the building.
Milly: What's all over the building?
Molly: The roof.

Monty: I can stay under water for
ten minutes.
Tony: Impossible.
Monty got a tumbler of water and
put it on his head.

Patient: Doctor, I'm very bothered about my breathing, Doctor.
Doctor: Oh, we'll soon find something to stop that.

Conceited pundit: Have you seen me on television?
Acquaintance: Yes, on and off.
Pundit: And how did you like me?
Acquaintance: Off.

Eddie: If two's company and three's a crowd, what are four and five?
Edie: Nine.

Buster: Why can't two elephants go into a swimming pool at the same time?
Lester: Because they have only one pair of trunks.

The family had enjoyed their
holiday on the farm and wrote again
the following year to book a
fortnight.
In his letter, Mr Brown wrote to the
farmer 'The only thing we didn't
enjoy was the noise the pigs made.'
The farmer wrote back, 'Don't
worry, sir, we haven't had any pigs
here since you left.'

Roger: Oh, he's a friendly dog, he'll
eat off your hand.
Lodger: That's what I'm afraid of.

Blondie: I'd like a knickerbocker
glory, with double creams,
raspberry syrup, chocolate chips,
and lots of ice cream.
Waiter: Would you like a cherry on
top?
Blondie: Oh no – I'm on a diet.

Des: Do you know why bears have
fur coats?
Les: Well, they'd look a bit silly in
plastic macs.

The Texan was showing Laird
Macintosh round his vast ranch, and
boasting that he had 4,000 head of
cattle.
'Well, man,' said the Laird – 'I have
5,000 cattle in my lands in Scotland.'
The Texan quickly replied, 'What I
meant, my lord, was that I have 4,000
head of cattle in the freezer.'

Shopper: What? 80 pence a pound
for butter? Down the road it's only
60 pence.
Grocer: Well, why don't you go and
get it there?
Shopper: Well, they're out of it.
Grocer: Well, when I'm out of it,
mine's only 50 pence a pound.

Householder (to insurance salesman)
Give me one good reason why I
should purchase your insurance
policy.
Insurance salesman: Well, last week
I sold a policy to a man near here,
and the following day he was
trapped under a lorry, and we paid
out £10,000. Just think, you might be
just as lucky.

The helicopter had been on its mercy mission combing the snowy wastes of Scotland. The pilot spotted a curl of smoke coming from a half-buried chimney, and descended. He called down through the chimney: 'Is there anybody there?'

'Yes. Who are you?'

'We're the mountain rescue helicopter and we're hovering over your house.'

'Well, go away, we bought a flat off you last year.'

Lecturer to Chairman: May I sit on your right hand?

Chairman: You may – but I'll need it later to ring the bell with.

1000 LAUGHS

Throughout **1000 LAUGHS** twenty-six
crazy characters will be starring in our
jokes. Meet them all now! They are:

ANN	NINA
BEN	OSCAR
CLARE	PAM
DAN	QUENTIN
EVE	ROSE
FRED	SIMON
GILLIAN	TINA
HARRY	ULRIC *1
IVY	VAL
JOHN	WILLIAM
KEVIN	XANTIPPE *2
LILY	YORICK *3
MARK	ZOE

1. The name **ULRIC** actually
   means 'ruler of wolves'.
2. You may never have heard of
   **Xantippe (pronounced Zan-
   tippy)**, but she was the wife of
   Socrates, the Ancient Greek
   philosopher, and by all accounts
   she was a bit of a joker!
3. **YORICK**, of course, was a fool
   and the king's jester, and said
   by many to a numbskull too!

CATEGORIES. . . . .

1. **CRAZY JOKES**
The craziest laughs in the whole wide world!

2. **ANIMAL CRACKERS**
From the dog with no nose that smells terribly to the elephant that went away to forget. . . .

3. **GRAFFITI**
Hilarious scrawls from the walls.

4. **VERSE — AND WORSE!**
Potty poems and loony limericks.

5. **APRIL FOOLS!**
Practical jokes to play on your friends!

6. **DOCTOR, DOCTOR!**
Medical mirth to prove that laughter is the best medicine.

7. **RIDICULOUS RIDDLES**
How did Bo-Peep lose all her sheep? She had a crook with her!

8. **DAFFYNITIONS**
   Daft definitions that you won't find in
   any dictionary!

9. **WAITER, WAITER!**
   Crazy cooks, weird waiters, riotous
   restaurants and dotty diners!

10. **MAKE 'EM LAUGH!**
    Practical ways of making people laugh
    from funny faces to silly walks.

11. **BOOKSHELF**
    Laughter-making titles that no library
    should be without!

12. **CRAZY INSULTS**
    All you need to insult your friends. . . .
    just for a laugh!

Good Manners: The noise you don't make when you're eating soup.

 How does an intruder get into your house?

ˑмopuᴉм ɹǝpnɹʇuI

 DOCTOR: *What's the matter with you?*
LILY: *I've got water on the knee?*
DOCTOR: *How can you be so sure?*
LILY: *I dropped a bucketful on it.*

 There was a young lady from Gloucester,
Whose parents thought they had lost her.
From the fridge came a sound
And at last she was found.
The problem was — how to defrost her.

 Take some extra strong glue (taking care not to get it on your hands) and stick a 5p or 10p coin to the pavement. All you have to do is hide and watch passers-by try to pick it up!

'I won't say she's got buck teeth, but the last time she used her electric toothbrush, she blew every fuse in the house.'

232

I take the bus home every day, but my mother always makes me bring it back.

How do you stop moles digging up your garden?

Hide the spade.

Take a piece of paper and write the word 'What?' on it. Put the piece of paper in your pocket and say to a friend: 'I know what you're going to say next.' Your friend is certain to say: *'What?'* You can then produce your piece of paper to show that you were right!

GROWING VEGETABLES *by Rosa Carrots*

YORICK: *Doctor, doctor, come quickly. We can't get into the house.*
DOCTOR: *Well, that's hardly my concern.*
YORICK: *Yes, it is. The baby's swallowed the door key.*

ZENA: *Does this train stop at Liverpool Street?*
TINA: *If it doesn't there'll be a big crash.*

Why did Ivy laugh when the cow slipped over in the ice?

She knew it wasn't any use crying over spilt milk.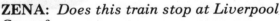

233

'*You've got beautiful hair. I wish you'd wear it more often.*'

'**Waiter, waiter, there's a flea in my soup!**'
'*Tell him to hop it!*'

WILLIAM: '*You know, Harry spends half his time trying to be witty.*'
GILLIAN: '*Yes. I suppose you could say he's a half-wit.*'

Traffic light: *A little green light that changes to red when your car approaches.*

NINA: '*Will you join me in a bowl of soup?*'
JOHN: '*Do you think there'll be room for both of us?*'

What do you give a pig with a sore trotter?

Oinkment.

234

DOCTOR: *Why did your wife hit you with a tennis racket?*
PATIENT: *Because she couldn't find her hockey stick.*

'Is that your real face, or are you still wearing a gas mask?'

Why do dragons sleep during the day?

Because they like to hunt knights.

There's only one thing wrong with Ann's face. It sticks out of her dress!

MARK: I once had a parrot for four years and it didn't say one word.
CLARE: It must have been tongue -tied.
MARK: No, it was stuffed.

Abundance: A party in a bakery.

DAN: *'Doctor, are you certain this bottle of medicine will cure my cold?'*
DOCTOR: *'Well, nobody's ever been back for a second bottle.'*

What would happen if an elephant sat in front of you at the cinema?

You'd miss most of the film!

235

Ulric had an extremely odd grandmother. In the winter, no matter how cold it was, she would go outside and get the coal in her nightie. Ulric bought her a shovel, but she said the nightie held more . . .

LILY: *It says in this book about food that Eskimos eat whale meat and blubber.*
OSCAR: *Well, you'd blubber too if you ate nothing but whale meat.*

GILLIAN: *Mummy, you know that vase that you said had been handed down from generation to generation?*
MOTHER: *Yes, dear.*
GILLIAN: *Well, this generation just dropped it.*

 IN THE COUNTRY *by Theresa Greene*

 I used to be a werewolf, but I'm alright nowoooooooooooooh!

 KEVIN: *You know that woman who moved next door? Well, she's got carrots growing out of her ears.*
TINA: *That must be awful for her.'*
KEVIN: *It's terrible. She planted cabbages.*

236

Where does it cost you £25 a head to eat?

In a cannibal restaurant.

You're probably not as stupid as you look. You couldn't possibly be.

 What's fishy and goes dot-dot-dash-dash and lives in Norway?

The Norse Cod.

QUENTIN: *There's a black cat in the dining-room.*
YORICK: *Black cats are supposed to be lucky.*
QUENTIN: *This one certainly is, he's just eaten your supper.*

 SIMON: *Doctor, doctor, I've just bitten my own ear!*
DOCTOR: *How on earth could you bite your own ear? It's impossible.*
SIMON: *No it's not. I stood on a chair so that I could reach.*

 Xantippe telephone the travel agent in London and asked:
'How long does it take to fly to Aberdeen?'
The travel agent said, **'Just a minute.'**
'Thank you,' said Xantippe and hung up.

'Have you ever been to the zoo? As a visitor I mean.'

 EASY MONEY *by Robin Banks*

 Motel: William Tell's sister.

There was a young lady named Perkins,
Who was extremely fond of small
    gherkins.
      One day at tea
      She ate fifty-three,
And pickled her internal workings.

IVY: *Doctor, doctor, my family think I'm mad.*
DOCTOR: *Why?*
IVY: *Because I like kippers.*
DOCTOR: *That's nonsense. I like kippers too.*
IVY: *You do? You must come round and see my collection, I've got thousands!*

 Who wears the biggest hat in the world?

The person with the biggest head, I suppose.

THE EXPLOSION *by Dinah Mite*

238

Place **TEN** matchsticks on the table and
challenge your friend to make a monkey
from them. When your friend gives up,
simply arrange the matches to spell the
word **A P E**, using two matches to make
the top of the letter **P**. You will have
made a monkey out of your friend!

BEN: *Why are you standing on one foot?*
DAN: *The doctor told me to eat a
balanced diet.*

Some people bring happiness wherever
they go; you bring happiness whenever
you go.

Dogmatic: A mechanical hound.

HARRY: *Waiter, waiter, what do you
call this?*
WAITER: *It's bean soup.*
HARRY: *I don't care what its been, what
is it now?*

VAL: *What's on the television tonight?*
PAM: *Same as always, a vase and the
goldfish bowl.*

CLARE: *'Mummy, are we
descended from apes?'*
MOTHER: *'I don't know,
dear, I never met your
father's family.'*

'Waiter, waiter, I want to complain about this disgusting meal. Bring me the chef at once.'

'I'm afraid I can't, sir. He's gone out to lunch.'

 THE FIRE ON THE GRASS by *Lorna Lite*

VICAR: *'Is this cricket ball yours?'*
SIMON: *'Did it do any damage?'*
VICAR: *'No.'*
SIMON: *'Then it's mine.'*

 To do a silly walk: Swing each leg as far forwards and backwards as it will go when you walk, and wave your arms up and down as you stride along.

 Did you hear about the woman that joined the Army rather than the Navy because she looked better in green than in blue?

 Why is a radio never complete?

It's always a wire-less.

A HOLE IN MY ROOF by *Lee King*

Aardvark: That which elderly people say the young don't like doing.

A bandy-legged policeman from Crewe
Said: 'I really don't know what to do.
I can stop without fuss
A car or a bus,
But bicycles simply go through.'

 I NEVER USED TO BE ABLE TO FINISH ANYTHING — BUT NOW I

How many letters are there in the alphabet on December 25th?

Twenty-five, because on that day we say No-el.

 'Is that your face or are you breaking it in for Frankenstein?'

'Doctor, doctor, I keep losing my memory.'
'When did this first happen?'
'When did what first happen?'

When did the waiter stop waiting?

When he got his just desserts.

Debate: What you put on a line to catch a fish.

Say to your friend on April 1st:
'Hey, Mark, you'd better keep your eyes open today.'
'Why?'
'If you don't you'll keep bumping into things!'

THE UNTIDY HAIRDRESSER *by Aaron Floor*

EVE: *What kind of dog is that?*
KEVIN: *It's a police dog.*
EVE: *Well, it doesn't look like a police dog to me.*
KEVIN: *It's in plain clothes, that's why.*

ROSE: *One more word from you, and I shall go home!*
FRED: *Taxi!*

Put your shirt and tie, or blouse, on back to front so that it looks as if your head has been turned around the wrong way. Then walk into a room with a perfectly straight face as if nothing is wrong, and see what happens!

What do you do with a wombat?

Play wom, of course!

XANTIPPE: *I feel dizzy every morning for half an hour when I get up. What can I do?*
DOCTOR: *Get up half an hour later.*

What do you call two vegetables that fall in love?

Sweethearts!

YORICK: *Well, doctor, how do I stand?*
DOCTOR: *I don't know. It's a miracle to me.*

THE OPTICIAN'S DAUGHTER
KEEPS MAKING A SPECTACLE OF
HERSELF.

FIRST DOG: *My name's Buster, what's yours?*
SECOND DOG: *I don't know, but I think it's Get-Down Boy.*

WHICH IS THE WAY OUT? *By Isadora Negsitt*

TEACHER: *Ann, will you tell me what the Order of the Bath is?*
ANN: *Well, miss, first there's Pam, then it's Dan, and then it's my turn to get in.*

 Denial: The main river of Egypt.

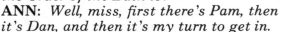

What's black and white and black and white and black and white?

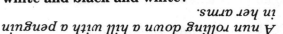

A nun rolling down a hill with a penguin in her arms.

'*Last night I dreamt I saw something in front of your house that made me very happy — a removal van.*'

'**Doctor, doctor, I keep thinking I'm a dog.**'
'*Sit down and tell me all about it.*'
'**I'm not allowed on the couch.**'

Lift-operator: '*We're at the first floor, you can get out now, son.*'
Quentin: '*Why did you call me son?*'
Lift-operator: '*Well, I brought you up, didn't I?*'

Sign in a restaurant in Holland:
'*Mothers, please wash your Hans before eating.*'

 I CAN TELL STORK FROM BUTTER — BUTTER CAN'T STAND ON ONE LEG.

Where did Humpty Dumpty put his hat?

Humpty Dumpet 'is 'at one the wall.

'*You can go back home now. They've finished cleaning your cage.*'

244

TEACHER: *Quentin, what is the outer part of a tree called?*
QUENTIN: *Don't know, miss.*
TEACHER: *Bark, boy, bark!*
QUENTIN: *Woof, woof.*

Impact: A theatrical show that imps perform.

 What is yellow and stupid?

Thick custard.

THE UGLIEST GIRL IN THE WORLD *by Ida Face*

What did the baby porcupine say when he backed into a cactus?

'Is that you, mother?'

VAL: *'Doctor, doctor, there's something wrong with my stomch.'*
DOCTOR: *'Well, keep your cardigan buttoned up an nobody will notice.'*

LILY: *'I haven't seen you for weeks.'*
IVY: *'Oh, so much has happened. I've had a tooth out and a new gas stove put in.'*

Hatchet: What a hen does to an egg.

245

Say that you will make the lunch.
Disappear into the kitchen and after five
or ten minutes call everybody to tell them
that lunch is ready. When they are seated
at the table, you will carefully carry bowls
of soup to them with a cloth, saying:
*'Now, be careful how you eat this because
it's very very hot.'*
Your victims will probably blow the soup
before tasting it. April Fools! They are in
for a shock because the soup is cold! You
haven't heated it at all.

There once was a man from Calcutta,
Who spoke with a terrible stutter.
At breakfast he said,
'Give me b-b-b-bread,
And b-b-b-b-b-b-butter.'

OSCAR: *'Waiter, why have you got your
thumb on my steak?'*
WAITER: *'Well, I don't want it to fall on
the floor again.'*

THE BANK ACCOUNT *by Xavier*
Munney

**What is white, has just one horn, and
gives milk?**

A milk float.

Fred rushed into his mother.
'*Mum,*' he puffed, '*is it true that an apple a day keeps the doctor away?*'
'**That's what they say,**' replied his mother.
'*Quick, give me an apple,*' said Fred, '*I've just broken the doctor's window.*'

'*I've got a minute to spare — tell me everything you know.*'

Why is the theatre a sad place?

Because the seats are in tiers.

How can you recognise rabbit stew?

It has hares in it.

PREVENT ACCIDENTS — START
DOING THINGS DELIBERATELY.

JOHN: '*I'll give this five pound note to anyone who is contented.*'
KEVIN: '*I'm very contented.*'
JOHN: '*Then you won't be needing this five pound note.*'

'*Is that your real face, or is today Hallowe'en?*'

ANN: '*Your dad's just shaved his beard off. That's the third time he's grown one then cut it off, isn't it?*'
IVY: '*Yes, mum's stuffing a cushion.*'

What is one of the hardest things to do?

Milk puddings.

Try these questions on a friend, or enemy!
'What is frozen water?' *'Ice.'*
'What is frozen cream?' *'Ice cream.'*
'What is frozen tea?' *'Iced tea.'*
'What is frozen ink?' *'Iced ink.'*
Well, have a bath then!

OOPS!

IF AT FIRST YOU DON'T SUCCEED
— GIVE UP SKYDIVING

VAL: *'My mum took me to the cinema last night.'*
LILY: *'Did you enjoy it?'*
VAL: *'No, I cried.'*
LILY: *'Why, was it sad?'*
VAL: *'No, they wouldn't let us in.'*

How do you catch a monkey?

Hang upside down from a tree and make a noise like a banana.

I sat next to the Duchess at tea,
It was just as I feared it would be.
Her rumblings abdominal
Were simply phenomenal
And everyone thought it was me!

248

Mischief: A red Indian's daughter.

A CHEAP BREAKFAST *by Roland Marge*

WAITER: *'Today I have pig's trotters, fried liver, boiled tongue, and stewed kidneys.'*
XANTIPPE: *'Don't stand there telling me your ailments, get me a menu.'*

Cannibal: Someone who is fed up with people.

What is Italian, 182 feet high and delicious?

The Leaning Tower of Pizza.

Hide under a bed or a cupboard until someone comes into the room and then, when they least expect it, make a noise like an elephant trumpeting or a pig grunting.

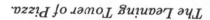

CLARE: *'I wish I had a penny for every boy who wanted to marry me.'*
HARRY: *'What would you do, buy a packet of polos?*

What can a whole apple do that half an apple can't?

Look round.

Coconut: Someone who is mad about chocolate.

THE DANGEROUS LION *by Claudia Armoff*

Who is short, afraid of wolves and uses bad language?

Little Rude Riding Hood.

FRED: *'Why does a monkey scratch himself?'*
ROSE: *'I don't know, why?'*
FRED: *'Because he's the only one that knows where it itches.'*

ULRIC: *'Waiter, waiter, there's a button in my salad!'*
WAITER: *'It must have fallen off while the salad was dressing.'*

GILLIAN: *Why can't you replace my lost budgie?*
PET SHOP OWNER: *Because I wouldn't fit into the cage.*

DOCTOR: *You must take one of these pills three times a day.*
WILLIAM: *How can I take the same pill three times?*

NEXT TIME YOU GET A SORE THROAT, BE THANKFUL YOU'RE NOT A GIRAFFE.

250

NEVER PLAY IN THE STREETS —
YOU MIGHT GET THAT RUN DOWN
FEELING.

**What do gorillas sing at
Christmas?**

'Jungle bells, jungle bells.'

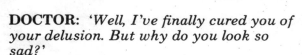

DOCTOR: *'Well, I've finally cured you of
your delusion. But why do you look so
sad?'*
PATIENT: *'Wouldn't you be sad if
yesterday you were the Queen of England
and the next day you were a nobody?'*

I'VE BEEN CURED OF INDECISION.
AT LEAST I THINK I HAVE.

*'If I gave you a going-away
present — would you?'*

What is a complete waste of time?

Telling a bald man hair-raising stories.

:PATIENT: *'Doctor, doctor, my hair's
falling out. Can you give me something to
keep it in?'*
DOCTOR: *'Here's a plastic bag.'*

251

Mr. Window Cleaner, you'll soon be well
After all, it wasn't far you fell.
You certainly received a nasty crack
Don't worry though you'll get your ladder
  back.

 When is a pie like a poet?

When it is Browning.

 Starfish: A creature that
comes out of the sea at night.

 DAN: *'Waiter, waiter, there's soap in this food.'*
WAITER: *'That's to wash the food down with.'*

 NINA: *'My cat's cleverer than yours.'*
ZOE: *'Why?'*
NINA: *'Well, to catch mice it eats cheese and then waits at a mousehole with bated breath.'*

What did the hen say when she saw a plate of scrambled eggs?

'What a crazy bunch of mixed-up kids.'

FANCY FOOD *by Della Katessen*

 Eclipse: What a gardener does to a hedge.

252

What is a hen's favourite TV programme?

Hatch of the Day.

WILLIAM: *'My dad bought mum a mink outfit for her birthday.'*
GILLIAN: *'Did he?'*
WILLIAM: *'Yeah. Two steel traps and a shotgun.'*

'Twas in a restaurant they met,
Romeo and Juliet.
He had no money to pay the debt
So Romeo'd and Juliet.

PASTE EARRINGS *by Faye Kearings*

What is a HIbVE?

A small bee in a big hive.

MARK: *'Pam, my dear, I am burning with love for you.'*
PAM: *'Come now, Mark, don't make a fuel of yourself.'*

OSCAR: *'I hate to say this, but the toast is very tough here.'*
LILY: *'You're eating the paper plate, dear.'*

Dynamite: A boom stick.

What did one sheep say to the other by the gate?

'After ewe.'

253

HELP AUSTRALIAN OAKS — PLANT AN ACORN UPSIDE DOWN

ULRIC: *How did you get on when you went on safari to Africa, doctor?*
DOCTOR: *Oh, it was very disappointing, I didn't kill anything. I would have been better off staying here in the hospital.*

Which song was sung when the yacht exploded?

Pop goes the wee sail.

'That's some perfume you're wearing. Who sold it to you, a skunk?'

IS TOLKEIN HOBBIT FORMING?

'Doctor, doctor, my husband thinks he's a car.'
'Well, bring him in.'
'I can't. He's double parked outside.'

Why are writers the strangest creatures in the world?

Because their tales come out of their heads.

What is black and white and noisy?

A zebra with a set of drums.

Endorse: The last nag in the race.

The rain makes all things beautiful,
The grass and flowers too.
*If rain makes **all** things beautiful,*
Why can't it rain on you?

VAL: *'In this restaurant you can eat dirt cheap.'*
ZOE: *'Yes, but who wants to eat dirt?'*

 VAN GOGH WAS EAR!

ROSE: *'Why do you like gravy so much?'*
MARK: *'Because the bones don't get stuck in my throat.'*

William heard a very good joke at school and was going to take it home, but he decided that was carrying a joke a little too far.

What did one rock pool say to the other rock pool?

'Show us your mussels.'

THE CLEVER COOK by *Maida Pie*

Sweet little Eileen Rose
Was tired and sought some sweet repose.
But her naughty sister Clare
Placed a pin upon her chair
And sweet little Eileen Rose!

255

'Doctor, doctor, I keep seeing double.'
'Just lie down on the couch.'
'Which one?'

What did the Eskimo waiter sing when
asked what was on the menu?

'Whale meat again . . .'

SHEARING SHEEP *by Sean Flocke*

How do you make German people jump?

Sneak up behind them and shout 'Hans up!'

KEVIN: *'What instructions did Noah
give his sons about fishing off the ark?'*
SIMON: *'I don't know. What?'*
KEVIN: *'Go easy on the bait lads, I've
only got two worms!'*

'Doctor, doctor, there's an Invisible Man
waiting outside.'

'Tell him I can't see him.'

BETTER TO FIND A HAIR IN YOUR
SOUP THAN SOUP IN YOUR HAIR.

THE TRICK CYCLIST *by Rhoda Biyke.*

Operator: Someone who hates operas.

How do you join the Navy?

Handcuff the sailors together.

Say to your friend:
*'Did you hear about the stupid fool that
goes around saying no?'*
'No.'
'Oh, it's you then is it!'

DOCTOR: *'Now I'm just going to give
you a small injection, you won't feel a
thing.'*
QUENTIN: *'Aaaaaaaaaaaaaaarrrgh.'*
DOCTOR: *'But I haven't put the needle
in yet, what's the matter?'*
QUENTIN: *'You're standing on my
foot!'*

**What runs around the forest making
other animals yawn?**

A wild bore.

'Is your dress too short, or are you in it too far?'

AN ELEPHANT NEVER FORGETS, BUT WHAT'S AN ELEPHANT GOT TO REMEMBER?

Did you hear about the really rich tree surgeon who had seven branch offices?

'The only thing you took up at school was space.'

How do you keep a skunk from smelling?

Hold his nose.

LILY: *'Do you sell dog's meat?'*
BUTCHER: *'Only if they are accompanied by an adult.'*

FRED: *'I heard a new joke the other day. Did I tell it to you?'*
JOHN: *'Is it funny?'*
FRED: *'Yes, very.'*
JOHN: *'Then you didn't.'*

'Waiter, waiter, you've got your thumb in my soup.'

'Don't worry, it's not hot.'

A charming young singer named Hannah,
Got caught in a flood in Savannah;
As she floated away,
Her sister — they say —
Accompanied her on the piannah!

What do you call a giraffe that steps on your foot?

Anything you like, it's head is too far away to hear you.

One of the oldest practical jokes is still one of the funniest. Simply balance a pillow on the top of a door that is slightly ajar. When the victim opens the door, the pillow will fall on their head. Never use anything heavier than a pillow.

Ice cream: Yell at the top of your voice.

What do you call mad fleas?

Loony ticks.

THE POST-SCRIPT *by Adeline Extra*

GIVE ANTS A BREAK, WALK ON ONE LEG.

TINA: *'Excuse me, but can you tell me if this play is very long?'*
NINA: *'Long! The interval is in July.'*

To make a funny noise: blow up a balloon and then let the air out again very slowly. It makes a marvellous sound. Try letting the air out quickly too and see what kind of funny noise it makes.

Why did the elephant tie a knot in his trunk?

So that he wouldn't forget.

DON'T DO HOMEWORK — NO TEACHER CAN BLAME YOU FOR SOMETHING YOU HAVEN'T DONE.

BEN: *'I must get myself a calendar.'*
DAN: *'Why?'*
BEN: *'Because yesterday I got sick so that I wouldn't have to go to school, and then I found out it was Saturday.'*

DOCTOR: *'I can't hide from you the fact that you are very ill. Is there anyone you would like to see?'*
YORICK: *'Yes. Another doctor.'*

If you ate five hot dogs and then ate three more, what would you have?

You'd have eight, and ate, and ate!

Why is Wales covered in water?

Because there are so many leeks.

GILLIAN: *'Did you hear about the woman who wore dark glasses all the time?'*
XANTIPPE: *'What about her?'*
GILLIAN: *'She took a dim view of things.'*

Why did the short-sighted chicken cross the road?

To go to the Bird's Eye shop.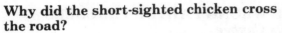

'She's got such a turned up nose, every time she sneezes her hat blows away.'

THE LOCAL MAGISTRATE by *Lady Lawdowne*

ZOE: *'The service in this restaurant is terrible.'*
PAM: *'If you think the service is terrible, wait until you see the food.'*

 Knob: A thing to adore (a door).

TEACHER: *'Ulric, why are you crawling into the classroom?'*
ULRIC: *'Because class had already started and you said: "Don't anyone dare* **walk** *into my lesson late." '*

261

THE NAUGHTY SCHOOLBOY
by Enid Spanking

What did the rake say to the hoe?

'Hi, hoe!'

THE WRONG PAIR OF TROUSERS *by*
Titus Canbee

IVY: *'I play the piano by ear.'*
OSCAR: *'Doesn't it interfere with your earrings?'*

BEN: *'I can lift an elephant with one finger,'*
ZOE: *'I bet you can't!'*
BEN: *'OK then, bring me a one-fingered elephant and I'll show you.'*

Study your friends' and see if they have any particular mannerisms, such as a very distinctive walk, or some characteristic by which you can recognise them, and see if you can copy it. It can be great fun to impersonate your friends, but be kind in your mimicry — it isn't funny if you upset them.

Jack and Jill went up the hill
To fetch a pail of water.
Jack fell down and broke his crown,
And squashed the farmer's daughter!

Lamb Stew: Much Ado About Mutton

A WINTER'S WIND by I.C.Blast

Take a piece of paper and say to your
friend: *'I can write with my left foot!'*
When you are challenged to do so, take a
pencil and write 'with my left foot' on the
paper.

LILY: *'Zoe's cooking lunch for us.'*
FRED: *'Oh dear, it will mean her
Enthusiasm Soup again.'*
LILY: *'Why do you call it Enthusiasm
Soup?'*
FRED: *'Because she put's everything
she's got into it.'*

*'That coat fits you like a glove. Pity it
doesn't fit you like a coat.'*

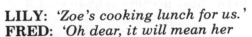

What do you call two chemists shops?

A pair of Boots.

VAL: *'You remind me of the sea.'*
KEVIN: *'Why, because I'm wild, reckless
and romantic?'*
VAL: *'No, you make me sick!'*

'Doctor, doctor, I feel like a race horse.'
'How long have you felt like this?'
'Ever since I won the Grand National.'

There once was an elegant Miss
Who said, 'I think skating is bliss.'
This no more does she state,
Since a wheels shot off her skate

¡siɥʇ ǝʞᴉl ƃuᴉɥʇǝɯos dn pǝpuǝ ǝɥs pu∀

AN APPLE A DAY KEEPS THE
DOCTORS AWAY, BUT AN ONION A
DAY KEEPS EVERYONE AWAY.

**What do the best doctors take to cure a
cold?**

·spunod ǝʌᴉɟ-ʎʇuǝʍʇ ɟo ǝǝɟ ∀

Sign in a restaurant:
Our tongue sandwiches speak for
themselves.

CLARE: *'The doctor has put Lily on a*
sea food diet.'
EVE: *'Is she sticking to it?'*
CLARE: *'Yes, now she only eats when*
she can see food.'

IF WE LEARN FROM OUR
MISTAKES, I'M GETTING A
FANTASTIC EDUCATION!

'Doctor, doctor, I feel like a cricket ball.'
'How's that?'
'Don't you start!'

264

TEACHER: *'Which is farthest away, Australia or the moon?'*
WILLIAM: *'Australia.'*
TEACHER: *'What makes you think that?'*
WILLIAM: *'Well, you can see the moon, but you can't see Australia.'*

A gentleman dining at Crewe
Found a rather large mouse in his stew.
Said the waiter: 'Don't shout
And wave it about
Or the rest will be wanting one too.'

What is approximately 39 inches long and watched by 5 million children?

Blue Metre.

'Don't worry if your mind wanders. It's too weak to go very far.'

VISITOR: *'You're very quiet, Gillian.'*
GILLIAN: *'Yes, well mum gave me 25p not to say anything about your red nose.'*

ACHES AND PAINS *by Arthur Ritis*

265

Why did the daft man like to be by himself?

Because he preferred to be a loon.

 Who went into the lion's den and came out alive?

The lion.

 Piggy Bank: Where pigs keep their money.

'Waiter, waiter, this meat is bad.'
'Who told you?'
'A little swallow.'

 JOHN: *'Our dog is just like one of the family.'*
MARK: *'Which one?'*

'Doctor, Doctor, will you give me something for my head?'
'Sorry, I've already got one.'

 THE FITTED CARPET by *Walter Wall*

 KEVIN: *'Nina, your hat is on the wrong way.'*
NINA: *'How do you know which way I'm going?'*

ULRIC: *'I'm feeding my dog garlic.'*
XANTIPPE: *'Why on earth are you doing that?'*
ULRIC: *'It makes his bark worse than his bite.'*

Locate: A greeting for Katherine (Lo, Kate!)

What is the difference between a railway shed and a tree?

One leaves its shed and the other sheds its leaves.

'You have that far-away look. The farther away you are, the better you look.'

What is yellow and goes 'Clunch!'?

A Chinaman eating crisps.

'Doctor, doctor, I keep thinking I'm a bird.'
'Well, perch yourself there and I'll tweet you in a minute.'

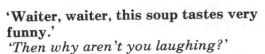

'Waiter, waiter, this soup tastes very funny.'
'Then why aren't you laughing?'

WHY IS WHISPERING NOT ALOUD?

Place your two index fingers in the corners of your mouth and pull them to give yourself a very wide grin. Now stick out your tongue as far as it will go, and try and look at the tip of your nose at the same time! The funny face you make will have your friends in stitches — but don't pull your mouth too hard or you will need stitches too!

PUT CEMENT IN YOUR LEMONADE AND HAVE A STIFF DRINK!

'Doctor, doctor, I want to thank you for curing the pain in my back. Was it a slipped disc?'
'No, twisted braces.'

AT THE SOUTH POLE *by Anne Tartic*

'Waiter, waiter, there's a funny film on this soup.'
 'What did you expect for 30p — E.T.?'

There was a young poet called Dan
Whose limericks never would scan.
When they said it was so,
he replied: 'Yes, I know,
But you see I make it a rule to always try
and get just as many words into the last
line as I possibly can!'

'Doctor, doctor, people keep being rude to me.'
 'Get out of here you silly fool.'

268

Who led 10,000 pigs up a hill and then back down again?

The Grand Old Duke of Pork.

He's so conceited, he goes out into the garden so that the flowers can smell him!'

Road sign in an Irish country lane:
WHEN THIS SIGN IS UNDER WATER, THE ROAD IS CLOSED TO TRAFFIC.

Say to a friend who is wearing a coat, *'I bet you can't button your coat up in one minute.'* He or she will naturally rise to the challenge and fasten the buttons to prove you wrong. You then say, *'There I knew you couldn't button your coat up!'* — because everyone buttons their coat from the top **down**.

'For a minute I thought you were crazy, but I was wrong.
You've been crazy much longer than that.'

What is French for dentures?

Aperitif.

'Doctor, doctor, will my measles be better next week?'
'I hate to make rash promises.'

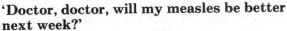

269

EVERY DOG HAS ITS DAY, BUT
ONLY A DOG WITH A BROKEN TAIL
HAS A WEAK-END.

'Waiter, waiter, this steak tastes like a
polystyrene tile.'
'That's why we charge ceiling prices, sir.'

XANTIPPE: *'You look exhausted.'*
YORICK: *'Well, they rang from the
hospital yesterday to say that I've got to
go in for a blood test, so I've been up all
night studying for it.'*

HYPOCHONDRIAC: *'Doctor, doctor,
I've got a pain in my neck.'*
DOCTOR: *'So have I, and you're it!'*

Lesson: Result of taking some clothes
off.

*Little Miss Muffet
Sat on her tuffet
Eating some Irish stew.
Along came a spider
And sat down beside her
So she gobbled him up too.*

Take a piece of sellotape and stick down
the receiver rest on your telephone and
replace the receiver. When the phone
rings and someone tries to answer it, it
will continue ringing.

What do you get if you cross an elephant with a bus driver?

A trunk an' driver.

'*Let's see what kind of an athelete you are. Try holding your breath for a few days.*'

Announce that you can sing under water. When you are challenged to perform this unlikely feat, you can either hold a glass of water over your head while you sing, or simply sing the words '*under water*' to a popular tune.

Diploma: The man who mends broken pipes.

ANN: '*How do you know your parents want to get rid of you?*'
BEN: '*Mum packs my sandwiches in a road map every day.*'

'*Doctor, doctor, there's something wrong with my ear.*
Every time I put my finger in it I go deaf....

THE BARGAIN TOY by *Adolphus Ayle*

'*I don't know — that must be a face, it has ears on it.*'

HARRY: '*Mum, where are the Andes?*'
MOTHER: '*If you put things away more carefully, you'd know where they were when you wanted them!*'

271

Out-of-bounds: A tired kangaroo.

 'Dad, I don't want to go to Australia!'
'Shut up, and keep digging. . . .

How do you get through life with only one tooth?

 You grin and bare it.

What happens when you cross a dog with a chicken?
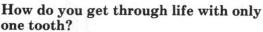
You get poached eggs.

'Doctor, doctor, I keep feeling that I'm covered in gold paint.'
'Don't worry, it's just a gilt complex.'

KEVIN: *'This restaurant must have very clean kitchens.'*
 WAITER: *'That's kind of you, sir, how can you tell?'*
KEVIN: *'Everything tastes of detergent.'*

GILLIAN: *'Mum, can I play the piano?'*
MOTHER: *'Not until you've washed your dirty hands.'*
GILLIAN: *'Oh, mum, I promise I'll only play the black notes.'*

GO AND BITE A FISHERMAN — HE MIGHT NOT HAVE HAD A BITE ALL DAY!

ACTOR: *'I hope the cameraman catches my best side.'*
 ACTRESS: *'Which is that?' The back of your head?'*

272

Say to your victim: *'Did you know that the Queen is going to open a new tellycost today?'*
'What's a tellycost?'
'Oh, about a hundred pounds.'

SIMON: *'Mum, can I have the wishbone from the chicken?'*
MOTHER: *'Not until you've eaten all your sprouts.'*
SIMON: *'But I want to wish I won't have to eat them.'*

THE BULLFIGHTER *by Matt Adore*

Which letters are bad for your teeth?

D K.

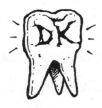

What do you call ducks that swim in milk?

Cream quackers.

BO PEEP DID IT FOR THE INSURANCE!

'Is it true that at Christmas they hang you up and kiss the mistletoe?'

Man: The only animal in the world that goes to bed when he isn't sleepy, and gets up when he is.

273

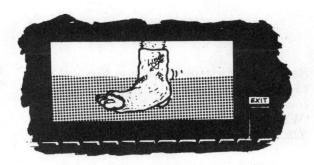

'Why did you call your first film *'The Broken Leg'*?
'Because it had a big cast.'

DOCTOR: *'Please breathe out three times.'*
YORICK: *'Is that so that you can check my lungs?'*
DOCTOR: *'No, it's so that I can clean my glasses.'*

DISENGAGED by *Lou-M.T.Now.*

HARRY: *'Last night I heard a funny noise in my ears.'*
LILY: *'Well, where else would you hear it?'*

To make a clown's nose: simply paint half a ping-pong ball bright red. Get an adult to drill a couple of holes in the 'nose' on either side so that you can thread a piece of elastic through, and you will be able to dress up as a clown!

QUENTIN: *'Tina's been told she must do more exercises to keep her weight down.'*
WILLIAM: *'What exercise is she doing?'*
QUENTIN: *'She pushes herself away from the table four times a day.'*

274

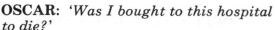

Newton heard a sort of plonk —
An apple fell upon his conk;
Discovering gravitations law
Shook poor Isaac to the core.

OSCAR: *'Was I bought to this hospital to die?'*
AUSTRALIAN NURSE: *'No, you were bought her yester-die.'*

Why do skunks argue?

They like raising a stink.

Zinc: Where you wash the zaucepans.

What is big, grey and mutters?

A mumbo jumbo.

'Is it true that when you go to the zoo, the monkeys throw peanuts at you?

'Doctor, doctor, I keep thinking I'm a clock.'
'Well, don't get wound up about it.'

KEVIN: *'That was some thunderstorm we had last night.'*
SIMON: *'It certainly was.'*
EVE: *'Why didn't you wake me up? You know I can't sleep when there's thunder and lightening.'*

275

TODAY: SPILT PEA SOUP!

'Waiter, waiter, is there soup on the menu?'
'No, madam, I wiped it off.'

Why is a kettle like an animal?

Because it is a water otter.

I'D TRAVEL BY TRAIN MORE OFTEN, BUT I'M SO AFRAID OF MEETING JIMMY SAVILLE.

GROCER: *'Can I help you miss?'*
PAM: *'Yes, how much are these tomatoes?'*
GROCER: *'Fifty pence a pound.'*
PAM: *'Did you raise them yourself?'*
GROCER: *'I certainly did. Yesterday they were forty pence a pound.'*

Do Indians wear skirts?

No, but sometimes they wear headdresses.

I shot an arrow in the air
It fell to earth, I know not where.
I lose all my arrows that way.

276

What did the hamburger say to the ketchup?

'I've had enough of your sauce!'

NEVER RACE TRAINS TO CROSSINGS — IF IT'S A TIE, YOU LOSE.

ANN: *'Do you let your dog lie on the couch?'*
EVE: *'Only when he visits a psychiatrist.'*

'Waiter, waiter, can I have a steak pie, please.'
'Anything with it, sir?'
'If it's like the last one I had, a hammer and chisel.'

How did Hiawatha?

With thoap and water.

Rose and Ivy went to pick flowers in a field on Farmer Brown's land, when suddenly they noticed a bull in the field. **'Is that bull safe?'** shouted Ivy.
'Off hand,' replied the farmer, *'I'd say he's a lot safer than you are.'*

'Doctor, doctor, I keep thinking I'm a strawberry.'
'You are in a jam, aren't you.'

'You have a pretty little head, and for a head, it's pretty little.'

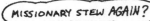

Why did the cannibal become a vegetarian?

Well, you can go off people, you know.

Juicy: Did you observe? e.g. *'Juicy what I just saw?'*

HARRY: *'Was it hot when you went on holiday?'*
OSCAR: *'I'll say it was. There were no trees, so we took it in turns to sit in each other's shadow.'*

AN APPLE A DAY KEEPS THE DOCTOR AWAY — IF AIMED RIGHT.

THE CHURCH STEEPLE *by Belinda Belfry*

Why doesn't the corn like the farmer?

Because he picks his ears.

'Doctor, doctor, what can I do about my insomnia?'
'Don't lose any sleep over it.'

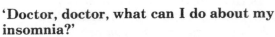

'She's got a baby's complexion, and quite frankly I think the baby was glad to get rid of it.'

278

ULRIC: *'How's your nose?'*
YORICK: *'Shut up!'*
ULRIC: *'So's mine. It must be the cold weather.'*

What would you call a highly educated plumber?'

uoǝƃɹns uıɐɹp ∀

MARK: *'Why do you make your dog sit so close to the fire?'*
JOHN: *'Because I like hot dogs.'*

Kidney: The knee of a baby goat.

What do you get if you cross a chicken with a cement mixer?

ɹǝʎɐlʞɔıɹq ∀

'Of course I'm listening to you. . . . can't you see me yawning?'

'Doctor, doctor, I keep thinking I'm a dustbin.'
'That's rubbish!'

A fly and a flea in a flue
Were imprisoned, so what could they do?
Said the fly, 'Let us flee!'
'Let us fly!' said the flea.
So they flew through a flaw in the flue.

LONG NECKED ANIMALS by G.Raffe

'Waiter, waiter, do you call this a three-course meal?'
'That's right, sir. Two chips and a pea.'

DR.FRANKENSTEIN WAS LONELY UNTIL HE LEARNT HOW TO MAKE NEW FRIENDS.

CLARE: *'Did you hear about the pickpocket that robbed the same man twice in one day?'*
GILLIAN: *'That's what I call returning to the scene of the crime.'*

'Your teeth are like the stars,' he said,
And pressed her hand so white.
He spoke the truth, for like the stars,
Her teeth came out at night.

What has four legs and can fly?

Two birds.

Say to your friend: *'Here's a piece of paper and a pencil. I want you to write a small letter I with a dot over it.'* Your victim will quite naturally think that this is easy and is certain to write 'i' on the paper, which is wrong! A small letter **I** with a dot over it looks like this: **i**

Gallows: a place where no noose is good noose.

'If I bought fifty loaves of bred for £1.00, what would each one be, Gillian?'
'Mouldy, miss.'

'Doctor, doctor, I keep thinking I'm a fly.'
'Well, come down off the ceiling and let's talk about it.'

HYPOCHONDRIACS MAKE ME SICK!

Why did the sailor grab a bar of soap when the ship sank?

To wash himself ashore.

 HOW TO APOLOGISE *by Thayer Thorry*

Why does the hamburger roll always say please and thank-you?

Because it is well-bread!

'Waiter, waiter, there's a fly in my soup.'
'Hang on a minute, sir, I'll call the RSPCA.'

right wrong!

 HOW TO MAKE AN IGLOO *by*
S.K.Mow

Some say that fleas are black,
But I know that is not so,
'Cos Mary had a little lamb
With fleas as white as snow.

 WILLIAM: *'It looks like rain.'*
GILLIAN: *'Well, I put six teabags in the*
pot. . . .'

 Does a giraffe get a sore throat if he gets
his feet wet?
Yes, but not until a fortnight later.

 NINA: *'Did you get a good place in your*
exams?'
TINA: *'Yes, right next to the radiator.'*

 'Doctor, doctor, this new banana diet you
gave me is having a strange effect.'
'Well, stop scratching and come down
from the curtains.'

 Which animal has a trunk and is found at
the South Pole?

A lost elephant.

Place your tongue **over** your bottom teeth and keep it there. Now try to speak. You will find it gives you a very funny voice. Try curling your tongue upwards too and press it against the roof of your mouth as you speak — your friends will be in hysterics, especially if you talk to them over the telephone.

ALL ABOARD THE SHIP *by Abel Seamann*

VAL: *'My cat swallowed a light bulb last night.'*
EVE: *'Is he alright?'*
VAL: *'He wasn't at first, but now he's de-lighted.'*

TUTANKHAMUN HAS CHANGED HIS MIND AND WANTS TO BE BURIED AT SEA.

'Am I as pretty as a picture?'
'Yes, but your frame is a mess.'

'You're so old that when you were at school history was known as current events.'

THE OPTICIAN'S DAUGHTER KEEPS MAKING A SPECTACLE OF HERSELF.

What did the robot say when it ran out of electricity?

'AC come, AC go.'

To fool your teacher, all you need is a scouring pad! One day tell your teacher that your mother's hobby is growing cacti, and that she has a unique specimen. The next day you take in one of these rare plants as a special present. In fact it is a scouring pad in a pot of real earth. Unless your teacher is an expert, he or she could look after this unique plant for years!

'Waiter, waiter, there's a dead beetle in my wine.'
'Well, you asked for something with a little body in it.'

A painter who lived in West Ditting
Interrupted two girls with their knitting.
He said with a sigh,
'That park bench — Well I
Just painted it, right where you're sitting!'

THE GREETING *by Howie Dewing*

BEN: *That's a realistic scarecrow.*
FARMER: *Yes, it's so good that the crows are bringing back corn they stole two years ago.*

284

'Doctor, doctor, what's the worst part of my operation?'
'Sewing you up. I can't see to thread the needle.'

KEEP THE CAT OUT OF THE KITCHEN — OTHERWISE IT WILL BE HOTPOT TOMORROW.

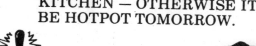

Shin: A device that man has to find objects in a dark room.

OUCH!!!

'I'll have my bill now please.'
'How did you find your steak?'
'I just moved a chip, and there it was.'

RESTORING OLD FURNITURE by Ann Teak

What did the electricity meter say to the 50p piece?

'Glad you dropped in, I was just going out.'

Bacteria: The rear entrance of a cafeteria.

FRED: 'How do you top a car?'
HARRY: 'Tep on the brake, 'tupid.'

285

'Does the undertaker know you're up and about?'

How many months have 28 days?

All of them?

ZOE: *'How did you break your arm?'*
PAM: *'I followed my doctor's prescription.'*
ZOE: *'How could you break your arm doing that?'*
PAM: *'It blew out of the window and I followed it.'*

GOING TO MARKET *by Tobias A.Cow*

'Waiter, waiter, what do I have to do to get a glass of water in this place?'
'Set yourself on fire, sir.'

THEY LAUGHED WHEN I DISCOVERED DYNAMITE, BUT WHEN I DROPPED IT, THEY EXPLODED.

XANTIPPE: *'I'll have an ice-cream sundae with two spoonfuls of chocolate-chip ice cream, one spoonful of vanilla ice-cream and one of raspberry ice-cream, all covered in fresh cream and with a chocolate flake on the top.'*
WAITER: *'Would you like a cherry on it?'*
XANTIPPE: *'No thanks, I'm slimming.'*

286

ZOE: *'Why did you give Ann two black eyes?'*
EVE: *'Because she told me my stockings were wrinkled.'*
ZOE: *'And were they?'*
EVE: *'I wasn't wearing any stockings!'*

'Doctor, doctor, my wife thinks she's a lorry.'
'Bring her in to see me.'
'I will when she gets back from delivering iron girders to Newcastle.'

I DISCOVERED A CURE FOR AMNESIA, BUT I'VE FORGOTTEN WHAT IT IS.

HER BIRTHDAY GIFT by Sheila Doritt

QUENTIN: *'I've just swallowed a bone.'*
OSCAR: *'Are you choking?'*
QUENTIN: *'No, I'm serious.'*

What is easy to get into, but hard to get out of?

Trouble.

Who has a parrot that shouts:
Pieces of four! Pieces of four!'?

 Short John Silver.

287

What did the boy octopus say to the girl octopus?

I want to hold your hand hand hand hand hand hand hand hand.

High chair: A friendly greeting to a piece of furniture.

'That's a nice outfit you're wearing. Pity they didn't have it in your size though.'

BABY SITTING *by Justin Casey Howls*

There was a young cannibal called Fred
Who used to eat onions in bed.
His mother said: 'Sonny,
That's not very funny.
Why don't you eat people instead?'

'Waiter, waiter, what do you call this?'
'Cottage pie, sir.'
'Well, I think I've just bitten on a brick.'

Quadruplets: Four crying out loud.

288

GOD MADE MAN, BUT THOUGHT HE COULD DO BETTER SO HE MADE LITTLE GIRLS.

Why is a cat on the beach like Christmas?

Because they both have sandy claws.

OWNING A PET *by Ivor Dogg*

LILY: *'Will you send for the flying squad, please.'*
POLICEMAN: *'Why, madam?'*
LILY: *'Because I've lost my budgie.'*

What do you call a by-pass in Wales?

A Dai-version.

'Do you have pig's feet?'
'Yes, I do.'
'Well, if you wear shoes, nobody will notice.'

'Mother Nature created you. Well, anyone can make a mistake.'

'Waiter, waiter, will my sausages be long?'
'About six inches, sir.'

CLARE: *'I invited you to come* **after** *dinner!'*
HARRY: *'That's what I've come after. . . . dinner.'*

'Doctor, doctor, are you still treating that man who thought he was a tailor?'
'Yes.'
'When are you going to cure him?'
'When he's finished making me a suit.'

THE OUT OF WORK CONJURER *by Trixie Coudden-Do*

SHAZAM!

'Waiter, waiter, what is this insect in my soup?'
'I wish you hadn't asked me — I can't tell one bug from another.'

What happens to a tree after it is chopped down?

¡dn pǝddoɥɔ sı ʇI

WELLINGTON'S WIFE WAS AN OLD BOOT!

Fungus: Someone called Gus who has a lot of laughs.

When do ghosts have the most fun?

When they are in high spirits.

'The only thing your head is good for is keeping your ears apart.'

To fool your Mother say to her:
'Mum, why did you drop that £5 note in the rubbish bin?'
The result will be a lot of frantic scrabbling and searching as she empties the rubbish bin all over the kitchen floor looking for the £5 note. After ten minutes you return and shout **APRIL FOOL!**

SCHOOL DINNERS *by R.E.Volting*

JOHN: *'Can you tell me the way to Bath?'*
MARK: *'Well, I always use soap and* *water.'*

ANN: *'That's a lovely coloured cow cover there.'*
PAM: *'It's a Jersey.'*
ANN: *'Is it really? I thought it was his skin...'*

TERRIBLE SHOT *by Miss.A.Lott*

'Waiter, waiter, there's a bird in my soup.'
'That's alright. It's birds nest soup.'

She stood on the bridge at midnight,
Her lips were all a-quiver;
She gave a cough, her leg fell off
And floated down the river!

THE ONLY WAY TO AVOID
MISTAKES IS TO GAIN
EXPERIENCE. THE ONLY WAY TO
GAIN EXPERIENCE. . . . IS TO MAKE
A MISTAKE.

'Doctor, doctor, I have a broken arm,
poison ivy, measles and a knife wound.'
'I know, there's a lot of it about.'

'Did you know that the most intelligent
person in the world is deaf?'
'Really, who is it?'
'Pardon?'

Archaeologist: A man whose career is in
ruins.

Play silly games to make people
laugh: Get someone to sit in a chair and
look as serious and straight-faced as they
can. He or she must remain serious while
you make every attempt to get them
laughing. Pull funny faces, tell jokes, and
keep on until the person laughs, then you
can change places.

Who tracks down lost vicars?

The Bureau of Missing Parsons.

What pets do pigs keep?

Hamsters.

MY ACHING LEGS *by Carrie M.Holme*

HARRY: *'My father is an old newspaper man.'*
SIMON: *'Is he doing well?'*
HARRY: *'Not really. Not many people want old newspapers.'*

'Doctor, doctor, what's good for biting fingernails?'
'Sharp teeth.'

ZOE: *'I think grandma needs new glasses.'*
PAM: *'Why's that?'*
ZOE: *'She's watching clothes going round in the washing machine and she thinks it's* **Crossroads.** *'*

WILLIAM: *'May I sit on your right hand at dinner?'*
XANTIPPE: *'I may need it to eat with, but you can sit on it for a while if you want.'*

PAM: *'I've played the piano for years — on and off.'*
VAL: *'Slippery stool?'*

293

How can you make a fire with only one stick?

Make sure it is a matchstick!

DAN: *'I went riding this afternoon.'*
IVY: *'Horseback?'*
DAN: *'Yes, two hours before I was.'*

 Despair: The extra tyre.

 'There's something about you I like. Give me a year or two and I might remember what it is. . . .'

What are hippies?

Something to keep your leggies up.

ARE LONDONERS DIM BECAUSE THE POPULATION'S SO DENSE?

TEACHER: *'Take this sentence, 'Let the cow be taken to the pasture.' Now, what mood?'*
TINA: *'The cow.*

294

'Doc-oc-octor, Doooo — oc-oc-tor, I ha-ve diff-i-cul-ty sp-sp-eak-ing.'
'*Sorry, I wasn't listening. Could you repeat that?*'

There was a young lady from Harrow
Whose mouth was exceedingly narrow;
She ate with a spoon
By the light of the moon,
But all she could eat was a marrow!

'Waiter, waiter, I think I'd like a little game.'
'*Ludo or tiddley-winks, sir.*'

WANTED: Mattress by a lady stuffed with horsehair.

'Doctor, doctor, what's the matter with me?'
'*Relax, Lady Crabtree, it's only a common cold.*'
'I can't have anything common! It must be an aristocratic cold!'

Why are astronomers like boxes?

They are always seeing stars.

 Stand in the street with a friend and point upwards towards the sky. Keep looking up and before long you will be joined by a crowd!

TARZAN (swinging through the jungle: *Aaahhaaaaaaaaaa.*
ELEPHANT TO FRIEND: *Sounds as if Tarzan's got cramp again.*

MOTHER: *'Gillian, there were two chocolate cakes in the larder and now there is only one. Why is that?'*
GILLIAN: *'It must have been so dark I didn't see the other one.'*

 BANK ROBBER: *'Stick 'em down!'*
CASHIER: *'Don't you mean stick 'em up?'*
BANK ROBBER: *'No wonder I haven't been making any money.'*

THOSE WHO THINK THEY KNOW EVERYTHING ARE ANNOYING TO THOSE OF US WHO DO.

'Waiter, waiter, bring me a cold fried egg,
some greasy chips and some sausages like
rubber.'
'We don't serve food like that, sir.'
'You did yesterday, what's changed?'

ZOE: *'Have you any idea how long the
next bus will be?'*
BEN: *'About six metres.'*

Say to your friend: *'I bet I can get you to
clasp your hands together in such a way
that you won't be able to leave the room
without undoing them.'*
When they accept the challenge you
simply clasp their hands around a piano
leg, or heavy piece of furniture. They
won't be able to leave the room without
unclasping their hands first!

*A kilted young man from Dumbarton
Claimed he could run like a Spartan.
On the fifty-sixth lap
His braces went snap,
And his face went as red as his tartan!*

LET OUT OF JAIL
by Freda Prisoner

What did the cowboy say when his dog fell over a cliff?

'Doggone!'

'*You're so short, when it rains you're the last to know.*'

'Doctor, doctor, these pills you gave me for my stomach ...'
'*What about them?*'
'They keep rolling off in the middle of the night.'

In which pantomime does the giant shout: '*Fe Fi Fo Fum, I smell the blood of a Scottish man*'?

Jock and the Beanstalk.

Depend: Not the shallow part of the swimming pool.

I kicked a ball into the air,
It fell to earth, I know not where.
And that is why I sit and dream
Upon the bench with the fourth-division team.

What kind of umbrella does the Queen
carry on a rainy day?

A wet one.

MOTHER: *'Why did you just kick Simon
in the stomach?'*
QUENTIN: *'It was his own fault, he
turned round.'*

THE HIGHLAND GAMES *by Eva
Kaber*

'Doctor, doctor, I think I'm going to die!'
*'Don't be silly, that's the last thing you'll
do.'*

Did you hear about the unlucky
princess who kissed a
handsome prince and he
turned into a frog?

YORICK: *'Zoe has just got engaged to
an X-ray technician.'*
XANTIPPE: *'I wonder what he sees in
her?'*

299

'Waiter, waiter, this milk is weak.'
'Sorry, sir, the cow got caught in the rain.'

BEN: *'I was in the jungle and all of a sudden I spotted a leopard.'*
DAN: *'You can't have done. They're born with spots.'*

Say to your friend:
'How many acorns grow on an average pine tree?'
What ever he or she replies, it will be wrong. Acorns don't grow on pine trees!

Why did the little girl say there was a black cat in the bath when it was really an elephant?

She was colour-blind.

Black eye: The result of a guided muscle.

What is made of chocolate, is wrapped in coloured paper and lies at the bottom of the ocean?

An Oyster Egg.

300

LILY: *'Could you see me across the road, Constable?'*
POLICEMAN: *'I could see you a mile away!'*

 'Doctor, doctor, I've broken my leg, what shall I do?'
'Limp.'

MOVING *by Ivor Newhouse*

An eager young fisher named Fisher
Once fished from the edge of a fissure.
A fish, with a grin,
Pulled the fisherman in —
Now they're fishing the fissure for Fisher!

 RICHARD COEUR DE LION — THE
FIRST HEART TRANSPLANT

What do you get if you cross a polar bear with an ice hockey player?

I don't know, but when it wants to score a goal, nobody tries to stop it.

'Doctor, doctor, I want you to remove four 20p pieces that I got stuck up my nose two months ago.'
'Two months ago! Why didn't you come to me before?'
'I didn't need the money until now.'

SHAKESPEARE MARRIED AN AVON LADY.

WHO'S THERE?
by Justin Quire

YORICK: 'Dad, what are these holes in the new fence?'
FATHER: 'They're knot-holes.'
YORICK: 'Yes they are, I can put my finger in them.'

What did the mother sardine say to her children when they saw a submarine?

'Don't worry, it's only a tin of people.'

HARRY: *'Doctor, doctor, how can I stop my nose running?'*
DOCTOR: *'Stand on your head.'*

'Waiter, waiter, this egg is rather small.'
'Give it a chance, it was only laid yesterday.'

KEVIN: *'Where were you born?'*
CLARE: *'Scotland.'*
KEVIN: *'Which part?'*
CLARE: *'All of me.'*

Why couldn't Humpty Dumpty be put back together again?

He wasn't all he was cracked up to be.

DON'T COMPLAIN ABOUT THE TEA, YOU MIGHT BE OLD AND WEAK YOURSELF ONE DAY.

Babysitter: Someone paid to sit on babies.

303

'Is it true that you won the King Kong lookalike contest?'

What is bright yellow, weighs one tonne, has four legs and sings?

Two half-tonne canaries.

A girl who weighed many an ounce
Used language I dare not pronounce.
For a person unkind
Pulled her chair out behind,
Just to see (so he said) if she'd bounce.

'Doctor, doctor, I feel like an old sock.'
'Well, I be darned.'

EVE: *'You've got your socks on inside out.'*
BEN: *'I know, but there are holes on the other side.'*

Performing magic tricks can be very funny, especially if they go wrong, so drop your pack of cards on the floor as you shuffle them. Tell people that you are going to pull a chicken out of a hat and pull a feather out of the hat instead, saying that the bird has flown!

What is the best way to catch a fish?

Get someone to throw one at you.

 'My dentist comes from abroad.'
'Oh, he's of foreign extraction then.'

HOW TO GET THERE QUICKLY *by*
Ridya Byke

TEACHER: *'If you lost four fingers what would you have?'*
FRED: *'No more piano lessons.'*

'You look like a nervous wreck. OK, so you're not nervous . . .'

Baldness: The best cure for dandruff.

305

How do you make soup gold?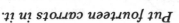

Put fourteen carrots in it.

DRINK VARNISH — IT GIVES YOU A
LOVELY FINISH.

 What invention allows you to see through walls?

A window.

 NINA: *'What do you think of Red China?'*
TINA: *'I don't mind it, if it doesn't clash with the tablecloth.'*

 LOOKING SMART *by Esme Socksagging*

Why did the farmer feed his cow batteries?

So that she could blow her horn.

HARRY: *'How did you get the job as a puppeteer?*
SIMON: *'I just pulled a few strings.'*

'You're a fine broth of a boy. Pity some of your noodles are missing.'

All you need for this practical joke is a needle and some cotton. Take your victim's pyjamas or nightdress and put a few stitches either in the sleeves or legs, so that when your victim attempts to put them on, they will find that they cannot get their arm or leg through. You will have a good laugh while they wriggle about trying to get inside — but don't sew them up too tightly or they'll never get in!

 Why did the monster give up boxing?

He didn't want to spoil his looks.

'Doctor, doctor, people keep ignoring me.'
'Next patient, please.'

A sleeper from the Amazon
Put nighties of his grandma's on.
The reason? That
He was too fat
To get his own pyjamas on.

 Oyster: What you shout when you want someone to lift your mother up.

What is a giraffe's favourite joke?

A tall story.

What did Noah say when he heard the rain coming down?

'Ark!'

LEGALISE TELEPATHY!
I knew you were going to say that!

 WHO KILLED COCK ROBIN *by*
Howard I.Know

Why did the mother kangaroo scold her children

 Because they ate biscuits in bed.

**SOME PEOPLE ARE LIKE BLISTERS
— THEY APPEAR WHEN THE WORK
IS DONE.**

How do you stop a dog from barking in the front sea t of your car?

Put him in the back seat.

Next time you have boiled eggs for breakfast, wash the empty shells carefully and save them. When you have boiled eggs again, put the empty shell upside-down in the egg cup so that it looks like a whole egg. When your victim smashes the top, he'll be in for a surprise!

CLARE: *'Answer the telephone.'*
HARRY: *'It's not ringing.'*
CLARE: *'Why must you leave everything until the last minute?'*

Sign in a flying school:
NO CRASH COURSES GIVEN HERE.

'Waiter, waiter, this lobster's only got one claw.'
'It's been in a fight, sir.'
'Well, bring me the winner then.'

OPTICIAN: *'Can you read the bottom line of the eye chart?'*
RUSSIAN: *'Read it, he's a friend of mine!'*

S
TA
LINWAS
ACREEP
!

CONSTRUCTING A HOUSE by Bill Ding

*There was a young man from Bengal
Who went to a fancy dress ball.
He thought he would risk it
And go as a biscuit,
But a dog ate him up in the hall.*

'Are you really leaving, or are you just trying to brighten my day?'

Where do goblins go to get fit?

To an elf farm.

Avoidable: What a matador
tries to do.

XANTIPPE: *'How did you find the
weather when you were on holiday?'*
WILLIAM: *'I just went outside and
there it was.'*

*The elephant is very large
They ought to have him shrunk,
And pack his great big body
Inside his little trunk.*

'Waiter, waiter, are the eggs fresh?'
*'Fresh? The chicken hasn't noticed
they've gone yet.'*

**What did the egg say when it
went to the monastry?**

*'I suppose it will be out of the
frying pan into the friar.'*

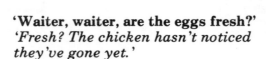

LOOKING FORWARD by Felix Ited

'Is that Braintree four, double 0, two, five?
'No, this is Braintree 4 0 0 2 5.'
'Oh, I'm so sorry to have bothered you.'
'That's alright, the phone was ringing anyway.'

'Waiter, waiter, have you ever been to the zoo?'
'No, sir, why?'
'You'd get quite a thrill watching the tortoises zipping by at such a speed.'

FRED: 'I don't think people like me.'
ROSE: 'What makes you say that?'
FRED: 'Every time we play hide and seek, I run off and hide and nobody bothers to look for me.'

'I just bought a Japanese radio.'
'How can you understand the language?'

THE FIVE BABIES by Bertha Quinns

What's a definition of a bad actor?

Tall, dark and some ham.

OSCAR: 'What do you get if you cross a computor with an elastic band?'
ULRIC: 'I don't know what you call it, but it makes snap decisions.'

311

What was Eve's telephone number in the Garden of Eden?

Adam 812.

Anthem: Very good looking e.g. Tall, dark and anthem.

'You don't need jewellery, there are plenty of rings under your eyes.'

 Which animal hibernates standing on its head?

Yoga Bear.

 LILY: *'Do you know the joke about the corn flakes and the rice crispies that had a fight?'*
ROSE: *'No.'*
LILY: *'I can only tell you a little — it's a serial.'*

We three Kings of Orient are
One in a taxi, one in a car,
One in a scooter, peeping his hooter,
Following yonder star.

IVY: *'Shall I tell you a joke about a pencil?'*
EVE: *'There's no point.'*

What do golfers use in Peking?

China Tees.

'You would look nice in something flowing — like a river.'

Yank: An American dentist.

ANN: *'What's the weather like?'*
PAM: *'I can't see for the fog.'*

What fur do you get from a skunk?

As fur away as possible!

ZOE: *'Why did the butcher put bells on his scales?'*
IVY: *'I don't know, why?'*
ZOE: *'Because he wanted to jingle all the weigh.'*

BOILED OR MASHED *by Po Taters*

'Waiter, waiter, I ordered hot chocolate.'
'That's what you've got — a bar of plain,
and a match.'

'Doctor, doctor, if this swelling gets any
worse in my legs my trousers won't go
on.'
'Here's a prescription.'
'What's it for?'
'A kilt.'

POLLUTION IS A DIRTY WORD!

YORICK: *'You've given me arsenic
instead of sleeping powder!'*
CHEMIST: *'So sorry, that'll be another
60p.'*

HARRY: *'Your dad is bow-legged, isn't
he.'*
KEVIN: *'Yes, mum has to iron his
underpants on a boomerang.'*

HOW TO AVOID ARGUMENTS *by*
Xavier Breath

What goes 'Ha, ha, ha, plop!'?

Someone laughing their head off.

 Tail wagging: A happy ending.

'You've got a heart of gold — cold and hard!'

Why does a nasty Russian called Alf stay indoors in wet weather?

dear.
Because Rude Alf, the Red, knows rain,

DAN: 'What is red, runs on wheels and
eats grass?'
ANN: 'I don't know. What?'
DAN: 'A bus. I lied about the grass.'

There was an old man of Vancouver
Whose wife got sucked into the hoover.
He said, 'There's some doubt
if she's more in than out,
But which ever it is, we can't move her.'

HELP!

SAY YOUR PRAYERS
by Neil Down

315

'Waiter, waiter, there's a dead fly in my soup.'
'It's the hot water that kills them.'

What is a butcher with five children called?

Daddy.

DR.JECKYL IS A
CHANGED MAN.

Sign in hospital cafeteria:
OUR SILVERWARE IS NOT MEDICINE — DON'T TAKE IT AFTER MEALS!

Epitaph on a gentleman's tombstone:
PARDON ME FOR NOT RISING WHEN YOU CAME IN.

TINA: *'My pet duck is very intelligent.'*
NINA: *'Prove it. Get it to make a few wise quacks.'*

Why can't a steam engine sit down?

Because it has a tender behind.

316

DOUBTS by R.U.SURE

'Your tongue is so long — you can seal an envelope after you've put it in the post box.'

Shout and scream: '*Aaaaaaaarrrggghhh! There's a horrible great big spider over there! It's huge!*' Everyone will leap up on to the table screaming and shouting: '*Help! Where is it!*' After a couple of minutes you shout: '**APRIL FOOLS!**'

ROUND THE MOUTAIN by Sheila B.Cummin

'When I want your opinion, I'll rattle your cage!'

Why did the ant elope?

Nobody Gnu.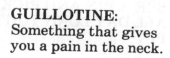

GUILLOTINE:
Something that gives
you a pain in the neck.

What is the best way to hunt bear?

With your clothes off.

'Doctor, doctor, I feel like a billiard ball.'
'Get to the back of the queue.'

'Waiter, waiter, how long have you worked here?'
'Two weeks, sir.'
'Oh, it can't be you that took my order then.'

Here I sit in the moonlight,
Abandoned by women and me,
Muttering over and over,
'I'll never eat garlic again.'

Flea: An insect that has gone to the dogs.

SEE A PIN AND PICK IT UP AND
ALL DAY LONG YOU'LL HAVE A
PIN . . .

How was the blind carpenter able to see?

He picked up a hammer and saw.

318

ANN: '*Have you heard what the sea said to the shore?*'
DAN: '*What?*'
ANN: '*Nothing. It just waved.*'

Dressing up in your parent's clothes is always fun, but try walking into a room wearing a very large hat or a baggy pair of trousers. Try and keep a straight face just as if the clothes you are wearing are perfectly normal.

FALLING OUT OF BED *by Eileen Dover*

Octopus: A cat with eight feet

'You ought to stop taking those tablets. They could be habit forming.'
'*Nonsense! I've been taking them for years.*'

GILLIAN: '*Mum, what was the name of the last station we stopped at?*'
MOTHER: '*I don't know. Don't bother me now, you can see I'm knitting.*'
GILLIAN: '*That's a pity, because my brother fell out there. . . .*'

319

IVY: *'Do you know your dog barked the whole night long.'*
VAL: *'Don't worry. He sleeps during the day.'*

 RESTAURANT MANAGER: 'Well, it's August again ... time to change the table cloths.'

 What did the man say when he staggered into the Queen's Arms?

'You shouldn't have bothered Your Majesty.'

 **ARE YOU A GENIUS** by Nora Mye

IF A JOB'S WORTH DOING YOU CAN ALWAYS FIND SOMEBODY TO DO IT FOR YOU.

How do you make a ham roll?

Push it.

Did you hear about the girl who was so shy she went to the bathroom to change her mind?

ULRIC: *'He's an M.D.'*
OSCAR: *'A medical doctor?'*
ULRIC: *'No, Mentally Defficient.'*

Unit: A term of abuse.

'Better to keep your mouth shut and let people think you are an idiot than to open it and remove all doubt.'

What is a ghost's favourite carol?

'I'm Screaming of a Fright Christmas.'

THE LONG WAIT *by Miss.D.Train*

A Professor named Benjamin Stet
Said, "Three things I always forget.
There's all my friends' names,
And the times of the trains
And the third one I can't recall yet.'

'Doctor, doctor, I feel like an apple.'
'Come over here, I won't bite you.'

What would happen if pigs could fly?

Bacon would go up.

MOTHER: *'Quentin, I want you to wash before your music teacher arrives.'*
QUENTIN: *'I have already.'*
MOTHER: *'Did you wash your ears?'*
QUENTIN: *'Well. . . . I washed the one nearest to her.'*

Ask someone to write down on a piece of paper eleven thousand, eleven hundred and eleven. They'll always give you the wrong answer. The correct way to write it is 12111.

TEACHER: *'There was the Ice Age, then the Stone Age, what came next?'*
WILLIAM: *'The saus-age?'*

Macaroni: Someone who invented the radio.

 Why did the judge sentence the comedian to ten years in prison?

Because he was involved in some funny business.

HYPOCHONDRIA IS THE ONLY DISEASE I HAVEN'T GOT.

 Did you hear about the woman that got her head stuck in a washing machine and ended up brainwashed?

'Waiter, waiter, why have you just been fired?'
'Because I'm too tough. I don't take orders from anyone.'

CAVEMAN 1: *'I hear you got hurt in an accident?'*
CAVEMAN 2: *'Yes, I sprained my back hunting Brontosaurus.'*
CAVEMAN 1: *'Did the dinosaur chase you?'*
CAVEMAN 2: *'No, I did it lifting the decoy.'*

Why was Lady Godiva a gambler?

She put everything she had on a horse.

Duck: A chicken wearing water flippers.

 GO TO NURSERY SCHOOL — IT'S ALL PLAY AND NO WORK!

'But Harry, this isn't our baby!'
'Shut up, it's a better pram.'

OPTICIAN: *'How many fingers am I holding up on my left hand?'*
PATIENT: *'Seven.'*
OPTICIAN: *'I don't know if it's your eyes or your arithmetic that's bad.'*

THE INSOMNIAC by *Eliza Wake*

Why was the baby girl christened 'glug-glug'?

The vicar fell in the font.

XANTIPPE: *'What was the new play like at the Civic Theatre?'*
YORICK: *'I didn't like the ending.'*
XANTIPPE: *'What was wrong with it?'*
YORICK: *'It was too far away from the beginning.'*

'Waiter, waiter, can I have a cup of coffee without cream.'
'Sorry, sir, we're out of cream, would you like it without milk?'

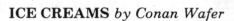

ICE CREAMS by *Conan Wafer*

What did the Ancient Egyptian boy say when his father was buried?'

'Goodbye Mummy.'

NINA: 'Everything I tell you seems to go in one ear and out of the other.'
MARK: 'I suppose that was why I was given two ears.'

'Waiter, waiter, what's wrong with these eggs?'
'I only laid the table. . . .'

 Why did the orchestra have bad manners?

It didn't know how to conduct itself.

DAN: 'I wish I had enough money to buy an elephant.'
ANN: 'What do you want an elephant for?'
DAN: 'I don't. I just wish I had the money.'

What do reindeer say before they tell a joke?

'This one will sleigh you.'

 'If I've said anything to upset you, do let me know. I might want to say it again.'

 Tulips: What you kiss somebody with.

'Doctor, doctor, I feel like a five pound note.'
'Go shopping. The change will do you good.'

DOCTOR: *'There is nothing wrong with your eyes.'*
LILY: *'What is it then?'*
DOCTOR: *'Your pigtails are too tight.'*

Did you hear about the worm that caught Egyptian 'flu?
It caught it from his mummy.

THE SWEET SHOP *by Annie Seedball*

During dinner at the Ritz
Father kept on having fits.
And, which made my sorrow greater,
I was left to tip the waiter.

SIMON: *'My brother has just opened a shop.'*
KEVIN: *'How's he doing?'*
SIMON: *'Six months. He opened it with a crowbar.'*

DEFINITION OF NOTHING:A
PEELED BALLOON.

'Doctor, doctor, you think I'm overweight, don't you?'
'Of course, not.'
'Then why during my check-up did you say 'Open your mouth and say Moooo. . . .'?'

*'Xantippe is a real drip. You can hear her,
but you can't turn her off.'*

**What happened when two geese collided
in mid-air?**

sdwnq ǝsooƃ ʇoƃ ʎǝɥ⊥

Net: Holes joined together with string.

'Waiter, waiter, my bill please.'
*'Yes, sir. And how did you find your
steak?'*
'With a magnifying glass.'

Say to your friend that you can show him
something he has never seen before and
will never see again. You then crack open
a peanut shell and show him the nut (he
will never have seen it before) and then
eat it (he will never see it again!).

NINA: *'I'd like to take a ship to
America.'*
FRED: *'Wouldn't it be more practical to
take a suitcase like everyone else.'*

*There was a young lady from Riga,
Who rode with a smile on a tiger.
They returned from the ride
With the lady inside
And the smile on the face of the tiger.*

327

CHILDHOOD IS WASTED ON THE YOUNG!

DOCTOR: *'Why is that Scottish patient complaining now?'*
NURSE: *'He says he got better before all the medicine was used up.'*

Trifle: A rifle with three barrels.

'I love the way you dress. Who wears your clean clothes?'

Why did the hen pour brandy sauce all over herself before laying an egg?

She wanted a Christmas brooding.

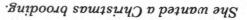

KEVIN: *'That star over there is Mars.'*
OSCAR: *'Which one is Pa's then?'*

'Did you hear the story about the germ?'
Never mind. I don't want to spread it around.'

HANDKERCHIEF
MANUFACTURERS ARE
THE ONLY ONES WHO
LIKE PEOPLE STICKING
NOSES IN THEIR
BUSINESS.

 What sort of lighting did Noah use on the ark?

Flood lighting.

A CHOICE OF MEATS *by Hammond* *Tongue*

 Monsoon: A small Frenchman

'I once ate in such a bad restaurant, I got food poisoning from opening the menu.'

In days of old girls went out to swim
Looking like Old Mother Hubbard.
Today they don't look quite so prim,
But a bit more like her cupboard!

What did Juliet say when she met Romeo in the balcony?

'Couldn't you get seats in the stalls?'

'No, I don't think you're a fool, but what's my opinion against a thousand others?'

Thread a needle with cotton on a cotton reel, and push the end of the cotton through your jacket so that just a couple of centimetres lay on the shoulder. Keep the rest of the cotton on the reel in an inside pocket. Sooner or later someone will notice a piece of cotton on your shoulder and will attempt to remove it for you. As soon as the victim takes hold of the loose end, walk away as fast as you can leaving them with a piece of cotton that is getting longer and longer and l-o-n-g-e-r!

FRED: *'Did you hear about the girl who was so ugly that boy scouts used to whistle at her as their food deed for the day.'*

WINNING ON THE ONE-ARMED-BANDIT
by Jack Potts

Why did the Invisible Woman take her invisible son to the doctor?

To see why he wasn't all there.

ARE PARISIAN SWIMMERS INSEINE?

What do you get if you dial 9737694630288554830936785?

A blister on your finger.

What bellows 'Eef If Of Muf!'?

A backward giant.

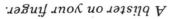

 'You missed being Miss. United Kingdom by two feet. Twelve inches on each hip.'

Throng: Not correct, as in 'That's the throng answer, thilly!'

Latin is a dead language
As dead as dead can be.
It killed off all the Romans
And how it's killing me!

331

'Doctor, doctor, I feel funny. What shall I do?'
'Get a job on television.'

'Waiter, waiter, if this is haddock I'm an idiot.'
'You're right, sir, it is haddock.'

TEACHER: *'Rose, if I was to say 'I have went' that wouldn't be right, would it?'*
ROSE: *'No, because you ain't went, you're still 'ere.'*

'I'd like a fur coat, please.'
'Certainly, madam, what fur?
'To keep warm, of course.'

I'M OFF MY HEAD
signed CHARLES I

WILLIAM: *'Daddy, were you in the last war?'*
FATHER: *'Yes, son, and I put up a very good fight . . . but they still made me go.'*

'You're the only person I know who forgot how to ride a bike.'

332

BANK ROBBER: *'Stick 'em up!'*
CASHIER: *'Stick what up?'*
BANK ROBBER: *'Look, don't get me muddled. This is my first job.'*

PSYCHIATRIST: *'As this is your first visit, and I don't know your problem, I suggest you start at the beginning.'*
PATIENT: *'Well, in the beginning I created Heaven and Earth . . .'*

 BEN: *'I've invented a new hearing aid that doesn't need batteries.'*
ANN: *'That's great, how does it work?'*
BEN: *'You hang a large sign around your neck saying: PLEASE SHOUT!'*

'You're so clumsy, if you fell down you'd probably miss the floor.'

 NO PROBLEM IS SO BIG THAT YOU CAN'T RUN AWAY FROM IT.

Kittens: Pets prepared to do a little mousework.

Who holds the record for staying underwater the longest?

Nobody knows. He hasn't come up yet.

SIGN IN AN OLD FOLKS HOME: *We're not deaf, we've just heard everything worth hearing.*

 JOHN: *'Stop the bus! An old lady's just fallen off!'*
CONDUCTOR: *'It's alright. She's paid her fare.'*

Tina went to the dentist to have a tooth pulled out. Because she was nervous the dentist gave her a tranquiliser.
'Do you feel better now?' he said.
'Much,' said Tina, *'I'd like to see anybody try and pull a tooth of mine out now!'*

Where is there a collection of records made by cows?

At the British Mooseum.

'Doctor, doctor, I've a very sore throat.'
'Will you go to the window and stick your tongue out.'
'Will that help my throat?'
'No, it's just that I don't like the neighbours.'

 THE TWO HIGHWAYMEN *by Angus Eyatt Dorne*

At Christmas, or on someone's birthday (especially if their birthday is on April 1st!) give them a huge present. When they undo one layer of paper they will find another layer, and another, and another, and another. There must be at least twelve layers, even a few boxes inside each other. In the centre of the parcel will be an old potatoe!

'Doctor, doctor, I snore so loudly that I wake myself up.'
'Well, sleep in another room then.'

'I hear you had to drop out of kindergarten. The work was too difficult for you, I suppose.'

'Waiter, waiter, you've got your tie in my soup.'

'Don't worry, it's non-shrinkable.'

ZOE: *'Why did you give up tap dancing?'*
PAM: *'I kept falling in the sink.'*

CENTRAL HEATING *by Ray D.Aitor*

 FRED: *'I saw the latest 'Superman' film last night and nearly died.'*
LILY: *'Why?'*
FRED: *'A piece of popcorn got stuck in my throat.'*

 THIS TOWN IS SO HEALTHY THEY HAD TO KILL SOMEONE TO START A CEMETERY.

 TODAY'S PROVERB: *A bird in the hand makes it difficult to blow your nose.*

Clock factory: A place where people are paid to make faces.

How does a flea get from one place to another?

By itch hiking.

 SIMON: *'Is it true that when you wake up in the morning you are on the floor?'*
ULRIC: *'Yes, I go to bed every night and I always drop off.'*

336

The reason she smiled, Mona Lisa,
Was seeing the Tower of Pisa.
They really did mean
To make thing lean,
'Cos they built it that way just to please
her.

What did the housewife say to the plumber when he mended her water cistern?

'Tanks so much,'

HOW TO MAKE CHAINS *by Lincoln Weldham*

'Now be a good boy and say 'Ah!' so that I can take my finger out of your mouth.'

What did the skunk say when the wind changed direction?

'It's call coming back to me now.'

'Let's wash the windows mother, the neighbours are straining their eyes.'

'Don't think it hasn't been nice knowing you — because it hasn't.'

GILLIAN: *'Do you keep dripping?'*
BUTCHER: *'I certainly do.'*
GILLIAN: *'It must be a dreadful nuisance.'*

337

Mary had a little lamb,
You've heard this tale before.
But did you know she passed her plate
And had a little more?

HARRY: *'When I was fishing in Wales I caught five jellyfish.'*
OSCAR: *'Cor! What flavours?'*

DOCTOR: *'Hello. I haven't seen you for months.'*
PATIENT: *'No, I've been very ill.'*

BEN: *'What a lovely fur coat you've got.'*
ZOE: *'It's my old tweed coat, but the dog always sleeps on it.'*

THE EMBARRASSING MOMENT *by Lucy Lastic*

Why did the schoolboy stand on his head?

He was turning things over in his mind.

Jargon: A missing container.

Take a piece of thick paper. Place a 5p piece on the ground and hide. When someone bends down to pick up the coin, tear the paper in half. Watch the embarrassed look on their faces when they think they have torn something!

> **TEACHER:** *'Where do fleas go in winter?'*
> **QUENTIN:** *'Search me.'*

The bomb he set went off too soon
And here his story ceases.
The bits we found are buried here —
And so he Rests In Pieces.

What is the motto of people who work in a fish and chip shop?

 If at first you don't succeed, fry fry again.

'So your doctor saved your life?'
'Yes, I rang him but he couldn't come.'

WHEN EVERYTHING SEEMS TO BE
COMING YOUR WAY, YOU'RE
PROBABLY IN THE WRONG LANE
OF TRAFFIC.

Take the inside pages from an old
newspaper and glue them all together.
When they are nicely stuck and you can't
open any of the pages, place them inside
the front pages of **TODAY'S** paper. Now
watch someone try to read the paper and
wonder why they can't open it up!

FOR SALE: *A piano that would suit a
beginner with chipped legs.*

**'Doctor, doctor, my wife thinks she's a
rubbish bin.'**
'Take her out tonight.'

**What did the princess say to the knight
when a dragon appeared?**

'Don't just stand there, slay something.'

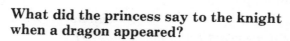

THE DOCTOR'S PROVERB: *When it comes to injections it's better to give than receive.*

YESTERDAY I COULDN'T SPELL EDUCATED, NOW I ARE IT.

'Waiter, waiter, this stew is terrible.'
'Our chef has been making stew since before you were born!'
'Then why did he have to save it for me!'

VAL: *'I told my mum and dad that I wanted to see the world.'*
TINA: *'What did they do?'*
VAL: *'They bought he an atlas.'*

A QUICK MEAL *by Tina Beans*

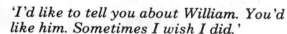

'I'd like to tell you about William. You'd like him. Sometimes I wish I did.'

MARK: *'Every Tuesday my dad used to take a pig to market but he never ever sold one.'*
JOHN: *'Why was that?'*
MARK: *'Market day was Friday.'*

Why didn't the man believe what the sardine said?

ʎɥsıɟ ooʇ pǝpunos ʇI

Garlic: The language Scotsmen speak.

IVY: *'Will you come with me to the nudist camp?'*
LILY: *'No thank you. The bare thought of it puts me off.'*

MABEL'S FALLING OFF THE CLIFF
by Caesar Titely

 What do two flags have when they get married?

Baby buntings.

'Doctor, doctor, what's a permenant cure for bunions?'
'Have your foot amputated.'

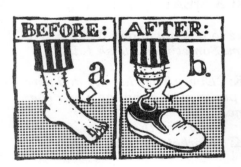

My goodness you've got the biggest mouth I've ever seen. The biggest mouth I've ever seen.'
'There's no need to repeat yourself.'
'I didn't. That was an echo.'

342

NOTHING IS ALL WRONG.
EVEN A BROKEN CLOCK
IS RIGHT TWICE A DAY.

'She's such a big girl, she wasn't just in the front row of the chorus, she was the front row of the chorus.'

Taxi Driver: Someone who does business by driving away customers.

DAN: *'What is the quickest way to the station?'*
PAM: *'Run like mad!'*

SCENT MANUFACTURERS PUSH THEIR BUSINESS INTO OTHER PEOPLE'S NOSES.

I THINK I'VE BEEN BITTEN *by A. Flee*

Old Bob is gone too soon, alas!
He tried to trace escaping gas.
With lighted match he braved the fates
Which blew him to the Pearly Gates.

Melancholy: A sad vegetable.

343

KEVIN: *'Do you want to know how I keep my head above water when I swim?'*
XANTIPPE: *'I know already. Wood floats.'*

What jumps from cake to cake and tastes of almonds?

uvdızɹvⱵ

'You have a very saintly face. The face of a Saint Bernard.'

YORICK: *'Nice to see you again! You haven't changed at all.'*
ULRIC: *'No, the laundry's been on strike.'*

TEACHER: *'Do you enjoy doing homework?'*
WILLILIAM: *'I like to do nothing better.'*

Polygon: A dead parrot.

'Your ears are so big, you look like a taxi cab with the doors open.'

How would you feel if somebody poured beer over your head? You would feel bitter.

FEEDING THE ELEPHANTS *by P. Nuts*

ZOE: *'Where did you learn to swim?'*
ANN: *'IN the water.'*

**How is a skunk different
from a rabbit?**

*The skunk uses cheaper
deoderent.*

REMEMBER: Anyone who goes to see a
psychiatrist ought to have their head
examined.

THE COWS ESCAPE *by Gay Topen*

ANN: *'Is that new horror film really
frightening?'*
DAN: *'I'll say it is! The ushers hold
hands when they walk down the aislex.'*

How does Count Dracula make a prison?

With blood cells.

TIME FOR SCHOOL *by R.U. Upjohn*

Doubloons: Daft twins.

'Doctor, doctor, I feel like a cat.'
'How long have you felt like this?'
'Oh, since about my fifth or sixth life.'

A steeple-chase jockey named John
A most obstinate horse sat upon.
Half-way around the course
'That's enough!' said the horse,
And she stopped while her rider went on.

What animal answers to a knock?

A doormouse.

LILY: *'You're looking all screwed up.'*
ROSE: *'Why do you say that?'*
LILY: *'You've been trying to get into the waste paper basket for the last half-an-hour.'*

What was the red-headed boxer's favourite drink?

Ginger punch.

RECEPTIONIST: *'Dr. Papadooblopolopolis is waiting to see you.'*
PATIENT: *'Which doctor?'*
RECEPTIONIST: *'Oh no, he's fully qualified.'*

'You must be 32 years old. I just counted the rings under your eyes.'

How can you make a snail fast?

Don't feed him.

IF YOU'VE A HEADACHE PUT YOUR HEAD THROUGH A WINDOW AND THE PANE WILL DISAPPERAR.

KEEPING CHEERFUL *by Mona Lott*

'Why is my cream cake flat? *'You said bring me a cream cake, and step on it!'*

Neighbour: People who knock on the door to borrow or the wall to complain.

 Why did the idiot go and touch a freshly painted pillar box?

He wanted his palm red.

ONE GHOST TO ANOTHER: *'Would you like to see where I had my apparition?'*

'Zoe, will you marry me?
'Yes, of course I will. Who is this speaking?'

What did one ghost say to the other?

Who was the ghoul I saw you with last night?'

1st GOAT: 'Who is that little goat over there?'
2nd GOAT: 'That's my kid brother.'

The baker's daughter, Fanny Jones,
Has lots and lots of fun,
For everytime she does her hair
She puts it in a bun.

PAM: 'Why does Dan walk around with his mouth open?'
EVE: 'He's so lazy, it saves him having to yawn.'

'Doctor, doctor, I've a terrible problem.
Will you help me out?'
'Certainly. Which way did you come in?'

There were ten people under one umbrella. Why didn't they get wet?

It wasn't raining.

HIT ON THE HEAD *by I.C. Starrs*

'You're such a bad cook, you're the only person I know who could burn a fruit salad.'

NINA: *'This disco is crowded tonight.'*
TINA: *'It certainly is. I fainted an hour ago and had to dance around for ten minutes before I could find a place to fall down.'*

Did you hear about the doctor who lost his patients?
He kept sticking the knife in.

A jovial fellow named Whacker
Pulled a joke from his Christmas cracker.
It said, 'If you're stuck
For a turkey, try duck —
You could say it's a real Christmas quacker!'

THE POST-SCRIPT *by Adeline Extra*

Year: What you hear with.

MOTHER: *'What do you want to do when you're as big as your father?'*
WILLIAM: *'Go on a diet.'*

How did Frankenstein eat his food?

He bolted it down.

'Doctor, doctor, do you make house calls?'
'Only if your house is really sick.'

 I GET ON WITH EVERYONE —
EXCEPT PEOPLE AND ANIMALS.

'The only time a man winks at her is if he's got something in his eyes.'

Why is it dangerous to do maths in the jungle?

·ǝʇɐ ʇǝ𝑔 noʎ 'ㄣ puɐ ㄣ ppɐ noʎ ɟI

'Doctor, doctor, I'm terrified of birds.
Even if I see a tiny sparrow I break out in a cold sweat.'
'But why are you afraid of birds?'
'Aren't all worms?'

'You have nice even teeth. It's just a pity the odd ones are missing.'

What monkey is like a flower?

A chimp-pansy.

MacPherson: *'Old MacTavish certainly knows how to put his drink away.'*
MacTartan: *'Yes, it's in the cupboard as soon as he sees visitors arriving.'*

Did you hear about the rich bank robber? He hired a secretary so that he could dictate his hold-up notes to her.

 PLEASE MAKE SURE YOUR BRAIN IS ENGAGED BEFORE PUTTING YOUR MOUTH INTO GEAR.

 Where is the best place to get a hair cut?

On the top of your head.

Which bird is always out of breath?

Puffin.

It is easy enough to be pleasant
When life flows round and round,
But the man worthwhile
Is the man who can smile
With his trousers falling down!

 'You're so thick. You're the closest thing to an idiot.'
'Do you want me to move away from you?'

Fission: What scientists eat with chips.

NEVER GIVE UP
by Percy Vere

SIGN IN A LION'S CAGE: *Trespassers Welcome For Dinner.*

'Is this new banana diet doing you any good?'
'Well, I haven't lost any weight, but you should see me climb trees!'

FRED: *'Next April Fools Day we're going to be very tired.'*
ROSE: *'How do you work that one out?'*
FRED: *'We will just have reached the end of a 31 day March.'*

*There once was a fat boy called Kidd
Who ate thirty jam tarts for a quid.
When asked 'Are you faint?'
He replied, 'No, I ain't,
But I don't feel quite as well as I did!'*

NINA: *'Your brother's very small isn't he?'*
TINA: *'Yes, he's only my half-brother.'*

BELL RINGING *by Paula Rope*

Can you carry water in a sieve?

Yes, if you freeze it first!

Pressing engagement: Two dry cleaners getting married.

What has a lot of money and makes a funny noise?

Lloyds Bonk.

OPERATIONS ARE FUNNY — THEY HAVE YOU IN STITCHES.

OSCAR: *'Ben is a mental tourist.'*
YORICK: *'A mental tourist?'*
OSCAR: *'Yes, his mind wanders.'*

 Pylon: To make a heap.

'Waiter, waiter, have you any wild duck?'
'No, but I've got a tame one I can irritate for you.'

Play silly games to make people laugh. For some strange reason, people always find the word '**Sausages**' funny! Get people to ask you questions, to which you can only reply '*Sausages*' **without laughing**. '*What do you hang on your Christmas tree?*' **Sausages**! '*What is that growing on the top of your head?*' **Sausages**! If you laugh, change places and ask the questions yourself.

POSTMAN: '*Is this your parcel, the name is obliterated.*'
WOMAN: '*No, my name is Boswell.*'

'**Waiter, waiter, the food in this restaurant is the worst I have ever tasted.**'
'*Sorry you didn't like it. Any other complaints.*'
'**Yes, the portions are far too small.**'

'The only thing you can keep in your head longer than a day is a cold.'

What do you call a midget novelist?

A short story writer.

'How did you get that nasty lump on your head?'
'I said to my workmate — "I'll hold the post and when I nod my head, hit it." and he did!'

354

DO POCKET CALCULATORS COUNT POCKETS?

Drive somebody crazy — walk up to a complete stranger and say: *'Lovely to see you again after all this time! So you've come into a fortune, eh? You lucky thing. Well, I'll see you at the reading of the will.'* and rush away!

LANDLORD: *'When are you going to pay me the rent Madame Zoe?'*
FORTUNE TELLER: *'Give me two pounds and I'll look in my crystal ball.'*

How do you milk a caterpillar?

··· *First, you get a very low stool* ···

TEACHER: *'Now, Kevin, I'm going to use my hat to represent the planet Jupiter. Have you any question?'*
KEVIN: *'Yes, is Jupiter inhabited.'*

WHY DOES CHRISTMAS ALWAYS COME AT A TIME WHEN THE SHOPS ARE SO BUSY?

THOUGHT FOR THE DAY: If you can't say something good about somebody, say something bad. It keeps the conversation going.

Fete: Boring garden party which is worse than death.

CLARE: *'How did you burn your ears?'*
GILLIAN: *'I was ironing when the telephone rang, and I answered the iron.'*
CLARE: *'But how did you burn the other ear?'*
GILLIAN: *'I just put the iron down when the phone rang again.'*

'Doctor, doctor, I'm losing my memory.'
'Oh, forget it.'

'Waiter, waiter, this soup isn't fit for a pig.'
'I'll take it back and bring you some that is.'

'I spend hours in front of the mirror admiring my beauty. Is it vanity?'
'No, a very vivid imagination.'

What kind of music do ghosts like?

Something with a haunting melody.

'Have you ever had German measles?'
'No, I've only ever been as far as the Isle of Wight.'

356

DELICIOUS MEALS FOR ONE by Eileen Joyitt

SCHOOL DINNERS SHOULD CARRY A GOVERNMENT HEALTH WARNING.

ZOE: *'What's wrong with your back?'*
BEN: *'I went for a check-up with the doctor. He told me I was fine, slapped me on the back and injured my spine.'*

CONSULT A DOCTOR — YOU'LL NEVER LIVE TO REGRET IT.

'Waiter, waiter, there's a beetle in my soup. Send the manager here at once!'
'That won't do any good. He's frightened of them as well.'

CLARE: *'Your dog looks pleased to see me, he's sitting up and wagging his tail.'*
HARRY: *'That's probably because you're eating off his plate.'*

·'I can play the piano by ear.'
'I wish you'd play it over there!'

FUN IN THE ARMY
by Major Laugh

LAUGH — THAT'S AN ORDER!!

POLICEMAN: *'Can I help you?'*
YORICK: *'Yes, I've lost my toffee.'*
POLICEMAN: *'I thought it was something serious.'*
YORICK: *'It is. My teeth are in it.'*

Revolving door: Where people go around together.

Why do undertakers go to Wembley?

For the Hearse of the Year Show.

 'I admit you're stronger than I am, but bad breath isn't everything.'

 What do people in China do when it rains?

Get wet.

Mouth: Something that is often opened by mistake.

EVE: *'I never drink anything stronger than pop.'*
ZOE: *'Yes, but Pop will drink anything you give him.'*

'Waiter, waiter, my tea is weak.'
'*What do you expect me to do, give it weight training?*'

When I die, bury me deep,
Bury my history book at my feet.
Tell the teacher I've gone to rest,
And won't be back for the history test.

Tortoise: What the teacher did.

 ULRICK: '*What's the difference between an elephant and upduck?*'
XANTIPPE: '*What's 'upduck'?*'
ULRICK: '*Nothing much, dearie.*'

What do Irishmen do with old apple peels?

Throw them away!

STRONG WIND *by Gail Force*

I USED TO BE APATHETIC, BUT NOW I JUST DON'T CARE.

'Your husband is very ill, why didn't you send for me sooner?'
'*I thought I'd give him a chance to get better.*'

 IF YOU CAN READ THIS

YOU'RE UPSIDE DOWN

359

MOTHER: *'Harry, now go and kiss Auntie Ethel good-bye.'*
HARRY: *'Why, I haven't done anything wrong!'*

'Waiter, waiter, is this chicken pie or minced beef?'
'Can't you tell the difference?'
'No.'
'Then does it matter?'

What's the difference between a hard ball and a soft ball?

 The difference between concussion and a lump.

'Waiter, waiter, I can't eat this soup.'
'Why not, sir?'
'I haven't got a spoon.'

Why are vampires unpopular?

Because they are a pain in the neck.

 EVERY MAN REAPS WHAT HE SOWS — EXCEPT THE AMATEUR GARDENER.

 'You're not yourself today, I noticed the improvement straightaway.'

Which animal never became famous
because he got off at the wrong station?

Waterloo Bear.

Ooey Gooey was a worm,
A wondrous worm was he.
He stepped upon a railway line,
A train he did not see.
                    Ooey gooey.

Catch a friend out by saying: *'There's*
only one way of making money.' He or
she is certain to reply: *'What's that?'* and
you say: *'I thought* **you** *wouldn't know*
it!'

Safety: A cup of drink
that won't hurt you.

SAFE-TEA
HELMET

I'VE GOT KLEPTOMANIA — WHAT
CAN I TAKE FOR IT?

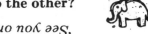

Two flies stood on Robinson Crusoes
head. What did one say to the other?

'See you on Friday.'

How do you stop a head cold from going to your chest?

Tie a knot in your neck.

BOTH OF US by *Ewan Mee*

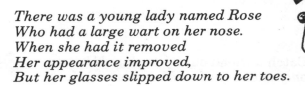

There was a young lady named Rose
Who had a large wart on her nose.
When she had it removed
Her appearance improved,
But her glasses slipped down to her toes.

When you meet your friend on April Fools Day, give him or her a welcoming handshake and watch the expression on their faces. What they won't know is that you have a spoonful of honey or jam in the palm of your hand!

ULRIC: *'Whilst we were hunting we saw a man-eating lion.'*
ZOE: *'Some people will eat anything.'*

THEATRICAL PRODUCER: *'Have you had any stage experience?'*
QUENTIN: *'I had my leg in a cast once.'*

362

A DISUSED CHURCH *by Pugh Bustead*

Antibody: Uncle's fat wife.

'Your menu says Cold Boiled Ham, what is that?'
'Ham that has been boiled in cold water.'

MARK: *'I told my girlfriend I would go to the ends of the earth for her.'*
JOHN: *'What did she say?'*
MARK: *'She told me to jump off when I got there.'*

'Doctor, doctor, I can't stop pulling funny faces.'
'That's not a serious problem.'
'But people with funny faces don't like it when I pull them.'

What is the worst month for soldiers?

A FRIEND IN NEED IS A PEST!

HARRY: *'Why did you have a fight with that masseur?'*
FRED: *'He just rubbed me up the wrong way.'*

'You've changed your mind? Does the new one work any better?'

Sickle: Just a little bit sick.

363

'Doctor, doctor, how can I cure myself of sleep walking?'
'Put drawing pins on the floor.'

I had written to Aunt Maud
Who was on a trip abroad,
When I heard she'd died of cramp
Just too late to save the stamp.

Which detective takes bubble baths?

Sherlock Foams

What do you get if you cross an elephant with a boy scout?

An elephant that helps old ladies across the street.

LILY: *'Aren't sardines stupid!'*
ROSE: *'Why do you say that?'*
LILY: *'They crawl into tins, shut themselves in and then leave the key on the outside!'*

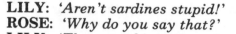

TINA: *'I went to the sea for my asthma.'*
NINA: *'Why, can't you get it here?'*

364

BROADEN YOUR MIND —
PUT A STICK OF
DYNAMITE IN EACH EAR.

'Doctor, doctor, my wife thinks she's a
cat.'
'*What can I do?*'
'Just stop her eating mice.'

What did Lady Hamilton say to Lord
Nelson?

'*You're the one-eye care for!*'

PSYCHIATRIST: '*And how long has
your husband thought he was Napoleon?*'
WIFE: '*Eversince Waterloo.*'

DO UNTO OTHERS BEFORE THEY
GET A CHANCE TO DO IT UNTO
YOU.

YORICK: '*I'll have some rat poison,
please.*'
CHEMIST: '*Shall I wrap it up for you,
sir.*'
YORICK: '*No, I'll send the rats down
here to eat it!*'

'You throw yourself into everything you
do. Why not go outside and dig a very
deep hole?'

Why are Egyptian children good?

Because they respect their mummies.

 Who is Welsh and fiendishly cunning?

Dai Abolical.

 What do you get if you cross an owl with a skunk?

Something that smells and doesn't give a hoot.

'I'll have to put some stitches in that cut.'
'*While you've got your needle out, can you sew this button on for me?*'

Sneeze: Much achoo about nothing.

LIVING ON EARTH MAY BE EXPENSIVE, BUT IT DOES INCLUDE AN ANNUAL FREE TRIP AROUND THE SUN.

Humpty Dumpty sat on a wall,
Humpty Dumpty had a great fall.
All the king's horses and all the king's men
Had scrambled eggs for dinner again.

TRAFFIC POLICEMAN: *'When I saw you driving down the road, I said to myself, 'Sixty-five at least'.*
LADY MOTORIST: *'Oh officer, it's just this hat makes me look older.'*

'Doctor, doctor, I can't sleep. Can you do anything for me?'
'Hold on to the phone. I'll sing you a lullaby.'

XANTIPPE: *'I've been cooking for five years.'*
QUENTIN: *'Didn't you soon ought to be done?'*

THE CALYPSO BAND by Lydia Dustbin

What is the difference between an elephant and a biscuit?

You can't dip an elephant into your tea!

 Zing: What you do with a zong.

367

I'm fairly gracious to the bore
Who tells me jokes I've heard before,
But he will find me glum and grim
Who tells me jokes **I told to him!**

'Waiter, waiter, will my pancakes be long?'
'No, madam, they will be round.'

 PRESERVE WILDLIFE — PICKLE A
WEASEL TODAY!

OSCAR: 'We have a new cook. A real marvel. Chicken, beef, pork, lamb, you name it and it makes no difference to her. She eats everything.'

'Doctor, doctor, how can I stop myself falling out of bed?'
'Sleep on the floor.'

 'Can you hear her singing?'
'Yes, we couldn't get the best seats.'

 EVE: *'What shall we do tonight? Stay at home?'*
JOHN: *'No, I've got a bad cough, let's go to the theatre.'*

368

BE ALERT, YOUR COUNTRY NEEDS LERTS.
Be aloof, we've got enough lerts.

'I'm sure we've met before. I don't remember your face, but I never forget a dress.'

IVY: *'Did anyone laugh when you slipped on the ice?'*
BEN: *'No, but the ice made a few cracks.'*

What do you call a mischievous egg?

ʌ pɹɐctᴉɔɐl ʎolɥɐɹ.

Nonsense: An elephant hanging over a cliff with its tail tied to a blade of grass. That's nonsense!

An apple landing on his head
Set Isaac Newton thinking, but —
It would have been a different tale
Had it been a coconut.

WHO SAW HIM LEAVE *by Wendy Go*

MOTHER: *'Ulric, have you got your shoes on yet?'*
ULRIC: *'All but one of them.'*

369

'Waiter, waiter, there's a fly in my butter.'
'No there isn't!'
'Yes, there is!'
'There isn't. That's a beetle and it's marge, not butter!'

'I don't think my psychiatrist really cares about listening to my problems.'
'What makes you think that?'
'Every time I go, he's wearing earmuffs.'

What did the modern undertaker call his funeral parlour?

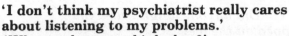

The Departure Lounge.

THE UGLY WOMAN *by Ida Fayce*

MY MUM'S GOT A PRETTY FACE IF YOU CAN READ BETWEEN THE LINES.

Lisp: When you call a spade a thpade.

'Doctor, doctor, I feel like a bar of soap.'
'That's life, boy.'

370

What did they call the baby
bear that was born bald?

Fred bear.

On a piece of paper write a message, such
as 'GIVE ME A KISS', and attach it to
someone's back with a piece of sticky
tape. Give them a friendly pat on the
back as you greet them, and they won't
notice. All day they will wander around
wondering why they are so popular!

END OF THE WEEK *by Gladys Friday*

NEVER HIT A MAN WHILE HE'S
DOWN — HE MIGHT GET UP AGAIN.

What is chocolate on the outside, peanut
in the middle, and sings hymns?

A Sunday School Treet.

Walk along swinging your right leg up as
high as it will go. You will get some very
funny looks as you walk down the street!

*'Do you know 'The Road to Mandalay?' I
don't mean sing it — I mean take it!'*

**'Doctor, doctor, I've got a bad liver. What
shall I do?'**
'Take it back to the butcher.'

GILLIAN: *'Why didn't you but that
colour television?'*
QUENTIN: *'Because of the black and
white price tag.'*

RESTAURANT MANAGER: *'Have you
had much experience of waiting?'*
JOB APPLICANT: *'Oh, yes, I've been
travelling by British Rail for years.'*

ANN: *'Do you like my cake?'*
DAN: *'It's very nice. Did you buy it
yourself?'*

VAL: *'How's your father?'*
IVY: *'He's suffering from fallen arches.'*
VAL: *'Bad feet, eh?'*
IVY: *'No, the railway viaduct fell on
him.'*

'Waiter, waiter, why are you crying?'
'I burnt my thumb in your soup.'

REMEMBER: AN EGG IS WHOLE
DAY'S WORK FOR A CHICKEN.

THE PAINTER *by R.T.Stick*

'I have a hunch.'
'*And here was me thinking you were just round-shouldered.*'

'Doctor, doctor, I'm very worried. This is the first operation I've ever had.'
'*Don't worry. This is the first operation I've ever done.*'

They used to call her Aphrodite.
Until they saw her in her nightie,
With face unpainted and hair all frizz.
Now they simply call her Liz.

What do koala's take on holiday?

All the bear essentials.

What do angry mice send each other at Christmas?

Cross mouse cards.

Pedestrian: Someone who should be seen and not hurt.

'Waiter, waiter, what's this fly doing in my ice cream?'
'*Winter sports?*'

Why did Eve never fear the measles?

Because she already Adam.

DENTIST: *Why did you just bit me?*
YORICK: *Because you go on my nerves.*

Why did the germ across the microscope?

To get to the other slide.

1000 RIDDLES

A farmer had eggs for breakfast every morning. He owned no chickens and didn't get eggs from anybody else. Where did he get the eggs?

From his ducks.

When will a net hold water?

When the water is frozen into ice.

Why is a Christmas pudding like the ocean?

It's full of currants.

What did the man say when he found he was going bald?

Hair today, gone tomorrow.

What's in the church, but not the
                    steeple,
The parson has it, but not the people.

The letter R.

If you saw a bird sitting on a twig, how could you get the twig without disturbing the bird?

Wait until the bird flew away.

What kind of bird is always around when there's something to eat or drink?

A swallow.

If a ton of coal costs £15, what will a ton of firewood come to?

Ashes.

Why is it more dangerous to go to the woods in springtime?

Because in the spring the grass has blades, the flowers have pistils, the leaves shoot, the cowslips about, and the bullrush is out.

Why is the letter P like a Roman emperor?

Because it is near O.

What is the difference between a bell and a cook?

One makes a din, the other a dinner.

A forest is two kilometres across. How far can you go into it?

One kilometre. After that, you will be going out.

Is it possible for a man to marry his widow's sister?

No – he'd be dead.

What will go up a chimney down, but won't go down a chimney up?

An umbrella.

Why did the butterfly flutter by?

Because it saw the dragonfly drink the flagon dry.

Three girls stood under an umbrella but none of them got wet? How was that?

It wasn't raining.

What can run but can't walk?

Water.

Mrs Bigger had a baby. Who was bigger?

The baby, because it was a little bigger.

Why do birds fly South?

Because it's too far to walk.

378

Why did Moses have to be hidden quickly when he was a baby?

Because it was a 'rush' job to save him.

What runs round the garden without moving?

The fence.

Why does the giraffe have such a long neck?

Because its head is so far from its body.

Your uncle's sister is not your aunt. Who is she?

Your mother

What does an artist like best to draw?

His wages.

If a boy ate his father and mother, what would that make him?

An orphan.

From what word of eight letters can you extract five and leave ten?

Tendency.

What musical key makes a good army officer?

A sharp major.

What has a head, can't think, but drives?

A hammer.

When is your mind like a rumpled bed?

When it isn't made up yet.

Why are first-class footballers like accomplished musicians?

Because they are very good players.

What has six legs, but only walks with four?

A horse with a rider.

What did the blackbird say to the scarecrow?

I can beat the stuffing out of you.

What kind of tunes do we enjoy most?

For-tunes.

Why did the man laugh after his operation?

The doctor put him in stitches.

Where was Solomon's Temple?

On the side of his head.

What river is ever without a
beginning and ending?

S—ever—N.

What goes all the way from Lands
End to John o'Groats without
moving?

The road.

Why are postmen clever people?
Because they are men of letters.

When will water stop running
downhill?
When it reaches the bottom.

Where are Kings and Queens usually
crowned?
On the head.

Why are your nose and your
handkerchief deadly enemies?
*Because they can't meet without coming
to blows?*

Why wasn't the elephant allowed on the aeroplane?

Because its trunk was too big to fit under the seat.

What animal eats and drinks with its tail?

All of them. They don't remove their tails for eating and drinking.

Why is a poor joke like an unsharpened pencil?

Because it has no point.

What question can never be answered by 'Yes'?

'Are you asleep?'

When is longhand quicker than shorthand?

On a clock.

Why can't the world come to an end?

Because it is round.

Why are heavy drinkers like heavy showers?

Because they usually begin with little drops.

Why is there no such thing as a whole day?

Because every day begins by breaking.

What didn't Adam and Eve have that everyone in the world has had?

Parents.

Why is it silly to buy coal?

Because instead of going to the buyer, it goes to the cellar.

What are the warmest months of the year?

September, November and December, because they all have embers in them.

Which is the strongest day of the week?

Sunday, because all the rest are week-days.

What 'bus' crossed the ocean?

Columbus.

What can you add to a bucket of water that will make it weigh less?

Holes.

How can you tell one sort of cat from another?

Look in the catalogue.

How can you go without sleep for seven days and not be tired?

Sleep at night.

Why are waiters good at sums?

Because they know their tables.

Why is a man who marries twice like the captain of a ship?

Because he has a second mate.

Why is a tall building dangerous?

Because it has a lot of flaws (floors) in it.

In what month do people eat the least?

February – it's the shortest month.

**Why was the
mother flea so
sad?**

*Because her children
were going to the
dogs.*

Shall
we walk
or...

**What did one flea say to the other
flea?**

'Shall we walk or shall we take the dog?'

**You can take away my first letter,
and my second letter.
You can take away all my letters, and
yet I remain the same.
What am I?**

The Postman.

What animal keeps the best time?

A watchdog.

**What lands as often on its tail as it
does on its head?**

A penny.

**Why is it that there is not a moment
that we can call our own?**

Because the minutes are not hours.

What wears shoes, but has no feet?

The pavement.

Why was the inventor of the safety match so pleased?

Because it was a striking success.

What has four legs and flies?

A dead horse.

What does a beard do for a man who seldom tells the truth?

It keeps him from being a bare-faced liar.

What kind of umbrella does the Prime Minister carry on a rainy day?

A wet one.

How do you make notes of stone?

Rearrange the letters.

What does everyone have that he can always count on?

His fingers.

What is the hardest thing about learning to roller-skate?

The ground.

Why did the baker stop baking bread?

Because he wasn't making enough dough.

Why is a black chicken smarter than a white one?

Because a black chicken can lay a white egg, but a white chicken can't lay a black one.

Who always goes to sleep with his shoes on?

A horse.

Do you know the story of the red-hot poker?

You couldn't grasp it.

What is the best way to eat spaghetti?

First, open your mouth.

Soldiers mark time with their feet. What does the same thing with its hands?

A watch.

When is a new baby not the usual delicate pink?

When he's a robust yeller.

Did you hear the story about the two holes in the ground?

Well, well.

387

its for You.

Why is waiting on the telephone like doing a trapeze act?

Because you have to hang on.

Why will the radio not take the place of newspapers?

You can't light the fire with a radio.

What is the longest view in the world?

Down a road with telegraph poles, because then you can see from pole to pole.

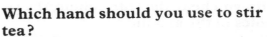

What do they do with a tree after they chop it down?

Chop it up.

Why is a traffic policeman strong?

Because he holds up heavy lorries.

Which hand should you use to stir tea?

Neither – it's best to use a spoon.

**What word of three syllables
contains twenty-six letters?**

Alphabet.

**What plays when it works, and works
when it plays?**

A fountain.

**How can you keep a rooster from
crowing on Sunday morning?**

Eat him for dinner on Saturday.

What is a boxer's favourite drink?

Punch.

Why is the theatre such a sad place?

Because all the seats are in tiers.

**How do you get in touch with
a fish?**

Just drop him a line.

**What did the boy say when
he opened his piggy-bank
and found nothing in it?**

I C U R M T

How many peas in a pod?

One P.

Why is tennis such a noisy game?

Because every player raises a racket.

A man had two sons and named them both Ed? Why?

He thought two eds were better than one.

What did the mother strawberry say to the baby strawberry?

Don't get into a jam.

What are the three easiest ways to spread rumour?

Telephone, telegraph – and tell a gossip.

What is black and white and read all over?

A newspaper.

What is the reddest side of an apple?

The outside.

What herb cures all diseases?

Thyme.

390

What runs around all day and then lies under the bed with its tongue hanging out?

Your shoe.

What is the difference between a thunderclap and a lion with toothache?

One pours with rain and the other roars with pain.

Why do you always start to walk with the right foot first?

Because when you move one foot, the other is always left behind.

Why did the boy wear two suits to the fancy dress party?

He went as twins.

What is the difference between a doormat and a bottle of medicine?

One is taken up and shaken, the other is shaken up and taken.

What did the judge say when he got home after work?

It's been another trying day.

What is it that increases the more it is shared with others?

Happiness.

Why is a room full of married couples empty?

Because there is not a single person in it.

Who is the strongest thief?

A shoplifter.

What often falls but never gets hurt?

Rain.

What is red and goes up and down?

A tomato in a lift.

What goes farther the slower it goes?

Money.

What is bought by the yard and worn by the foot?

A carpet.

Why is a penny like a policeman?

They're both coppers.

What happened when the steam-hammer was invented?

It made a great hit.

What has a foot at each end and a foot in the middle?

A yardstick.

What do all ships weigh, regardless of size?

Anchors.

Why is a herring like a cemetery?

Because it is full of bones.

If twelve makes a dozen, how many make a million?

Very few.

Why do we dress baby girls in pink and baby boys in blue?

Because they can't dress themselves.

What is it that everyone needs, everyone gives, everyone asks for and very few take?

Advice.

Why shouldn't you tell secrets when there's a clock in the room?

Because time will tell.

Where does Thursday come before Wednesday?

In a dictionary.

What kind of house weighs the least?

A lighthouse.

What is it that the man who makes it does not need, the man who buys it does not use for himself, and the person who uses it does so without knowing?

A coffin.

Why is an island like the letter T?

Because it is in the middle of water.

To whom does every man take off his hat?

His barber.

What is lengthened by a cut at both ends?

A ditch.

What did the burglar say to the lady who caught him stealing her silver?

'I'm at your service, madam.'

What is it a girl looks for but hopes she won't find?

A hole in her tights.

Why do surgeons wear masks during operations?

Because if they make a mistake, no one will know who did it.

What did the Eskimo say when he'd built his igloo?

'Ours is a nice house, ours is.'

Why did the man hit the clock?

Because the clock struck first.

What is pronounced like one letter, written with three letters, and belongs to all animals?

Eye.

What kind of robbery is the easiest?

A safe robbery.

Why does your sense of touch suffer if you are ill?

Because you don't feel well.

Why should you never tell secrets in a cornfield?

Because the corn has ears.

Why would a sixth sense be a handicap?

Because it would be a new sense.

What is filled every morning and emptied every night, except once a year when it is filled at night and emptied in the morning?

A stocking.

What does a garden say when it laughs?

Hoe, hoe, hoe.

Why do you always find something in the last place you look?

Because when you find it, you stop looking.

In what liquid does the Queen take her medicine?

Inside her (cider).

Do you believe in clubs for young people?

Only when kindness fails.

396

Why can't anyone stay angry long with an actress?

Because she always makes up.

What is easy to get into but hard to get out of?

Trouble.

Why is a week-old loaf like a mouse running into a hole?

Because you can see it's stale.

What is better than presence of mind in a road accident?

Absence of body.

What grows larger the more you take away?

A hole.

Why should a greedy man wear a tartan vest?

To keep a check on his stomach.

Why did the lobster blush?

Because it saw the salad dressing.

What's the easiest way to
get on TV?

Sit on your set.

What does a hard-working
gardener always grow?

Tired.

What is another name for a
butcher's boy?

A chop assistant.

What is boiled then cooled,
sweetened then soured?

Iced tea with lemon.

What should we do instead of
complaining when it rains?

Let it rain.

When a boy falls into water, what is
the first thing he does?

Gets wet.

When is it correct to say, 'I is?'

'I is the letter after H.'

Why is it a mistake to put on a shoe?

Because you're putting your foot in it.

What happened when the Eskimo
girl fell out with her boyfriend?

She gave him the cold shoulder.

How many beans can you put in an
empty bag?

One. After that the bag isn't empty.

What happened to the boy who ran
away with the circus?

The police made him bring it back.

Why wouldn't the parrot talk to the
Chinaman?

Because he only spoke pigeon English.

From what number can you
take half and leave nothing?

*The number 8. Take away
the top half and o is left.*

Why are horses not needed
in the Isle of Wight?

*Because visitors prefer
Cowes to Ryde?*

Why is the Prince of Wales
like a cloudy day?

Because he is likely to reign.

What is the difference between a glass of water and a glass of whisky?

About 40 pence.

What can be measured, but has no length, width or thickness?

The temperature.

Why does the Indian wear feathers in his hair?

To keep his wigwam.

Why is a warm day bad for an icicle's character?

Because it turns into an eavesdropper.

What did one angel say to the other angel?

'Halo.'

400

What gets harder to catch the faster you run?

Your breath.

Why should you not swim in the river at Paris?

If you did you would be in Seine.

Which Member of Parliament wears the largest hat?

The one with the largest head.

What sits on the bottom of the sea and shakes?

A nervous wreck.

Why is a girl extravagant with her clothes?

When she has a new dress she wears it out the first day.

If the green house is on the right side of the road, and the red house is on the left side of the road, where is the white house?

In Washington, USA.

What's the best place for a motorist to get a nice 'cuppa'?

At a T junction.

Why should you not upset a cannibal?

Because if you do, you might find yourself in hot water.

What did one windshield wiper say to the other windshield wiper?

'Isn't it a pity we seem to meet only when it rains?'

Why did the man keep a ruler on his newspaper?

Because he wanted to get the story straight.

Why is a doctor less likely to be upset on an ocean voyage?

Because he is accustomed to see sickness.

What did the necktie say to the hat?

'You go on ahead, I'll hang around for a while.'

Why is a bad cold a great humiliation?

Because it can bring a proud man to his sneeze.

What animal is grey and has a trunk?

A mouse going on holiday.

Why is a clock like a river?

Because it won't run for long without winding.

What kind of fall makes you unconscious but doesn't hurt you?

Falling asleep.

Why do women make good post office workers?

Because they know how to manage the males.

What turns everything round but doesn't move?

A mirror.

Why does the stork stand on one leg only?

If he lifted it, he would fall down.

Why do some people press the lift
button with the thumb and others
with the forefinger?

To signal the lift.

How many acorns grow on the
average pine tree?

None. Pine trees don't have acorns.

What day of the year is a command
to go forward?

March fourth.

If Harry's father is Bob's son, what
relation is Harry to Bob?

Bob is Harry's grandfather.

What is always behind the times?

The back of a clock.

When is a car not a car?

When it turns into a garage.

What can turn without moving?

Milk – it can turn sour.

What is the best way to
remove paint?

Sit down on it before it's dry.

How did the inventor discover gunpowder?

It came to him in a flash.

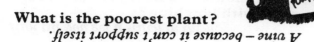

What is a bacteria?

The rear entrance of a cafeteria.

What is the poorest plant?

A vine — because it can't support itself.

What comes with a car, is of no use to a car, and yet the car can't run without it?

Noise.

How many weeks belong to the year?

Forty-six; the other six are only Lent.

Why did the Romans build straight roads?

Because they didn't want to drive their horses round the bend.

What kind of clothing wears the longest?

Underwear, because it is never worn out.

Why is a crossword puzzle like a quarrel?

Because one word leads to another.

405

What is the biggest ant?

An elephant.

What happens when the police take a burglar's fingerprints?

It creates a very bad impression.

What should you do if you split your sides with laughing?

Run till you get a stitch in them.

A lady who works in a sweet shop in Cambridge has measurements of 40–26–40. She is 5 feet 4 inches tall and wears a size 9 shoe. What do you think she weighs?

She weighs sweets.

During what season do ants eat most?

Summer. That is when they go to a lot of picnics.

What animals didn't come on the ark in pairs?

Worms. They came in apples.

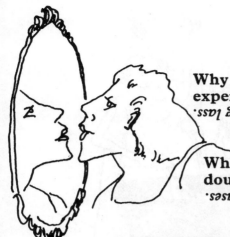

Why is a pretty girl like an expensive mirror?
Because she is a good looking lass.

What is the surest way to double your money?
Fold it — you'll find it increases.

Which Musician had the largest family?
Beethoven — he was known as the father of German music.

If a rooster laid a brown egg and a white egg what kind of chicks would hatch?
None. Roosters don't lay eggs.

Where did Caesar go on his thirty-ninth birthday?
Into his fortieth year.

Did you hear the story about the peacock?
It's a beautiful tail.

If you were to throw a white stone into the Red Sea, what would it become?
Wet.

What kind of person is fed up with people?

A cannibal.

What was the largest island before Australia was discovered?

Australia.

When is a poor church collection like a policeman's helmet?

When it has just one copper in it.

If a man is born in Italy, grows up in England, goes to America and dies in Baltimore, what is he?

Dead.

Why is a garden like a story?
They both have plots.

What is the last thing you take off when you go to bed?
Your feet from the floor.

If an electric train travels 90 miles an hour in a westerly direction and the wind is blowing from the north, in which direction is the smoke blowing?
There is no smoke from an electric train!

What is round and has a bad temper?
A vicious circle.

What is found in the middle of both America and Australia?
The letter R.

If cheese comes after dinner, what comes after cheese?
A mouse.

What gets wetter the more it dries?
A towel.

Why can't a deaf man be sent to prison?

Because you can't condemn a man without a hearing.

How many letters are there in the alphabet?

Eleven, T-H-E-A-L-P-H-A-B-E-T.

When does a bed grow longer?

At night, because two feet are added to it.

If thirteen birds were sitting on a telephone wire, and you shot one, how many would be left?

None. They would all fly away.

How did the boy feel after being caned?

Absolutely whacked.

Why do lions eat raw meat?

Because they don't know how to cook.

How can you make money fast?

Glue it to the floor.

What pets make exciting music?

Trumpets.

What is the best way to get fat?

Go to the butcher's shop.

What would happen if an elephant sat in front of you at the movies?

You would miss most of the picture.

What is oil before it is discovered?

A well-kept secret.

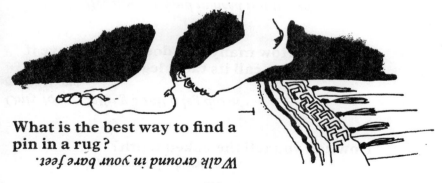

What is the best way to find a pin in a rug?

Walk around in your bare feet.

411

Why is a Viking like a cavalry officer?

Because he's a Norseman.

What do well-behaved young lambs say to their mothers?

'Thank ewe!'

Why did the jam roll?

Because it saw the apple turnover.

What beats a good wife?

A bad husband.

Why is a poor friend better than a rich one?

Because a friend in need is a friend indeed.

How many legs does a mule have if you call its tail a leg?

Only four. Calling a tail a leg doesn't make it one.

How can you tell the naked truth?

By giving the bare facts.

Why is mayonnaise never ready?

Because it is always dressing.

What has cities with no houses, rivers without water, and forests without trees.

A map.

Spell extra wise in two letters

YY (2 y's)

What two vegetables begin and end with two letters in the same order?

Tomato and onion.

How many wives can an Englishman have?

Sixteen: for better, for worse, for richer, for poorer.

What do baby apes sleep in?

Apricots.

413

If you are locked out of the house, how would you get in?
Sing until you get the right key.

Why are goal-keepers thrifty?
Because saving is their job.

Why is Westminster Abbey like a fireplace?
Because it contains the ashes of the great.

What does the Queen Mary weigh just before leaving harbour?
Anchor.

What do we all put off till tomorrow?
Our clothes, when we go to bed.

Why did the orange stop in the middle of the road?
It ran out of juice.

How many months have 28 days?
All of them.

Why shouldn't you tell a joke while you are ice skating?
Because the ice might crack up.

How can you leave a room with two legs and return with six legs?

Bring a chair back with you.

What do you lose every time you stand up?

Your lap.

Why were the elephants thrown out of the swimming pool?

Because they couldn't hold their trunks up.

Why is the letter S like thunder?

Because it makes our milk sour milk.

Why is a single person like borrowed money?

Because he is alone.

What is very light but can't be lifted?

A bubble.

What is an astonomer?

A night watchman with a college education.

If an egg came floating down the Thames, where would it come from?

From a chicken.

My first means equality; my second inferiority; and my whole superiority.

Match-less.

When you take away two letters from this five-letter word, you get one. What word is it?

Stone.

Why is a pig in the house like a house on fire?

Because the sooner you put it out, the better.

Why can't it rain for two nights in a row?

Because there is a day between.

What has a neck but no head?

A bottle.

What did one tap say to the other tap?

You're a big drip.

What is the difference between the North Pole and the South Pole?

The whole world.

What can speak in every language but never went to school?

An echo.

Why did Henry the Eighth have so many wives?

He liked to chop and change.

When is the weather worst for rats and mice?

When it rains cats and dogs.

Why did the man buy a set of tools?

Everyone said he had a screw loose.

What colours would you paint the sun and the wind?

The sun rose and the wind blue.

Why would a squeaking shoe be a good song-writer?

Because it has music in its sole.

Why is a tramp like a balloon?

Because he has no visible means of support.

What amount of money can be divided fifty-fifty between two persons giving one person a hundred times more than the other?

Fifty pounds and fifty pence.

Which has more legs, a horse or no horse?

No horse. A horse has four legs but no horse has six legs.

What will stay hot in the refrigerator?

Mustard.

What goes up and never comes down?

Your age.

What word of four letters still has five left when three of the letters are taken away?

Love. From this word take away L, O and E, leaving V, the Roman number five.

What letter is nine inches long?

The letter Y. It is one quarter of a yard.

418

What should you say when you meet a monster with three heads?

'Hello, hello, hello!'

Why did the butcher put bells on his scale?

Because he wanted to jingle all the way (weigh).

How do you spell blind pig?

B–L–N–D P–G – A blind pig had no eyes.

What man always find things dull?

A knifegrinder.

Why did the farmer feed money to his cows?

He wanted rich milk.

What is the difference between a retired sailor and a blind man?

One cannot go to see, the other cannot see to go.

What branch of the army do babies
join?

The infantry.

When do clocks die?

When their time is up.

What is the difference between a
thief and a church bell?

*One steals from the people, the other
peals from the steeple.*

Why is Derbyshire a good place for
pet dogs?

Because it is the Peak (peke) district.

What letters are invisible, but never
out of sight?

I and S.

Why did the girl sit on her watch?

She wanted to be on time.

What two words have thousands of
letters in them?

Post Office.

What 8-letter word has one letter in
it?

Envelope.

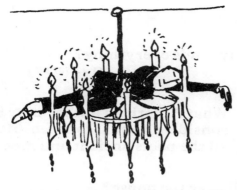

Why did the man climb up to the chandelier?

He was a light sleeper.

Why is a rifle like a lazy worker?

Because they can both get fired.

If a papa bull eats three bales of hay and a baby bull eats one bale, how much hay will a mama bull eat?

Nothing. There is no such thing as a mama bull.

What is the difference between a dog and a flea?

A dog can have fleas but a flea can't have dogs.

Why has a horse got six legs?

Because he has forelegs in front and two legs behind.

Why do you go to bed?

Because the bed will not come to you.

421

What always ends everything?

The letter G.

What American author may be considered equal to three-fifths of all the poets ancient and modern?

Poe.

What is all over the house?

The roof.

What is the difference between maximum and minimum?

When a boy named Maxi won't talk, that is maximum; when a girl named Mini won't talk, that's minimum.

What is the difference between a bright scholar and a shoe-cleaner?

One shines at the head, the other at the foot.

What 7-letter name has only 3 letters?

Barbara.

When a shoemaker makes a shoe, what's the first thing he uses?

The last.

What was the highest mountain before Mt. Everest was discovered?

Mount Everest.

What is the difference between a donkey and a postage stamp?

One you lick with a stick, the other you stick with a lick.

What is the best thing to put into a pie?

Your teeth.

What is the shortest month?

May. It has only three letters.

What is the difference between a hungry man and a greedy man?

One longs to eat and the other eats too long.

Why are the days long in summer and short in winter?

Because heat expands things, and cold contracts them.

Why did the pigeon fly over the racecourse?

Because it wanted to have a flutter on the horses.

Why are dentists artistic?

Because they are good at drawing teeth.

What do purcupines have for dinner?

Prickled onions.

What is the longest word in the English language?

'Smiles,' because there is a 'mile' between the first and last letters.

From a word of five letters take two and leave one.

Alone less A–L gives one.

What can a whole apple do that half an apple can't do?

It can look round.

What code message is the same from left to right, right to left, upside down and right side up?

S O S

What is the difference between a cat and a match?

One lights on its feet, the other lights on its head.

What is a foreign ant?

Important.

What is the difference between a cashier and a schoolmaster?

One minds the till, the other tills the mind.

Why are mosquitoes annoying?

Because they get under your skin.

What happened to the discoverer of electricity?

He got a nasty shock.

Where do squirrels go when they have nervous breakdowns?

To the nuthouse.

Why is O the only vowel that is sounded?

Because all the others are in audible.

What kind of animal needs oiling?

A mouse. It squeaks.

When Adam introduced himself to Eve, what three words did he use which read the same backwards and forwards?

'Madam, I'm Adam.'

What is junk?

Something you save for years and throw away just before you need it.

How many times can 16 be subracted from 160?

Only once, because any later subtractions would not be from 160, but from a smaller number.

**What does not move when it is fast
but moves when it is not fast?**

A motorboat tied up at a dock.

Why is a lady's belt like a dustcart?

*Because it goes round and round and
gathers the waist.*

**What is green and can jump a mile a
minute?**

A grasshopper with hiccups.

**What is it that a man can use for
shaving, cleaning his clothes and
sleeping in?**

A razor, a brush and a pair of pyjamas.

**Where do cars get the most flat
tyres?**

When there is a fork in the road.

**What is the difference between a cat
and a comma?**

*A cat has claws at the end of its paws, a
comma has a pause at the end of its
clause.*

427

If all Ireland should sink, what city would remain afloat?

Cork.

Why is a piano like an eye?

Because they are both closed when their lids are down.

What is it that everyone wishes for, and yet wants to get rid of as soon as it is obtained?

A good appetite.

How can you keep from getting a sharp pain in your eye when you drink your tea?

Take the spoon out of the cup.

Why is a field of grass older than you?

Because it is past-ur-age.

What is the best way to keep fish from smelling?

Cut off their noses.

428

What trees do fortune-tellers look at?

Palms.

Why is a race at a circus like a big fire?

Because the heat is in tents.

What gives milk and says, 'Oom, oom'?

A cow walking backwards.

Why did the mad chef watch the lazy cow?

He liked to see the meat loaf.

What is the difference between a beached vessel and a wrecked airplane?

One grounds on the land, the other lands on the ground.

What is the difference between an organist and a cold in the head?

One knows the stops, the other stops the nose.

What did the fireman say when the church caught fire?

"Holy smoke!"

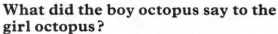

What did the boy octopus say to the girl octopus?

"I want to hold your hand, hand, hand, hand, hand, hand, hand."

Why doesn't the piano work?

Because it only knows how to play.

Why are cooks cruel?

Because they beat the eggs and whip the cream.

What word when deprived of a letter makes you sick?

Music.

Why are a fat man's braces like a big traffic jam?

Because they are both big hold-ups.

What do most gardeners not like to grow?

Old.

What did Columbus see on his right hand when he discovered America?

Five fingers.

How do we know that S is a scary
letter?

Because it makes cream scream.

What did the big watch hand say to
the little watch hand?

'Don't go away, I'll be back in an hour.'

Little Nancy Etticoat,
In a white petticoat
And a red nose,
The longer she stands
The shorter she grows.

A candle.

Where can you always find money?

In the dictionary.

What is the difference between a
beautiful girl and a mouse?

*One charms the he's, the other harms the
cheese.*

Why did the greedy boy pick all the white meat off the chicken?

To make a clean breast of it.

What dish is out of this world?

A flying saucer.

What should you always keep because nobody else wants it?

Your temper.

How can you place a pencil on the floor so that no one can jump over it?

Put it next to the wall.

When are eyes not eyes?

When the wind makes them water.

What is the difference between a man and a running dog?

One wears trousers, the other pants.

Why are policemen like the days of man?

Because they are numbered.

What kind of clothing does a pet dog wear?

A petticoat.

Why is a bride always out of luck on her wedding day?

Because she never marries the best man.

What is the difference between a jeweller and a jailer?

One sells watches, the other watches cells.

Why does a man's hair turn grey before his moustache?

Because it's older.

Can you spell Brandy with three letters?

B, R, and Y.

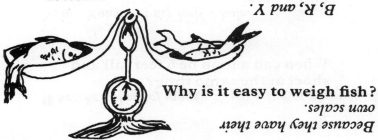

Why is it easy to weigh fish?

Because they have their own scales.

What is dark but made by light?

A shadow.

What is the best thing to make in a hurry?

Haste.

Why is scandal like the letter W?

Because it makes ill will.

What happens when a flea gets very angry?

It gets hopping mad.

Two men dig a hole in five days. How many days would it take them to dig half a hole?

None, You can't dig half a hole.

When can a man be 6 feet tall and short at the same time?

When he's short of money.

Why is a manicurist sure to get rich?

Because she makes money hand over fist.

Who drives away all his customers?

A taxi-driver.

How can you come face-to-face with a hungry, angry lion, dare him to fight, and still be unafraid?

Walk calmly to the next cage.

Why did the gardener throw roses into the burning building?

He heard that flowers grew better in hot houses.

What part of London is in France?

The letter N.

Why is an empty purse always the same?

Because there's never any change in it.

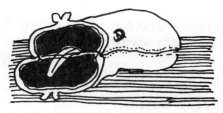

If two wrongs don't make a right, what did two rights make?

An aeroplane.

What extraordinary kind of meat is to be bought in the Isle of Wight?

Mutton from Cowes.

Where does a two-ton gorilla sleep?

Anywhere he wants to.

What man must have his glass before he starts to work?

A glazier.

When do 2 and 2 make more than 4?

When they make 22.

What is free speech?

When you can use someone else's telephone.

What would happen if you swallowed your tea-spoon?

You wouldn't be able to stir.

What 5-letter word has 6 left when you take 2 letters away?

Sixty.

What is a button?

A small event that is always coming off.

What is black when it is clean and white when it is dirty?

A blackboard.

Why is food that does not agree with you like a cook's apron?

Because it goes against the stomach.

If you found a £5 note in every pocket of your coat, what would you have?

Someone else's coat.

How do you stop a dog from barking
in the back seat of a car?

Make him sit in the front.

Why would a drummer in a swing
band make a good policeman?

Because he's used to pounding the beat.

What is the latest thing in dresses?

A nightdress.

What increases its value by being
turned upside down?

The number 6.

Why did Robin Hood rob the rich?

Because the poor didn't have any money.

Why would a compliment from a chicken be an insult?

Because it would be fowl language.

What is the best way to hunt bear?

With your clothes off.

What is a piece of pie in Italian?

A pizza pie.

Why is a lame dog like a boy adding six and seven?

Because he puts down three and carries one.

What is the difference between an oak tree and a tight shoe?

One makes acorns, the other makes corns ache.

What's the difference between the
business of a removal firm and a
shop that sells notepaper?

One's moving, the other's stationary.

Have you heard the story
about the Manx cat?

There's no tale to tell.

Why did Moses lose the race?

Because the Lord told him to come forth.

Why was Winston Churchill buried
in Oxfordshire?

Because he was dead.

What is a doughnut?

A person who is crazy about money.

There was a girl in our town,
Silk an' satin was her gown,
Silk an' satin, gold an' velvet;
Guess her name, three times I've
telled it.

Anne.

What would you call two bananas?

A pair of slippers.

What can a man give to a woman
that he can't give to a man?

His name.

What part of a clock is always old?
The second hand.

**What is the most disagreeable
month for soldiers?**
A long March.

**Why couldn't the mountain climber
call for help?**
Because he was hanging by his teeth.

**What happened when the little pussy
swallowed a penny?**
There was money in the kitty.

**How many books can a student put
into an empty school satchel?**
One; after that the bag will not be empty.

How can you make a slow horse fast?
Don't give him any food.

What part of a fish weighs the most?
The scales.

Why did the wife understand her invisible husband so well?

Because she could see right through him.

Why is snow different from Sunday?

Because it can fall on any day of the week.

If your watch is broken, why can't you go fishing?

Because you haven't the time.

What three letters does a wise man carry around with him?

A.Y.Z. (A wise head)

What did one fish say to the other?

If you keep your big mouth shut, you won't get caught.

What do you get if you cross an elephant with a Boy Scout?

An elephant who helps old ladies across the street.

441

Which eye gets hit the most?

A bullseye.

What is the difference between an old man and a cow?

One lives in the past, the other in the pasture.

What is the difference between a soldier and a young lady?

One faces the powder, the other powders the face.

What is the best way to win a race?

Run faster than anybody else.

What is the difference between a china shop and a furniture shop?

One sells tea-sets, the other sells settees.

What happened when the man sat on a pin?

Nothing; it was a safety pin.

What is the difference between the Prince of Wales and the water in a fountain?

One is heir to the throne, the other is thrown to the air.

Is it dangerous to swim on a full stomach?

Yes, it is better to swim in water.

Why is 4,840 square yards like a bad tooth?

Because it is an acre.

Why did the old lady who mended basins go crazy?

She was around cracked pots too long.

Why didn't the girl go to work in the wool factory?

Because she was too young to dye.

Why is an underground coal miner like a beautician?

Because they are both face workers.

Why is a shoemaker like a clergyman?

Both try to save soles.

What kind of band doesn't make music?

A rubber band.

What time is it when the clock strikes thirteen?

Time to have the clock repaired.

What is a dimple?

A pimple going the other way.

Why did the spy pull the sheets over his head?

He was an undercover agent.

Why do cows wear bells?

Because their horns won't work.

What time is it when a pie is equally divided among four hungry boys?

A quarter to one.

What is the difference between a dressmaker and a farmer?

A dressmaker sews what she gathers, a farmer gathers what he sows.

How long will an eight-day clock run without winding?

It won't run at all without winding.

What did the pig say when the butcher grabbed him by the tail?

'That's the end of me!'

Why is a group of convicts like a deck of cards?

Because there is a knave in every suit.

Which is heavier – a pound of lead or a pound of feathers?

They both weigh the same.

Why do white sheep eat so much more than black ones?

Because there are more of them.

A man was driving a black lorry. His lights were not on, the moon was not out. A lady was crossing the street. How did the driver see her?

It was a bright, sunny day.

What can you break without touching?

A promise.

What does the word 'minimum' mean?

A very small mother.

Why did Sarah marry the acrobat?

Because he was head over heels in love with her.

What happened when the wheel was invented?

It caused a revolution.

Why is Buckingham Palace the cheapest palace ever built?

Because it was built for one sovereign and furnished for another.

What animal makes the most of its food?

The giraffe. It makes a little go a long way.

Why does the butcher's wife always keep the books?

Because the business is a joint affair.

Why are oranges like bells?

You can peel both of them.

Why is a duke like a book?

Because he has a title.

What is most like a hen stealin'?

A cock robin.

**What did the chimney and the door
do when the house caught on fire?**

The chimney flue and the door bolted.

Why is a pig's tail like 5 a.m.?

They are both twirly (too early).

**What animal would you like to be on
a cold day?**

A little otter.

**When is a schoolboy like a postage
stamp?**

When he is licked and put in a corner.

Why does a dentist seem moody?

*Because he always looks down in the
mouth.*

**How did Little Bo-peep lose her
sheep?**

She had a crook with her.

What is a good way to get wild duck?

Buy a tame one and annoy it.

447

Who dares to sit down in front of the
Queen with his hat on?

Her chauffeur.

When they take out an appendix, it's
an appendectomy; when they
remove your tonsils, it's a
tonsillectomy. What is it when they
remove a growth from your head?

A haircut.

Why is a pony like a
person with a sore throat?

Because they are both a little ho(a)rse.

How do you know when night is
nigh?

When the 'T' is taken away.

What do people in America call little
black cats?

Kittens.

What would you call the life story of
a car?

An autobiography.

When is a sailor not a sailor?

When he's aloft.

Why is a ferryboat like a good rule?

Because it works both ways?

If the Forth Bridge were to collapse,
what would they do?

Build a fifth.

What does a dog get when it
graduates from dog school?

A pedigree.

What is a parasite?

Something you see in Paris.

Why is a newborn baby like a storm?

Because it begins with a squall.

Why was the United Nations worried
when the waiter dropped a platter of
turkey on the floor?

*It meant the fall of Turkey, the ruin of
Greece, and the break-up of China.*

Why did the man ring up the
dentist?

Because he was aching to meet him.

What is black, shiny, lives
in trees and is very
dangerous?

A crow with a machine gun.

Why are blacksmiths undesirable citizens?

Because they forge and steel.

If you are going for a hike in the desert, what should you carry?

A thirst-aid kit.

What do you get if you cross a chick and a guitar?

A chicken that makes music when you pluck it.

Why are British soldiers not to have bayonets any longer?

Because they are long enough.

Why did the girl tear the calendar?

Because she wanted to take a month off.

Who earns his living without doing a day's work?

A night watchman.

What would happen if you ate yeast and polish?

You would rise and shine.

When does a boat show affection?

When it hugs the shore.

450

**What is the difference between a
tailor and a horse trainer?**

One mends a tear, the other tends a mare.

Why do they call it a libel suit?

*Because you're liable to win and you're
liable to lose.*

What is hard to beat?

A drum with a hole in it.

**A word five syllables contains;
Take one away – not one remains.**

*Monosyllable. Take away MO and leave
NO SYLLABLE.*

Why did the boy take a ruler to bed?

He wanted to see how long he slept.

**What's the difference between an
orchestral conductor and an oven?**

*One makes the beat. The other bakes the
meat.*

**Who was the first man
in space?**

The man in the moon.

**Who often has his
friends for lunch?**

A cannibal.

What was the greatest invention in the world?

The wheel because it got everything rolling.

What time is the same spelled backward or forward?

Noon.

Make one word from the letters in NEW DOOR.

One word.

What two things can't you have for breakfast?

Lunch and dinner.

What's the difference between a Peeping Tom and a child just out of the bath?

One is rude and nosey, the other's nude and rosy.

Why did the man have to repair the horn of his car?

Because it didn't give a hoot.

What did the big chimney say to the little chimney?

'You are too young to smoke.'

What is the longest sentence in the world?

'Go to prison for life.'

What does Mexico produce that no other country produces?

Mexicans.

Why was the dog chasing his tail?

He was trying to make both ends meet.

Why are money and secrets both alike?

They are both hard to keep.

Which moves faster, heat or cold?

Heat; you can catch cold.

When does a wooden floor feel cold?

When it is parquet (parky).

What sick bird is unlawful?

An ill-eagle.

A man drove from London to Dover with a flat tyre. Why didn't he find this out?

It was his spare tyre.

Why is the letter K like a pig's tail?

Because it is the end of pork.

Why do ducks look sad?

When they preen their feathers they get down in the mouth.

We travel much, yet prisoners are,
And close confined to boot;
We with the swiftest horse keep pace,
Yet always go on foot?

Spurs.

What kind of bell doesn't ring?

A dumbell.

What can be right but never wrong?

An angle.

How was it that a dog tied to a 12-foot rope, managed to walk 30 feet?

The rope wasn't tied to anything.

What is too much for one, enough for two, but nothing at all for three?

A secret.

How could you fall off a ten metre ladder and not be hurt?

Fall off the bottom rung.

Why were the elephants the last animals to leave the ark?

They had to pack their trunks.

What happens to people who slim?

They have a thin time.

What is the best exercise for losing weight?

Pushing yourself away from the table.

What is the difference between an ice cream cone and a bully?

You lick one, the other licks you.

What is full of holes, yet holds water?

A sponge.

What is it that occurs four times in every week, twice in every month, and only once in a year?

The letter E.

What kind of clothes do lawyers wear?

Lawsuits.

Why is your heart like a policeman?

Because it has a regular beat.

What is it that is given to you alone, but used more by other people?

Your name.

Some ducks were walking down a path. There was a duck in front of two ducks, a duck behind two ducks, and a duck between two ducks. How many ducks in all?

Three ducks, waddling single file.

What did the violin say to the harp?

'May I string along with you?'

What must you keep after giving it to somebody else?

Your word.

Why does a dog wag his tail?

Because no-one else will wag it for him.

Why do nudists have plenty of time to spare?

Because they have nothing on.

Why did the girl call herself an experienced actress?

She broke her leg and was in a cast for six months.

What happened when the dentist and manicurist fell out?

They fought tooth and nail.

With what do you fill a bucket to make it lighter than when empty?

Holes.

Why do two fivers make a singer?

Because together they make a tenner (tenor).

457

What did the cannibal have for lunch?

Baked beings.

What relation is a child to its own father when it's not its own father's son?

Daughter.

Why did the silly boy go into the road with his bread and butter?

He was looking for the traffic jam.

Why did the same boy put his bed in the fireplace?

So he could sleep like a log.

What profession did the parrot decide to follow after she swallowed the clock?

Politics.

What did Cinderella say when her photos didn't arrive?

'Some day my prints will come.'

Why can two very thin people not become good friends?

They must always be slight acquaintances.

What did the 10 pence piece say when it got stuck in the slot?

'Money's tight these days.'

What dance represents two containers?

The can-can.

What happened to the fat man who sat on a flagpole to reduce?

He fell off.

Why is a railway patriotic?

Because it is bound to the country with the strongest ties.

When is a sailor not a sailor?

When he's aboard.

Why were the man's socks full of holes?

Because he didn't give a darn.

What's the difference between a sunbather and someone who lives in the Sahara?

One gets tanned by the sun, the other gets sand by the ton.

Did you hear the story about the dust-cart?

It was a load of rubbish.

What is a distant relative?

An uncle in Australia.

Why do bees hum?

Because they don't know the words.

What has a head, a tail, four legs, and sees equally from both ends?

A blind mule.

What is the difference between a bare head and a hair bed?

One flees for shelter, the other is shelter for fleas.

What can't you name without breaking it?

Silence.

What do you call an uneducated ant?

Ignorant.

What is an easy way to make your money bigger?
Put it under a magnifying glass.

What is the difference between 100 and 1000?
Naught.

Why is the letter D like a wedding ring?
Because you cannot be wed without it.

How can a leopard change his spots?
Move to another place.

Why is a river a good place for getting money?
There is a bank on either side.

Why is the letter A like noon?
Because it's the middle of day.

What did the old man do when he thought he was dying?
He moved to the living room.

If a farmer raises wheat in dry weather, what does he raise in wet weather?
An umbrella.

If you want to learn to fight, what book should you read?

A scrapbook.

Is life worth living?

It depends on the liver.

Why did the waiter look grumpy?

Because he had a chip on his shoulder.

What smells most in a chemist's shop?

The chemist's nose.

What are the most unsociable things in the world?

Milestone; you never see two of them together.

What insect is religious?

A praying mantis.

What kind of ant can count?

An accountant.

Why did the tightrope walker carry his bankbook?

In order to check his balance.

Why are teachers rather special?

Because they are in a class of their own.

What is in fashion but always out of date?

The letter F.

When is a woman deformed?

When mending socks, because she then has her hands where her feet should be.

When is a newspaper like a delicate child?

When it is weekly.

When is a black dog not a black dog?

When it's a greyhound.

Why should you tickle a mule?

You might get a big kick out of it.

Why is a cash register like someone who can't pay his bills?

Because it is pressed for money.

What is black and yellow and goes zzub, zzub?

A bee going backwards.

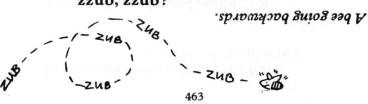

What did Adam first plant in the Garden of Eden?

His foot.

What creature becomes healthier when beheaded?

The whale – hale.

What is better than an idea?

You, dear.

What do you get if an axe hits your head?

A splitting headache.

Why is an optician like a teacher?

They both test the pupils.

Why does a cow go over a hill?

Because she can't go under it.

Which of your relatives are dependent upon you for a living?

Your aunts, uncles and cousins, for without U they could not exist.

Why are birds poor?

Because money doesn't grow on trees.

What is the best way to turn people's heads?

Go to the theatre late.

When should a pub landlord go to an iron foundry?

When he wants a barmaid.

What makes a road broad?

The letter B.

What runs along the streets in New York?

The kerb.

Why can a locomotive not sit down?

Because it has a tender behind.

On which side of a country church is the graveyard always situated?

The outside.

Why is a mirror like a resolution?

Because it is so easily broken.

How do sailors get their clothes clean?

They throw them overboard and they wash ashore.

When you look around
on a cold winters day,
what do you see on
every hand?

A glove.

Why are scales like
road-maps?

*Because they indicate
the 'weigh'.*

When is a chair like a woman's
dress?

When it is satin.

Why is the food one eats on a tossing
ship like a difficult conundrum?

One is obliged to give it up.

Why has a shoemaker great powers
of endurance?

Because he holds on to the last.

When is the only time a man is really
immersed in his business?

When he is giving a swimming lesson.

How do you keep food on an empty
stomach?

Bolt it down.

466

How do they dance in
Saudi Arabia?

Sheik-to-sheik.

What person helps to bring up
hundreds of people?

The lift attendant.

If butter is 70p a pound in Oxford,
what are window panes in
Staffordshire?

Glass.

What is the hardest thing for a bald
man to part with?

A comb.

Can you make a fire with only one
stick?

Yes, providing it's a matchstick.

Why did the man put a clock under
his desk?

He had decided to work overtime.

Why is the condition of a sick man
improved by having a flutter on the
Derby?

It makes him a little better.

467

What does the evening wear?

The close of day.

Why does a policeman's coat have brass buttons?

So he can button it up.

Why was Adam known to be a good runner?

He was the first in the human race.

Why is an MP like somebody queuing outside a cinema?

Because he stands in order to get a seat.

A cabbage, a tap and a tomato had a race. How did it go?

The cabbage was ahead, the tap was running, and the tomato tried to ketchup.

Why is a pig the most amazing animal in the farmyard?

Because first he is killed, then he is cured.

Why is Madame Tussaud's a disagreeable place to visit?

Because you will meet with plenty of wax (whacks).

What is a banged-up used car?

A car in first-crash condition.

What is a sleeping bull?

A bulldozer.

Do you know how long cows should be milked?

In the same way as short ones.

Why is U the merriest letter?

Because it is always in the midst of fun.

If Wellington's wife went to Waterloo while Wellington's washerwoman washed Wellington's woollies, how many W's are there in all.

None. There are no W's in 'all'.

Why is the nose on your face like the V in civility?

Because it is between two eyes.

What always happens at the end of a dry spell.

It rains.

What kind of music does a ghost like?

Haunting melodies.

469

What is the difference between a dog losing his hair, and a man painting a small outhouse?

One sheds his coat, the other coats his shed.

Why was the man standing on the railway bridge with a rod and line?

He was waiting to catch the train.

Why are boardinghouse keepers called *land*-ladies?

Because they charge the earth.

How do you make an egg roll?

Push it.

How was the blind carpenter able to see?

He picked up his hammer and saw.

What happened when the icicle landed on the man's head?

It knocked him cold.

What did the dentist say to the golfer?

'You have a hole in one.'

What has a name of three letters, but still has its name when two of the letters are taken away?

Tea or Bee.

What did the jack say to the car?

'Can I give you a lift?'

Why are golfers like cavemen?

Because they walk around with clubs in their hands.

Why did it take three Boy Scouts to take the old lady across the street?

Because she didn't want to go.

Why did the chicken cross the road twice?

Because it was double-crosser.

If you fell downstairs, what would you fall against?

Against your will.

When does an MP feel girlish?

When he makes his maiden speech.

When does a timid girl turn to stone?

When she becomes a little bolder.

471

Why was the young lady angry to receive a burning kiss from her boyfriend?

He had forgotten to take the cigarette out of his mouth.

If a girl falls into a well, why can't her brother help her out?

Because he cannot be a brother and assist her too.

Why is a volcano like an irritable person?

From time to time it blows its top.

Why is a lie like a wig?

Because it's a falsehood.

What travels around the world but stays in a corner?

A stamp.

How do you make a Maltese Cross?

Stick your finger in his eye.

If you were swimming in the Atlantic and an alligator attacked you, what would you do?

Nothing. There are no alligators in the Atlantic.

472

What men are most aboveboard in their movements?

Chessmen.

Why is a thief like a thermometer on a hot day?

Because they are both up to something.

How can you always find a liar out?

By going to his house when he isn't in.

Why are men going bald at an older age these days?

Because they're wearing their hair longer.

Which burns longer a wax candle or a tallow candle?

Neither : they both burn shorter.

What did the Children of Isreal eat while they were in the desert?

The sand which is there.

Why is the Pacific like an idea?

Because it's just a notion.

How do you know that carrots are good for the eyes?

Well, have you ever seen a rabbit wearing spectacles?

What nationality is Santa Claus?

North Polish.

A knight in armour had a pain. When and where was it?

In the middle of the (k)night.

What's the difference between a good footballer and a industrious man?

One times his passes well, the other passes his time well.

Why can't you remember the last tooth that you had extracted?

Because it went right out of your head.

Why did the chauffeur never have any trouble with 'back seat' drivers?

He drove a hearse.

Why does a bald-headed man have no use for keys?

Because he's lost his locks.

Why do women put their hair in rollers?

To wake curly in the morning.

What did Robert the Bruce do when he saw the spider climbing up and down?

He went and invented the yo-yo.

What do liars do after they die?

Lie still.

**Pray tell me, ladies if you can,
Who is that highly favoured man,
Who though he's married many a wife,
May yet be single all his life?**

A clergyman.

Why did the girl keep running round her bed?

She wanted to catch up on her sleep.

What is it of which the common sort is best?

Sense.

When is a man two men?

When he's beside himself.

Why did the boy's mother knit him three socks for Christmas?

Because he had written to say he'd grown another foot.

Why did the golfer wear two pairs of trousers?

In case he got a hole in one.

Why was Solomon so in love with his 999th wife?

She was one in a thousand.

Why does a dog chasing a rabbit resemble a bald-headed man?

He makes a little hare go a long way.

What fish has the lowest voice?

A bass.

Why was the worker fired from his job at the bed-factory?

He was caught lying down on the job.

As long as I eat, I live; but when I drink, I die. What am I?

Fire.

What do they call the man who winds up Big Ben?

A big time operator.

What is it that someone else has to take before you can get it?

Your photograph.

Where are there more nobles than at court?

In the library. All the books have titles.

What kind of pine has the sharpest needles?

A porcupine.

What's the difference between a pianist and sixteen ounces of lead?

One pounds away, the other weighs a pound.

When do crooks wear braces?

When they are hold-up men.

Is it safe to write a letter on an empty stomach?

Quite safe, but better to write on paper.

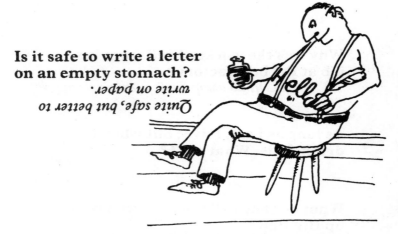

What is the difference between a man with no money and a feather bed?

One is hard up, the other is soft down.

What's the difference between a music maker and a corpse?

One composes, the other decomposes.

Why are country people smarter than town people?

Because the population is denser in towns.

What is the difference between a baby and a shipwrecked sailor?

One clings to his ma, the other clings to his spar.

Why is a new baby like a diamond?

Because it's a dear little thing.

478

Why did the orchestra have bad manners?

Because it didn't know how to conduct itself.

What happens to a boy who starts home to dinner and misses his bus?

He catches it when he gets home.

What is a person called who doesn't have all his fingers on one hand?

Normal. Fingers should be on two hands.

What ailment afflicts the oak tree?

A corn.

How many sides has a rugby ball?

Two – inside and outside.

What happened when the electric guitar was plugged into the lamp standard?

It played light music.

Why is a Member of Parliament like a shrimp?

Because he has MP at the end of his name.

Did you hear the story about the influenza germ?

Never mind. I don't want to spread it.

When can't astronauts
land on the moon?
When it is full.

Why was the chicken sick?
It had people-pox.

Why is a chef to a royal household
like a bucketful of coal?
Because he feeds the great.

What did the policeman say after
booking a dozen motorists for illegal
parking?
'I've done a fine day's work'.

What is the worst kind of fare for
men to live on?
Warfare.

Why is a cannon like a lady's make-
up case?
Because it is useless without powder.

What did the Egyptians do when it
got dark?
They turned on the Israelites.

Why did the doctor give up his
practice?
Because he lost his patience.

480

What's the difference between a water butt and a poor cricket fielder?

One catches the drops, the other drops the catches.

When did the fly fly?

When the spider spied her.

What's the difference between the end of a queue and a letter-box?

One makes the tail, the other takes the mail.

What animal doesn't play fair?

The cheetah.

What's the most important use for cowhide?

To hold the cow together.

When is a cow not a cow?

When she is turned into pasture.

481

What is drawn by everyone without
pen or pencil?

Breath.

What did the kangaroo say when her
baby was missing?

'My pockets' been picked !'

How can you double you money?

Look at it in a mirror.

Why is a man who's always
complaining the easiest man to
satisfy?

Because nothing satisfies him.

What is a calf after it is six months
old?

Seven months old.

Why are the fourteenth and fifteenth
letters of the alphabet of more
importance than all the others?

Because we cannot get on without them.

Luke had it first, Paul had it last;
boys never have it; girls have it but
once; Miss Polly had it twice in
the same place, but when she
married Peter Jones she never had
it again.

The letter L.

What is a sound sleeper?

Someone who snores.

What kind of star wears sunglasses?

A film star.

What's the difference between an ornithologist and a bad speller?

One's a bird watcher, the other's a word botcher.

What's the difference between here and there?

The letter 'T'.

What remains down even when it flies up in the air?

A feather.

What's the first thing you do in the morning?

You wake up.

What country makes you shiver?

Chile.

What kind of tree do you find in the kitchen?

A pantry.

What's the difference between a hard-hitting batsman and a flea?

One's a ball smiter, the other's a small biter.

What does a caterpillar do on New Year's day?

Turns over a new leaf.

Why did the twenty-stone girl marry the thirty-stone man?

She wanted a big wedding.

What is the opposite of restaurant?

Workerant.

Why are a star and an old barn both alike?

They both contain r-a-t-s.

What does C.I.D. stand for?

Copper in disguise.

Why is an old car like a baby playing?

Because it goes with a rattle.

484

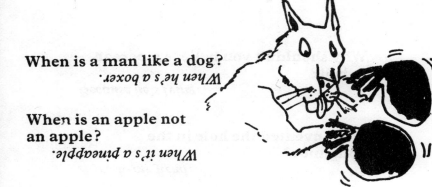

When is a man like a dog?
When he's a boxer.

When is an apple not an apple?
When it's a pineapple.

What's the difference between a clock and a partnership?
When a clock is wound up it goes; when a partnership is wound up, it stops.

What vegetable is it dangerous to have aboard ship?
A leek.

Why are five-star hotels so-called?
Because the bill is astronomical.

What gets around everywhere?
Belts.

What is another name for a telephone kiosk?
A chatterbox.

What's the difference between a simpleton and a Welsh Rarebit?
One's easy to cheat, the other's cheesy to eat.

Why shouldn't you believe a person in bed?

Because he's lying.

Who invented the hole in the doughnut?

A fresh-air fiend.

What can you hold without touching it?

A conversation.

What is the difference between a boy going upstairs and a boy looking upstairs?

One is stepping up the stairs, the other is staring up the steps.

Why couldn't the young witch write a decent letter?

She couldn't spell properly.

486

Why do windows squeak when you open them?

Because they have panes.

What did the Vikings use to keep in touch with one another?

The Norse Code.

What is the difference between a bus driver and a cold?

One knows the stops, the other stops the nose.

Why is twice ten like twice eleven?

Because twice ten is twenty, and twice eleven is twenty-two (twenty too).

**I went to a field and couldn't get through it,
So I went to a school and learned how to do it.**

Fence.

On the way to a water hole a zebra met 6 giraffes. Each giraffe had 3 monkeys hanging from its neck. Each monkey had 2 birds on its tail. How many animals were going to the water hole?

Only the zebra. The others were coming away from it.

487

Why is an acrobat like a whisky glass?
Because they are both tumblers.

What lives on its own substance and dies when it devours itself?
A candle.

The more there is of it, the less you see it. What is it.
Darkness.

If five boys beat up one boy, what time would it be?
Five to one.

Why is the letter R essential to friendship?
Because without it friends would be fiends.

What did Father Christmas's wife say during a thunderstorm?
'Come and look at the rain dear'.

When can you jump over three men without getting up?
In a game of draughts.

**Born at the same time as the world,
will live as long as the world, yet
never five weeks old? What is it?**

The moon.

What makes a tree noisy?

Its bark.

**Why do you brush your hair before
going to bed?**

To make a good impression on the pillow.

What is the best thing out?

An aching tooth.

**When is it bad luck to have a black
cat following you?**

When you are a mouse.

**What is always before you, yet
you can never see it?**

Your future.

**What's the difference between a man
parking his car and a man smashing
dishes?**

*One sets the brakes, the other breaks the
sets.*

What makes a pair of shoes?

Two shoes.

Why was Mr Smith not pleased to bump into his old friend?

They were both in their cars at the time.

Why did the silly boy try to lock his father in the fridge?

Because he liked cold pop.

What is the best way to make trousers last?

Make the coat and waistcoat first.

When the circus giant asked the dwarf to lend him a pound note, what did the dwarf say?

'I'm sorry, but I'm terribly short.'

What sound do two porcupines make when they kiss?

'Ouch!'

Why does a chef wear a tall white hat?

To cover his head.

What has neither flesh or bone, but has four fingers and a thumb?

A glove.

490

What are the little white things in your head that bite?

Teeth.

Where are Chinese boats stored?

In a junkyard.

Why is measles like a steel trap?

Because it is catching.

Why would someone in jail want to catch chicken-pox?

So he could break out.

What did the zookeeper see when the elephant squirted water?

A jumbo jet.

What makes everyone sick except those who swallow it?

Flattery.

What kind of cake do small boys dislike?

A cake of soap.

Why did the silly nurse always tiptoe past the medicine cabinet?

She didn't want to waken the sleeping pills.

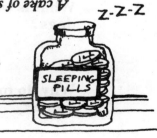

What happened to Lady Godiva's horse when he saw she had no clothes on?

It made him shy.

Why was there no standing on top of the bus?

It was a single-decker.

Why was young Sam a born leader?

He was always first away when school was over.

Why were the girl's holiday snaps not ready when she called for them?

The photographer was a late developer.

Why are good intentions like fainting ladies?

They need carrying out.

What is worse than raining cats and dogs?

Hailing taxi-cabs.

Why do most footballers play the game?

They do it for the kicks.

What is a pony with a sore throat?
A little hoarse.

Which is better, an old five-pound note or a new one?
Any five-pound note is better than a one-pound note.

When is a captain of a ship in love?
When he seeks a mate.

What man makes his living only at put-up jobs?
A paper-hanger.

How can you tell a sausage doesn't like being fried?
Because it spits.

What did the surgeon say to the patient after he'd finished the operation?
'That's enough out of you.'

What professional man works with a will?
A solicitor.

Why do Irish farmers wear capes?

To 'cape' them warm.

Why should a sailor know best what is going on in the moon?

Because he has been to sea.

What salad do lovers prefer?

Lettuce alone.

Why is an onion like a ringing bell?

Because peel follows peel.

With what vegetable do you throw away the outside, cook the inside, eat the outside, and throw away the inside.

Corn on the cob.

Why is a greedy man like one with a short memory?

Because he is always for getting.

Why is a lucky gambler a charming fellow?

Because he has such winning ways.

Why is dancing like new milk?

Because it stengthens the calves.

494

What did the sardine call the submarine?

A can with people in it.

What has a big mouth but can't talk?

A jar.

Why is a song by a very bad singer like an old man's head?

Because it is likely to be terribly bawled.

Why are storytellers strange creatures?

Because tales come out of their heads.

How can you get a quart of milk into a pint-pot?

Condense it.

What do you step into when it rains cats and dogs?

Poodles.

What is the only kind of pain of which one makes light?

A window-pane.

Why did Mrs Newrich buy a Ming vase?

To go with her ming coat.

495

How do fireflies start a race?

Somebody says, 'Ready, steady, glow !'

What did the coward say to the stamp?

'I can lick you.'

Why does Father Time wear sticking plaster?

Because day breaks and night falls.

Why should a fainting lady have more than one doctor?

Because she must be brought to.

What did Dick Turpin say after he'd finished his famous ride to York?

'Whoa!'

Why are spiders like tops?

Because they are always spinning.

What's the difference between a whale-hunter and a happy dog?

One tags his whale, the other wags his tail.

Why didn't the man believe the sardine's story?

It sounded too fishy.

You've heard of a flying fox – what is
a flying dog?

A Skye Terrier.

What kind of dog would you ask to
tell you the time?

A watch-dog.

Why is a tonic like an ambulance?

*Because you take it when you're run
down.*

What do you do to stop your nose
from running?

Put your foot out and trip it up.

What kind of animal has red spots?

A leopard with measles.

Why did the fireplace call the
doctor?

Because the chimney had the flue.

Why is a trampoline act a tricky way
of earning a living?

Because it's full of ups and downs.

What kind of kitten works for the St
John's Ambulance Brigade?

A first-aid kit.

Why are doctors good-natured?
*Because they don't mind if you stick your
tongue out at them.*

**What is the difference between a
blacksmith and a safe mare?**
*One is a horseshoer, the other is a sure
horse.*

What is a country seat?
A milking stool.

Why is it vulgar to sing by yourself?
Because it is so-lo.

**What do you have to know to be an
auctioneer?**
Lots.

**Why did the girl like her work in the
towel factory?**
She found the job very absorbing.

Why are pianos noble?
Because they are upright and grand.

What is the difference between a gardener and a billiard player?

One minds his peas, the other minds his cues.

Why is an acrobat an agreeable person to know?

He is always doing a good turn.

Where are all people equally beautiful?

In the dark.

Why is a busybody like tallow?

Because he makes scandals.

Why does a water melon have so much water in it?

Because it is planted in the spring.

What paper should make the best kites?

Fly paper.

What is a lawyer's favourite pudding?

Sue-it.

Which animal has wooden legs?

A timber wolf.

Why was Shakespeare able to write so well?

Because where there's a Will there's a way.

Where do all good turkeys go when they die?

To oven.

Why is a heavy fall of snow easily understood?

One can see the drift.

Why did the mother put her baby on the record-player?

It had an automatic changer.

What instruments do you carry in your ears?

Drums.

Why do portraits of George Washington always show him standing?

Because he would never lie.

CROAK

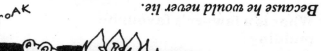

What happened to the frog when it died?

It just croaked.

What should you do if you see two snails fighting?
Leave them alone and let them slug it out.

What is the most suitable dance to wind up a frolic?
A reel.

Where can you always find diamonds?
In a pack of cards.

When do you get that run-down feeling?
When a car hits you.

Why did the small boy stamp on his letter?
He had been told you have to stamp them or they won't get taken by the post office.

Why did the ant-elope?
Nobody gnu.

Why did the sleepy boy throw away his alarm clock?
It kept going off when he was asleep.

501

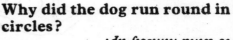

Why did the dog run round in circles?

He was a watchdog and wanted to wind himself up.

What is yellow, smooth and dangerous?

Shark-infested custard.

Why are playing cards like wolves?

Because they come in packs.

Which is greater, six dozen dozen or half a dozen dozen?

Six dozen dozen; it is 864, while the other is 72.

Why are sheep like pubs?

Because they are full of baas.

Why were the Dark Ages so dark?

They had more knights in those days.

What did the ram say to his girlfriend?

'I love ewe!'

What always comes into a house through the keyhole?

A key.

What miracles happened when Mr Stone and Mr Wood watched a pretty girl pass by?

Stone turned to Wood and Wood turned to Stone. They both turned to look, and the girl turned into a restaurant.

Why was the dentist not interested in his work?

He found the drilling boring.

Why is Saturday night important to Julius's girlfriend?

That's when Julius Caesar.

What are government workers called in Seville?

Seville servants.

What horses keep late hours?

Nightmares.

What bird can lift the most?

A crane.

What is the difference between a man with an unnatural voice and one with unnatural teeth?

One has a falsetto voice, the other a false set o' teeth.

What is the difference between a king's son, a monkey's mother, a bald head and an orphan?

The king's son is the heir apparent, a monkey's mother is a hairy parent, a bald head has no hair apparent, and an orphan has nary a parent.

What is the difference between a crazy rabbit and a counterfeit coin?

One is a mad bunny, the other is bad money.

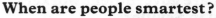

When are people smartest?

During the day because when the sun shines everything is brighter.

Why did the motorist drive his car in reverse?

Because he knew the Highway Code backwards.

What's the difference between Noah's ark and Joan of Arc?

One was made of wood, the other was Maid of Orleans.

Which two letters of the alphabet have nothing between them?

N and P; they have O between them.

Captain Cook made three voyages round the world and was killed on one of them. Which one?

The last one.

If an African lion fought an African tiger, who would win?

Neither. There are no tigers in Africa.

If a band plays in a thunderstorm, who is most likely to get hit by lightning?

The conductor.

What invention allows you to see through walls?

A window.

Why is a seascape artist like a large ship?

Because he draws so much water.

Why is the wheel of a motor car like a lazy person?

Because it's always tired.

Did the rooster fall in love with the hen at first sight?

Not really – she egged him on a bit.

Why may we doubt the existence of the Blarney Stone?

Because there are so many shamrocks in Ireland.

Why is an interesting book like a heavy drinker's nose?

Because it is read to the end.

Where did Noah keep his bees?

In the ark hives.

Why can you always believe a ruler?

Because it is on the level.

When you go to bed why are your shoes like deferred tasks?

Because they are put off till the next day.

What has four legs like an elephant, a trunk like an elephant, looks just like an elephant, but is not an elephant?

A picture of an elephant.

506

How is a pig like a horse?

When a pig is hungry he eats like a horse, and when a horse is hungry he eats like a pig.

On which side does a chicken have most feathers?

On the outside.

Why is a guitar like a turkey being made ready for the oven?

They both have to be plucked.

What is the difference between a banana and a bell?

You can only peel the banana once.

What animals are poor dancers?

Four-legged ones, because they have two left feet.

If the Prime Minister went to the circus and a lion ate him, what time would it be?

Ate P.M.

When is it easiest to see through a man?

When he has a pain in his stomach.

What did the patient say to the anaesthetist?

'Because of you I've been considerably put out.'

What is as round as the moon, as black as coal, and has a hole in the middle?

A gramophone record.

What's the difference between a jigsaw expert and a greedy boy?

One's a good puzzler, the other's a bad puzzler.

Why did the little girl put her head on the piano?

She wanted to play by ear.

Which is better: 'The house burned down or the house burned up?

Neither: they are both bad.

What happened when the dwarf applied for a job in the circus?

He was put on the short list.

Why are waiters always willing to learn?

Because they are always ready to take tips from people.

508

What is the difference between a pen and a pencil?

You push a pen, but a pencil has to be lead.

What does a lamppost become when the lamp is removed?

A lamplighter.

What trade is it in which no man will get on unless he sticks to it?

Bill-posting.

What ship is always managed by more than one person?

Partnership.

When does water resemble a gymnast?

When it makes a spring.

What is the difference between a greedy person and an electric toaster?

One takes the most and the other makes the toast.

509

What has a head but no brain?
A cabbage.

What is a bulldozer?
Someone who sleeps while a politician is making a speech.

Where do vampires keep their money?
In blood banks.

What's a bikini?
A space suit.

What is the difference between a milkmaid on the farm and a seagull?
One skims milk, the other skims water.

What are the best kind of stockings for crickets to wear?
Stockings with runs in them.

What is it that is alive and has only one foot?
A leg.

Why is coffee like a dull knife?
Because it has to be ground before it can be used.

Why might a man with indigestion hope for a long life?

Because he can't digest—yet.

Why did Adam bite the apple that Eve gave him?

Because he had no knife.

What happened to the girl who swallowed a spoon?

She couldn't stir.

Why did the boy put his trousers on backwards?

Because he didn't know if he was coming or going?

Why did the spy speak in a whisper?

Because he was on a hush-hush mission.

What is more to be admired than a promising young man?

A paying one.

What do historians talk about when they meet?

Old times.

If I dig a hole two feet square and two feet deep, how much dirt is in the hole?

None.

Why should birds in a nest always agree?

Otherwise they would fall out.

What person tries to make you smile most of the time?

A photographer.

What words can be pronounced quicker and shorter by adding another syllable to them?

'Quick' and 'short'.

What is worse than biting into an apple and finding a worm?

Finding half a worm.

I can be heard and caught but never seen. What am I?

A remark.

What is the hardest key to turn?

A donkey.

512

**What is as big as an elephant
but doesn't weigh anything?**
An elephant's shadow.

**At what sports do
waiters excel?**
*Tennis. They really know
how to serve.*

**What is it that you can take away the
whole and still have some left?**
The word 'wholesome'.

**What is the best thing to take when
you are rundown?**
The number of the car that hit you.

**Why did the waiter stamp on his
customer's beefburger?**
*Because the customer was in a hurry and
told the waiter to step on it.*

**What nail does a carpenter not like
to hit?**
His fingernail.

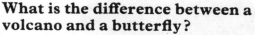

What is the difference between a volcano and a butterfly?

In one the lava comes out of the crater, in the other the crater comes out of the larva.

What is neither inside a house nor outside a house, but no house would be complete without it?

A window.

Why must a dishonest man stay indoors?

So no one will find him out.

What overpowers you without hurting you?

Sleep.

What did the porcupine say to the cactus?

'Are you my mother?'

How do you get down from an elephant?

You don't get down from an elephant; you get down from a duck.

When is a horse like a bad egg?

When it's addled (saddled).

514

What kind of tea makes you feel brave?

Safety.

What person always falls down on the job?

A paratrooper.

Why wasn't the girl afraid of the shark?

Because it was a man-eating shark?

What is the difference between the earth and the sea?

One is dirty, the other is tide-y.

A policeman saw a lorry-driver going the wrong way down a one-way street, but didn't stop him. why not?

The lorry-driver was walking.

Why is a false friend like the letter P?

Because although the first in pity, he's always the last in help.

Why is the letter G like the sun?

Because it is the centre of light.

515

Why should a clock never be put upstairs?

It might run down and strike one.

At this moment everyone in the world is doing the same thing? What is it?

Getting older.

If a doctor fell into a well, what should he have done instead?

Attended to the sick, and left the well alone.

Why did the pretty schoolteacher marry the caretaker?

Because he swept her off her feet.

What musical key cannot vote?

A-minor.

Why did the burglar take a bath?

So he could make a clean getaway.

What is it that you cannot hold for ten minutes, though it is lighter than a feather?

Your breath.

When was the boy twins?

In a picture taken when he was two.

Who invented spaghetti?

*An Italian who used
his noodle.*

**If you were walking in a jungle and
met a lion, what time would it be?**

Time to run.

**What asks no questions but gets a
great many answers?**

A doorbell.

**How can you jump off a 50-foot
ladder without getting hurt?**

Jump off the bottom rung.

**What is the difference between a
book and a bore?**

You can shut up a book.

What letter should you avoid?

The letter A because it makes men mean.

**What are the most disagreeable
articles for a man to have on hand?**

Handcuffs.

**What can be broken without being
hit or dropped?**

A promise.

What artist puts money away for a rainy day?

A pavement artist.

How does the letter A help a deaf woman?

It makes her hear.

What is worse than being with a fool?

Fooling with a bee.

What is a prickly pear?

Two porcupines.

What did the city commuter miss most living out in the country?

The last train home at night.

Why was Cinderella thrown out of the football team?

Because she ran away from the ball.

What kind of doctor treats ducks?

A quack.

1000 TWISTERS

Gyles Brandreth
warmly welcomes
you to his

Tremendous
tome of
tip — top
tongue-twisters —
terrifically tantalising,
teasingly testing,
ticklishly tormenting!

If you can say TINTINABULATION ten times in
quick succession without faltering, fluffing, or falling on the carpet in a faint, this is the book for you!
If you can't, this is still the book for you — because
it is quite simply the biggest and best collection of
tongue-twisters ever known!

Pester your parents!
Tease your teachers!
Fool your friends!

With 1000 tongue-twisters, you'll have a 1000
wonderful ways to get the tongues of the world
well and twuly tristed!

Six savoury sausages sizzling.

Would Winnie wish to come
a-wassailing?

Robin Robson was robbing Dobbin
Dobson and was nabbed by Dobbin's
godson.

Mr. Miller mills merrily with a miller's
millstone.

Greta Grubshore grabbed Gordon
Godwin with gratitude.

Stupid Stella Stubbins stifled Stephen
Stubbing.

Will Willie Wilkins be willing to wish
Willis welcome words?

Good gardeners grow great gherkins.

Amazing Annie Ashford asks for four frightening flashes.

Can Carol croon carols?

Betty Botter battered batter better
than Betty Bitter buttered butter.

Anthony Ackroyd had adenoids, acne
and hammer-toe.

Has Hannah ever had her hair
hennaed?

Pretty Pansy Parker parked her pram
in people's pantries.

Sulky Suki sucked sugar and sherbert
through straws.

Every Easter Ernie ignores Easter
eggs and eats almonds.

Handy Andy's got his Sunday undies
on!

Perky Polly planted pretty precious
pot plants.

'Are you copper-bottoming 'em, my
    man?'
'No, I'am aluminiuming 'em, Ma'am!'

Grinning Gregory grunts graciously.

Gormless Gertie grabbed great gladioli.

Red lorry, yellow lorry.

Rush the washing, Russell.

Great Gladys grinned gladly.

Tim, the thin twin tinsmith.

A ship saileth south soon.

Beautiful Bonnie Bliss
blows blissfully
beautiful bubbles.

The shepherds share the Shetland
shawl.

Quick quiet quills quote Queeny's
quarrels.

If a Hottentot taught
    A Hottentot tot,
To talk ere the tot could totter,
   Ought the Hottentot tot
Be taught to say 'ought' or 'naught',
   Or what ought to be taught her?

The winkle ship sank and the shrimp
ship swam.

            I'm a critical cricket critic.

She says she shall sew a sheet.

My Miss Smith lisps and lists. She
lisps as she talks and she lists as she
walks.

The cruel ghoul's cool gruel.

'Aye! Aye!' said the Ear.
'Hear! Hear!' said the Eye.

A glowing gleam glowing green.

Give George Green gloves
and gleaming galoshes.

Say this sharply, say this sweetly,
Say this shortly, say this softly,
Say this sixteen times in succession.

Wiles and snares and snares and wiles
of a snary, wily world.

Thelma was thoroughly thankless.

Gay gallants gambolling on the green
grass.

Good blue blood, bad black blood.

The hedge hindered the homicide from hurting himself.

Students study stencilling steadily.

The tracker tracked and tricked and trapped the tricky trickster.

The big black-backed bumblebee.

Ninety-nine naughty knitted nick-nacks were nicked by ninety-nine naughty knitted nick-nack nickers.

Rotten writing is written rotten.

Mixed biscuits.

There was an old lady from Ryde,
Who ate apple cider and died.
　　　The apples fermented
　　　Inside the lamented
And made cider inside her inside.

Blame the big bleak black book.

Six Scots soldiers shooting snipe.

Oswald Owl occupies the ancient old
oak.

Ted threw Fred three free throws.

The new King's queen,
The new Queen's king.

He hath eaten hot apples and haddock
hastily.

Roads close, so snow slows shows.

Brian blatantly boasted and bragged
of his blank verse and his black
pudding.

She was a thistle-sifter
And she sifted thistles.
She had a sieveful of sifted thistles,
And a sieveful of unsifted thistles.
The sieveful of unsifted thistles
She had to sift
She was a thistle-sifter.

Theresa tried on twenty-three silver
thimbles.

Twenty-two thundering trains flashed
through thirty tunnels.

Keep clean socks in a clean sock stack.

Blonde Blodwin Blossom
blushes bashfully.

Reds rule. Blue rules.

I shot three shy thrushes.
You shoot three shy
thrushes.

Sarah Snifter sneezes
sniffily.

Pretty Priscilla presses pillow-slips.

Urgent detergent.

Thirty theatrical thespians threatened
frolicsome theatre.

Cruel cannibals carelessly cooked the quaking cricketer from Chelmsford.

Curly Colin Cluster clips chrysanthemum clumps carelessly. If curly Colin Cluster carelessly clips chrysanthemum clumps, where are the chrysanthemum clumps curly Colin Cluster carelessly clips?

A thousand freckles was a feature of his face.

Please, Paul, pause for applause.

Timothy thanked Thomas Threlfall
for his thoughtfulness although
Father Threlfall had threatened him
fearfully.

Gladys' glamorous grannie grew more
and more garrulous.

Master Maston must miss his mascot
the mastiff.

The goats gravitated to the grazing
ground and gravely gathered grass.

If a wood chuck could chuck wood,
How much wood
  would a woodchuck chuck,
If a woodchuck could chuck wood?

Lucky Lillie likes to lighten her load
when her load isn't too heavy to
lighten.

Uriah Heep sounded servile,
obsequious and smarmy.

Steer clear of scythes, shears, scissors
and sharp steel spears, shun
stalactites and stalagmites, stagnant
pools, stale sausages, scorpions and
stag beetles.

Five fashionable females flying to
France for fresh French fashions.

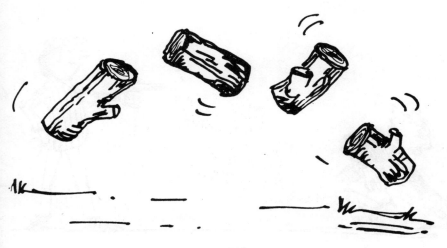

Olive oil ointment.

Ned Nott was shot
And Sam Shott was not.
So it is better to be Shott
    than Nott.
Some say Nott
    Was not shot.
But Shott says
    he shot Nott.
Either the shot Shott shot at Nott
    Was not shot,
    or
    Nott was shot,
If the shot Shott shot shot Shott,
    then Shott was shot,
    not Nott.
However,
    the shot Shott shot shot not Shott—
    but Nott.

Little Willie's wooden whistle
wouldn't whistle.

A clipper shipped several clipped
sheep.
Were these clipped sheep the clipper
ship's sheep?
Or just clipped sheep shipped on a
clipper's ship?

Betty beat a bit of
butter to make a
better batter.

I go by Blue Goose bus.

Naughty Nigel nearly knocked Norah
needlessly.

Married name. Maiden name.

Quixotic topic.

Through six thick swamps stumbled
Sammy.

I snuff shop snuff.
Do you snuff shop snuff?
I snuff enough snuff to stock shop
    snuff.

Richard gave Robin a rap in the ribs
for roasting the rabbit so rare.

A shy little she said 'Shoo!'
To a fly and a flea in a flue.

The religious relic reposed in the
reliquary.

She saw shiny soap suds sailing down
the shallow sink.

The hare's ears heard ere the hair
heeded.

The conundrum constructed by the
communist was catastrophical.

His shirt soon shrank in the suds.

She chews cream cheese and fresh
cress sandwiches.

My dame hath a lame tame crane,
My dame hath a crane that is lame.
Pray gentle Jane, let my dame's tame
   crane
Feed and come home again.

Elevating eleven elephants.

A cricket critic cricked his neck at a
critical cricket match.

Red rubies round ring.

Now nine nice nurses need necklaces.

Bees hoard heaps of honey in hives.

Educated Eliza elephant enjoys
everything elegant.

Stan slid in his sled and slithered to a
stop.

Sing songs sung sadly Sammy.

Better batter. Bitter butter.

Harold Aitch calls Aitch Haitch.
If Harold Aitch calls Aitch Haitch,
then Harold Aitch becomes Harold
Haitch.

I leaned over the fence to see Eileen
Dover's eyes peer over.

Mrs. Pipple-Popple popped a pebble in
poor Polly Pepper's eye.

Is there a pleasant peasant present?

Barry Berry buries Barry's beret.

Robin Redbreast's bad breath.

Can you imagine,
an imaginary menagerie manager
imagining managing an imaginery
menagerie?

Five French friars fanning a fainted
flea.

A dozen double damask dinner napkins.

Three thrice-freed thieves.

Loopy Lottie Lonnie-Dolly loves
licking lovely lollies.

Was that your ewer of yore?

The crew unscrewed the screws and
clipped the sheet to the clews.

A shadow sometimes settled on the
settle where Sheila sat her Suluki.

The brown cowes in Cowes chew more
cud than the white cows in Cowes.
There are more brown cows in Cowes
than white cows in Cowes.

Twelve tall tulips turning to the sun.

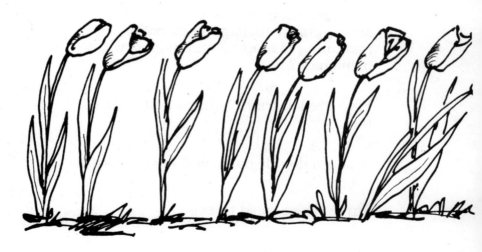

The bailiff brought the birds for
breakfast.

Strange strategic statistics.

'Manners maketh man,' mocked
Mark.

Down the slippery slide they slid
Sitting slightly sideways;
Slipping swiftly see them skid
On holidays and Fridays.

Black dog
danced on
the barn floor
barefoot.

How high His Highness holds his
haughty head!

The troops tread the toilsome trail.

'Cheep cheep,' chirped the cheery
chaffinch.

Wheedling, weeping Winnie wails
wildly.

Fetch fifty-five foils.

Bring back the *Brighton Belle*.

Big brown bulb-bowls.

How many cuckoos could a good cook
cook if a cook could cook cuckoos?

Nine numb ninnies notice nine dumb
nannies.

They thanked them thoroughly.

Neddy Noodle nipped his neighbour's
  nutmegs.
Did Neddy Noodle nip his
  neighbour's nutmegs?
If Neddy Noodle nipped his
  neighbour's nutmegs,
Where are the nutmegs
Neddy Noodle nipped?

Typical tropical trivial trite trash.

The bottle of perfume that Willie sent
was highly displeasing to Millicent.
Her thanks were so cold, they
quarrelled, I'm told, through that silly
scent Willie sent Millicent.

The poor dog's paw poured water
from every pore.

Four fat friars frying fat fish.

Twixt Trent and Tweed.

Sheila sewed shirts seriously.

Naughty Nelly's knitting knotted
nighties for the navy.

Miss Ruth's red roof thatch.

The sceptic questioned the schedule
closely scrawled by the science master
and seemed to suggest it should be
scrapped.

Red roses rustle rurally.

Peter Piper picked a peck of pickled
   peppers.
Did Peter Piper pick a peck of
   pickled peppers?
If Peter Piper picked a peck of
   pickled peppers,
Where's the peck of pickled peppers
   Peter Piper picked?

The wire wound around a reel.

Poor Peter's poodle was pulled out of
a puddle by a paddle.

The wild wolf roams the
wintry wastes.

The sloth loafs among the low slopes.

Quixote Quicksight quizzed a queerish
 quidbox.
Did Quixote Quicksight quiz a
 queerish quidbox?
If Quixote Quicksight quizzed a
 queerish quidbox,
Where's the queerish quidbox
 Quixote Quicksight quizzed?

They threw three thick things.

The Wye wound right around the rye
field.

Quick kiss! Quicker kiss! Quickest kiss!

Three thrice-freed thieves threw thousands of thick thistles.

As the roaring rocket rose, the restless roosters rollicked.

The savour of the silly scent the sentry sent to Millicent.

Eli eats the eels from Ealing.

Ten tiny tortoises talk to twenty
timid toads.

Last year I could not hear with either
ear.

Cheerful children chant charming
tunes.

Elizabeth lisps lengthy lessons.

A fly flew past Flo's flat,
And a fly flew past fat Flo.
Is the fly that flew past fat Flo,
The same fly that flew past Flo's flat?

I thought a thought.
But the thought I thought wasn't
   the thought I thought I thought.
If the thought I thought I thought
   had been the thought I thought,
I wouldn't have thought so much.

If Harry hurries, will hairy Henry
hand him a hundred hammers?

Quinine quickly quells the quaking
and cools the quesay quivers.

Miserable Martha mumbles madly.

Cuthbert was caught coughing in his
coffin.

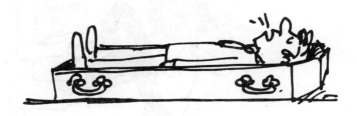

Percy Poppled played the pipes
So prettily he tooted
But presently his lips were sore
So Percy's toots were muted.

Big black bluebottles buzzed
boisterously below Billy's nose.

Crunch crispy crisps quickly.

Shipshape suit shops ship shapely
suits.

Blissful Brenda blithely backing
Britain.

Peggy Pringle's posture at the piano
was painful and practically impossible
when she practised on the piccolo.

The duchess danced gracefully and daintily and drew delightful glances.

It is imperative to institute immediate investigations into the incident at the hydrodynamics institute.

The suitability of a suet pudding without superfluous plums is a superstition presumably due to Susan's economy.

Rabbits rarely ravage red earth but render ruin in the rural regions.

Sixty-seven sacks of salt sitting side by side.

Crusts and crumbs and crunchy cake with clotted cream and custard and Christmas crackers.

The accountant cut along to the counting house — out of countenance as his cash didn't tally with his careful calculations.

The lachrymose lamprey looked lingeringly at the limpet lolling on the rock.

The dragnet dragged deliberately downstream and discovered the drowned duke

Miss. Misty Morris misses Mr. and Mrs Morris' mistletoe.

The sunshine sends shadow shows.

Pitter-patter
pitter-patter,
rather than
patter-pitter
patter-pitter.

Jolly holidays.
Merry jolly days.

Tom turned to Ted.
Told Ted to try
To tie the tie
Tom tried to tie.

Brenda bites Bourbon biscuits
briskly.

Can Christmas come twice? If
Christmas can come twice when else
can Christmas come?

Architectural assets assist accurate
accounting.

Good, better, best,
Never let it rest,
Till your good is better,
And your better best.

Ignatius Higginbottam was indignant
at the irregular hours which made him
irredeemably irritable.

A truly rural frugal ruler's mural.

The Sunday school sings spiritual
songs spiritedly.

My master said that 'that' is the right
'that' in that particular place.

Tommy Tickle tickled his teacher.
Where did Tommy Tickle's teacher
tickle Tommy?

Five flashy flappers
Flitting forth fleetingly
Found four flighty flappers
Flirting flippantly.

Three thumping tigers tickling trout.

'I know you believe you understand
what you think I said, but I am not
sure you realise that what you heard
is not what I meant.'

'Oh Horace, ain't it horrid when
you're hot and in a hurry and you
have to hold your hat on with your
hand.'

Great green gooseberries growing.

I was barbarously barbarised by the
barbarity of a barbarian barber in a
barber's barbarising shop.

Frisky Felix feeds on freshly fried
fishes.

A tooter who tooted a flute
    Tried to tutor two tooters to toot.
Said the two to their tutor,
    'Is it harder to toot or
To tutor two tutors to toot?'

Bright blows the broom on the
brook's bare brown banks.

Mr, Mrs, Master and Miss Moth met
Miss, Master, Mrs and Mr Moss.

Seven shaggy sheepdogs shook sand
everywhere.

Three Scotch thistles in the thicket.

Diligence dismisseth despondency.

How many cans
Can a canner can,
If a canner
Can can cans?
A canner can can
As many cans
As a canner can,
If a canner can
Can cans!

Tiny Tommy Tortoise talked to Tessie
Turtle on the telephone ten times
today.

Battling Bill bullied the blustering
brigand beside the bunker.

Plain plump Penelope played picquet
pleasantly.

This crisp crust crackles crunchily.

Plenty of potatoes and tapioca
pudding make people plump and pale.

Fiona felt the French film was fatuous
and flashy.

Six silly sisters sell silk to six sickly
senior citizens.

Red leather!
Yellow leather!

Chloe was coquettish and considerate
and skilfully contemporary, except
when she had the collywobbles.

The rat-catchers can't catch caught
rats.

Simon Short — Smithfield's Sole
Surviving Shoemaker Shoes Soles —
Sewed Super-finely.

The horse's hard hooves hit the hard
high road.

Nina needs nine
knitting needles
to knit naughty
Nita's knickers
nicely.

This lute, with its flute-like tones, was
captured in the loot of a great city,
and its luminous sides are made of
unpolluted silver.

Mixed metaphors muddle middling
minds.

Proud Percival pestered the Pastor for
a promised prayer.

The glow-worm's gleam glitters in
glade and glen.

The truants tramp trustingly towards
Truro.

Six Swiss ships swiftly shift.

Dauntless Doris Davis does a dozen
daring dives daily.

There are thirty thousand feathers on
that thrush's throat.

Two tubby teddies toasting tasty
teacakes.

A monk's monkey mounted a
monastry wall munching mashed
melon and melted macaroni.

Old Dunn,
Young Dunn,
And Old Dunn's son.

Young Dunn,
Will be Dunn,
When Old Dunn's done.

The short sort shoot straight through.

They tried to tempt the tattered
tramps to take the treacle tarts.

Pretty Pamela
Parker picked
pink petunia
posies.

Thin sticks;
thick bricks.

Lulu likes
lemon lollies
least.

The minx mixed
a medical mixture.

Inigo Impey itched for an Indian
    image.
Did Inigo Impey itch for an Indian
    image?
If Inigo Impey itched for an Indian
    image,
Where's the Indian image Inigo
    Impey itched for?

Thelma Thistlethwaite saw thick
thistles in the thatch.

She stops at the shops where I shop,
And if she shops at the shops where I
    shop
I won't stop at the shop where she
    shops!

The gun glue grew glum.

        You can have—
        Fried fresh fish,
        Fish fried fresh,
        Fresh fried fish,
        Fresh fish fried,
        Or fish fresh fried.

    I saw Esau kissing Kate,
    I saw Esau, he saw me.
    And she saw I saw Esau.

Our great-grand-gran is a greater
great-grand-gran than your great-
grand-gran is.

    My wife gave Mr. Snipe's wife a
    swipe.

        The twenty-two-to-two train to
        Tooting tooted tunelessly as it tore
        through the terrible tunnel.

Crime cuts cut crime.

Thirty thrifty whistling washers
witchingly whistling, wishing washing
was washed.

The tiresome wireless man's fireless,
Whilst the fireless wirelessman's
    tireless.

Many merry moments made many
Misses mischievous.

Mr. Matthew Mathers, my maths
master, munches mashed marmalade
muffins.

The school coal in the school coal
scuttle was scattered by a cool
scholar.

Lazy Lionel Lippet loves lovely Lucy
Locket.

A big beadle placed a body in a big
black bag.

Swedish sword swallowers shift short
swords swiftly.

A fat-thighed freak
fries thick steak.

Tiny orang-utan
tongues.

The threaded
thimbles thrilled
Thelma.

Sheep shouldn't sleep in shaky
shacks, should they?

Plenty of Poltergeists prance around
Pitlochry.

Now a sleeping car's known as a
   sleeper,
And sleepers for sleepers they keep,
And sleepers run under the sleepers
In which those sleepy sleepers sleep.

Dopey Denis dances dangerously in
Denmark.

Then the thankless theologian thawed
thoroughly.

Fearless Frank flew fast flights to
Frankfurt.

Outrageous Olive eats eight oranges hourly.

Can Colin climb chimney stacks carefully?

Steady stallions stride strongly.

A portion of plum pudding was put before Peter Pratt who promptly put it down his pudding-chute.

Artful Alex aimed eight awful arrows.

Colin cuddled Cora in the car and
caught his camera on the clutch.

A sudden sibilant whisper shouldn't
make one shudder, should it?

Malaria is a malady many men meet
when meeting mosquitoes in
Malaysia.

The sordid slum sent shivers down her
sensitive spine.

Florence Freeman fell forward and
frightened her father frightfully.

The customs official whistled at the
concealed contraband.

Lesser leather never weathered lesser
wetter weather.

The scandal-monger uttered scurrilous
statements until someone threatened
to sue him for slander.

Flora's fan fluttered feebly and her
fine fingers fidgeted.

Billy's big blue badly bleeding blister.

How has Harry hastened so hurriedly
to the hunt?

Christmas crackers create a cracking
Christmas.

Beautiful babbling brooks bubble
between blossoming banks.

A bearded peer on the pier appeared
to peer into the pier glass.

Coffee chocolate toffee apples.

Nice nieces nestle nicely in Nice.

Sixty-seven senior citizens sitting on a
seat.

A maid with a duster
Made a furious bluster
Dusting a bust in the hall.
When the bust it was dusted
The bust it was busted,
The bust it was dust, that's all.

Riotous Ricky Wiley really wrote
Rocking Robin rottonly.

'Please cook crooked crabs, Cook.'

Hungry Henry Hobson hurries home.

When all else fails, say 'Hail to all
ales!'

Cool pools are foolproof pools for
washing wool.

Billy Bolton buttoned his bright
brown boots and blue coat before
breakfast began.

Broad beamed Bertha breathes bad
breath.

Ranjit, the runner from Rangoon, ran
round the ramparts during Ramadan.

The seething sea ceaseth seething.

This myth is a mystery to me.

Nobby knew Noddy better than
Noddy knew Nobby.

George Gibbs grabs crabs,
Crabs George Gibbs grabs.
If George Gibbs grabs crabs,
Where are the crabs George Gibbs
    grabs?

Rubber baby-buggy bumpers.

Ned needed to name no new names.

A purely rural duel truly plural is
better than a purely plural duel truly
rural.

There was an old lady called Carr,
Who took the 3.3 for Forfar;
    She said, 'I believe
    It's sure to leave
Before the 4.4 for Forfar.'

Greek grapes.

Deeply dreadful dreams.

Thadeus sang his thrilling song for
the theatrical songsters.

Kenneth put the kibosh on the chow
when he caught him and kept him in
the kennel.

Jonathan jerked on his jerkin for his
jogging jaunt and jogged around
Jarrow.

Mortimer, the mess steward, made a
mish-mash of the mushrooms and
murdered the mulligatawny.

Cautious Carol choked carelessly on a
chunk of chocolate.

Swim, Sam, swim,
Show them you're a swimmer!
Six sharp sharks are out to take your
    liver,
So swim, Sam, swim!

Ian's irksome over icy icicles.

I wonder whither the weather will
    waft the wherry wherein the weather is,
And whether the wherry will
    weather the weather.

Julia Jenkins jumped joyfully, while
Jenny Johnson jeered.

Messy May Messant may,
but musing Maisie May mustn't.

Rita relishes Russian radishes.

Freckled-faced Florence frowned
furiously.

Chris, unfurl your kiss-curl!

'Night, night, Knight,' said one
Knight to the other Knight the other
night. 'Night, night, Knight.'

Daring Dan dashed dizzily down the
dale doing damaging deeds as he
went.

The cat-catchers can't catch caught
cats.

All I want is a proper cup of coffee
Made in a proper copper coffee pot.
You can believe it or not,
But I just want a cup of coffee
In a proper coffee pot.
Tin coffee pots
Or iron coffee pots
Are no use to me.
If I can't have a proper cup of coffee,
In a proper copper coffee pot,
I'll have a cup of tea!

A box of biscuits,
A box of mixed biscuits,
And a biscuit mixer.

Should Sheena shout 'Sheila', or
should Sheila shout 'Sheena'?

Judy Jordan jumped joyously during
Juliana's jubilee jamboree.

Once I heard a mother utter,
'Daughter, go and shut the shutter.'
'Shutter's shut,' the daughter uttered,
'For I can't shut it any shutter.'

Fearless Frank following in
Fanallioni's feuding family's
footsteps.

'Walter, get water from the waiter!'

Is this Hamlet here, heir to Piglet
there?

Could Queenie's callers come quietly,
Clarence?

Many mincing maidens meandered
moodily moorwards.

United States twin-screw steel
cruisers.

Who will wet the whetstone while
Willy whistles wistfully?

Gyles just jostled James.

Our black bull bled black blood on our
blackthorn flower.

Christian Christabel's Christmas
crackers.

Swift Sam Smith and Shifty Sidney
Smithers shouldn't send silly signals.

Dashing Daniel defied David to
deliver Dora from the dawning
danger.

Meek Morris Morrison made weak
Matthew Matthews many milkshakes.

A roving raven on the roofing —
raving!

Andrew Airpump asked his Aunt her
ailment.
Did Andrew airpump ask his aunt her
ailment?
If Andrew Airpump asked his Aunt
her ailment,
What was the ailment of Andrew
Airpump's Aunt?

The Leith police dismisseth us.

Bring back bright brand-new British
brushes from breezy Bridlington.

Flee from fog to fight 'flu fast.

Any noise annoys an oyster,
but a noisy noise annoys an oyster
most.

The mighty master murdered the
maddened magistrate.

Proud Pedro Papadopolous planted
plum and apple pips.

Walter Wooster worshipped
Worcester Sauce.

Lucy lingered, looking longingly for
her lapdog.

Many million mini-minors merrily
milling around Milthorpe.

Sally Wally dilly dallies daily.

I'm anti Auntie.

The new nuns knew the true nuns
knew the new nuns too.

Ten tame tadpoles tucked tightly
together in a tall thin tin.

The masts mask the majestic
mansions and the multitudinous
minarets.

Tony, try telling twenty thrilling tales
to twenty tiny tots.

Slim satellites sending scintillating
signals.

Tonight is a light night,
So you mustn't light a night light
On a light night like this.

His beard descending swept his aged
breast.

Miss Maggie MacGregor makes
magnificent macaroons.

Phone Phyllis to ask how fresh fish is,
Phil.

Mumbling bumblings. Bumbling
mumblings.

Can Kitty cuddle Clara's kitten?

Lily's lovely lolly cost a lot of Lily's
lovely lolly!

Little Boy Blue a big blue bubble
blew.

The two-twenty tore through town.

A Glasgow glazier's glorious gleaming
green glass gasglobes.

And ere the ear had heard,
Her heart had heard.

Yellow yo-yo's.

'Whose shoe?' sighed Sue.
'My shoe,' lied Lou.
'Here's your shoe Lou,' cried Sue.
'Shucks, Sue, thank you,' Lou sighed.
'My shoe,' cried Blue, 'I'll sue Lou
and Sue!'

Five frantic fat frogs fled from fifty
fierce fishes.

Three blue beads in a blue bladder;
rattle blue beads, rattle blue bladder.

Oswald Whittle's whistle outwhistles
all other whistler's whistles in
Oswaldtwistle.

Of all the felt I ever felt
I never felt a piece of felt
That felt the same as that felt felt
When I first felt that felt.

'Gone, gone, gone, gone, gone,'
groaned the grumpy greengrocer.

Eleven elves in Hell.

Quinn's twin sisters sing tongue
twisters.

Violet vainly viewed the vast, vacant
vista.

If a hair net could net hair,
How much hair could a hair net net,
If that hair net could net hair?

Gay Gladys glanced bravely at grave
Greta and glided glitteringly past
guilty Grace at the glorious garden
gala.

Sarah saw a sash shop full of showy,
shiny sashes.

The busy bee buzzed busily around
the busy beehive.

To sit in solemn silence
In a dim dark dock
Awaiting the sensation
Of a short sharp shock
From a cheap and chippy chopper
On a big black block.

From *The Mikado* **by W.S.
  Gilbert**

Do breath tests test breath?
Yes, that's the best of a breath test.
So the best breath stands the breath
  test best!

Shadows shade the sheltered shallows.

Real red rose rosettes.

Lots of little London lamplighters
light London's lot of little lamps.

Though a kiss be amiss,
She who misses the kisses,
As Miss without kiss,
May miss being Mrs!

The grotto underground was guarded
at the gates by a glowing-eyed guard-
dog.

She stood on the balcony
inexplicably mimicking him hiccuping
and welcoming him in!

Anthea and Andy ate acid apples
accidentally.

Lemon liniment.

The Pope poked a poker at the piper.
So the piper poked some pepper at the
Pope.

'Hark, an aardvark.' Mark barked for
a lark.

I'd rather lather father
Than father lather me.
When father lathers
He lathers rather free.

A black backed bath—brush.

The strenuous struggle strangles the
strong.

Many an anemone sees an enemy
anemone.

Some think Tom Thumb's plumb
dumb.

One old ox
opening
oysters.

Put the cut pumpkin in a pipkin.

Truly rural.

A sick sparrow sang six sad Spring
songs sitting sheltering under a squat
shrub.

The hare's ears heard ere the hares heeded.

Let Lionel Lion lie on the lounger.

Don't run along the wrong lane.

Mrs. Mixer mixes mixes in the mixer.

Blame the big bleak black book.

The quaint queen quickly quelled the quarrelsome Quaker!

There's the Mayor's mayoral mare.

If neither he sells seashells,
Nor she sells seashells,
Who shall sell seashells?
Shall seashells be sold?

'Have you got the knack of the new
knapsack strap, Nat?'

Babbling Brian blames Bertha.

Sad Cinderella cried sweeping cinders.

Lovely lilacs line Lee's lonely lane.

If you shoot three shy thrushes, I'll
shoot three shy thrushes.

You see yonder's Yorkshire's
youngsters.

Steady Stan! Stand steady!

Was Roger wrong, Rita?

Rapidly Red read what Ned wrote in
red water colour.

One hundred air-inhaling elephants.

A lively young fisher named Fischer.
Fished for fish from the edge of a
    fissure.
A fish with a grin
    Pulled the fisherman in!
Now they're fishing the fissure
    For Fischer.

        Dimpled Diana danced in dainty
        dimity down the dunes.

'Have you prepared the gooseberries,
    Mary?'
'No, I'm just topping and bottoming
    them, Ma'am.'

Sad Sam Smither's in a dither about
Sid Withers.

The heir's hair gets into the heir's ear
here.

Augustus Green got angry at the
garrulous gardener gazing at his
grandmother's gazebo.

A plethora of pigeons plied between
the pillars of the pier.

A poor pauper paused on purpose to
pawn a porpoise.

I see seven seagulls soaring south-
wards silently.

Shave a cedar shingle thin.

Pre-shrunk shirts for thrifty shoppers.

Goofy gophers gobble goodies gladly.

Don't miss the maths master's
messages.

Pretty pink pyjama patterns.

Must mussells have muscles?

Libby Lobster loves cute Quentin
Quail.

Will Wilma want Will on Wednesday
week, Willie?

Cherry Chocolate Cups.

Softly, silently, the scythe
Slithered through the thick sweet
    sward;
Seething, sweating, sad serfs writhe,
Slicing swathes so straight and broad.

Often, always, ever, ever, often,
always.

An oyster met an oyster and they
  were oysters two;
Two oysters met two oysters and
  they were oysters too;
Four oysters met a pint of milk and
  they were oyster stew!

A sloven in a shawl shovelled soft
snow slowly.

Heather was hoping to hop to Tahiti
to hack a hibiscus to hang on her hat.

Pink peas please plump porkers.

Chief Sheik, sheep section.

Slim Sam slid sideways on the slope.

Peter Pringle printed press paragraphs.

'Mortars may not match my magic,' muttered the magician menacingly.

Reading bells ring rapidly as reeds rustle round rivers.

The Archbishop's cat crept craftily into Canterbury Cathedral crypt causing cataclysmal chaos in clerical circles by keeping cunningly concealed.

A lump of red leather, a red leather lump.

Old oily Olly oils old oily autos.

I caught my tongue on a twister,
Cor, what a terrible pain!
What with 'effs' and 'iths' and 'ishes'
It'll never be straight again!

Peggy Babcock, Peggy Babcock,
Peggy Babcock.

Seven level streets with several level
crossings.

Once a feller met a feller
In a field of fitches,
Said a feller to a feller,
'Can a feller tell a feller,
Where a feller itches?'

The cox crew rowed at cock's crow.

We eat what we can and what we
can't, we can.

Let little Nellie run a little longer,
Lottie.

Lame lambs limp.

Benny Butler bought bitter butter in
a brass bell but broke it.

'Which switch, miss, is the switch for
Ipswich, miss?'

Tender tendrils twist through Ted's
trellis.

A laurel-crowned clown.

Ships lie shattered on the shingle.

I was looking back
To see if she was looking back
To see if I was looking back
To see if she was looking back at me.

Agnes looked askance at Horace's tie
which was awry and at Hilda's skirt
all askew.

Pheasant shooters had a pleasant
shoot.

A dozen droopy damsels dawdled
despondently down the docks.

Thrice times three, twice times two.

Swan, swim over the sea.
  Swim, swan, swim!
Swan, swim back again!
  Well swum, swan.

Merry mermaids murmer mainly in
the main.

The lieutenant's lady loved liqueurs
and liked to linger late with lots of
crême-de-menthe.

Twenty tiny tots twisting through the
turnstiles.

Maybe baby bees
bounce in baby
buggy buggies.

Languorous Lillie Lill looked
lugubriously at the lowering clouds
and longed for lighter nights.

Naughty Nigel knotted tearful Tina's
tights tightly in a knot.

There was a buzz in the bazaar when
the Arab from Arabia biffed the
Berber from Beirut on the back of the
bonce.

Claire collected
the cabbages,
carrots,
courgettes and
macaroni cheese.

Peter piles pink pails on pewter pots.

Milly Micklethwaite met a man
minding a monkey for a millionaire.

As I went into the garden,
  I saw five brave maids
Sitting on five broad beds
  Braiding broad braids.
I said to these five brave maids
  Sitting on five broad beds
Braiding broad braids,
  'Braid broad braids, brave maids.'

Although degraded, Drake denied his dereliction of duty.

The heiress found the heirloom haphazardly hanging from the high shelf.

Oh, don't groan at gentleman Gyles, the jolly jester.

THE JESTER

Timothy Tiddles twiddled tightly
twisted twine ten times to test it.

Seth hoes Beth's rows.

Valiant vassels vexed Victoria.

Mrs Snelling selling six sick
six-shilling sheep.

A man from Grantham broke a big
chrysanthemum, mum.

Shears have sharp shining points.

Curious quiet calm.

Snow slight: no snipe.

Pink silk socks with shot silk spots.

Shy Susie Simpson sewed the seams
of Sammy's Sunday shirts.

Simon and Steven slept blissfully and
securely side by side.

The raucous corncrake created a
querulous cacophony.

Gloria Groot glued a groat to
Gregory's goat.

Monday lunchtime: Lundi
Munchtime.

He ran from the Indies
To the Andes
In his undies.

My mother made Mary, Minnie and
Molly march many times round the
room to martial music.

Quick, whitewash wicket quite white.

Lean
Linny
Long
loves
long
Lenny
Lean.

Knott was not in.
Knott was out
Knotting knots in netting.
Knott was out,
But lots of knots
Were in Knotts knotty netting.

British 'Back Britain' badges and
brooches.

Some shun sunshine.

Cold cream clings in clottish clods.

The dim don dropped the drum.

Pure food for four pure mules.

Cows graze in droves on grass which
grows in grooves on groves.

An elevator on Everest: an Everest
elevator.

'Gee whiz, show biz,' said Miss Dixie
Fizz.

Oporto, a port in Portugal, exports
port.

Ron Watts runs rat races.

Vera was very vulnerable and the
vulgar verbosity of the volatile
Venetians vitiated her vocabulary.

How Harry hates hounding hares.

Chimes challenged the changing year.

Steady stallions stride strongly.

The broom blooms when the bluebell
blooms.

A wine van ran through the vine.

The dude dropped in at the Dewdrop Inn for a drop to drink.

We surely shall see the sun shine soon.

The frozen fishermen threw their fish back in again.

Twine twisted twigs twenty twirls.

With a shovel Sarah slowly shifted
sifted cinders.

Sweet Sheila Shoxtock sells sugar
shakers to Sheiks.

Black bug's blood.

Weak writers want white ruled
writing paper.

The sun shines on shop signs.

The lone leavers leave the leafy lane.

Mrs. Cripp's cat crept
into the crypt,
crept around and
crept out through a
crack.

Whistle for the thistle sifter.

Tommy Tye
Tried to tie his tie,
But tugging too tight
Tore his tie.

Amidst the mists and coldest frosts,
With barest wrists and stoutest
    boasts
He thrusts his fists against the posts,
But still insists he sees the ghosts.

The host in Ulster uttered an oath,
What was the oath the Ulster host
    uttered?

Two tugs toil Tynewards.

Una put your ewer in your yard.

Silver thimbles. Silver thimbles.

A selfish shellfish smelt a stalefish.
If the stale fish was a smelt
Then the selfish shellfish smelt a
    smelt.

Dressed in
drip-dry
drawers.

Nosey Norah
nosed
noiselessly.

DRIP DRY
DRAWERS
VERY
GOOD FOR
TRAVELLERS

Eager Edward educated Edgar in
economic eccentricities.

Did Diddy David dawdle down the
dale, or did Dale dawdle down to
Diddy David's.

Hungry Harry's homely uncle.

She says she shall sew a sheet.

Unique New York.

The myth of Miss Muffet.

Vile Willy's wily violin.

High roller.
Low roller.
Lower a roller.

LOW ROLLER

HIGH ROLLER

LOWER ROLLER

A gaggle of geese gobbled
gluttonously.

Twenty tinkers took two hundred tintacks to Toy Town.
If twenty tinkers took two hundred
tintacks to Toy Town,
How many tintacks to Toy Town
did each of the twenty tinkers going
to Toy Town take?

The sleepless sleeper seeks sleep.

The sinking steamer sunk.

Let us go together to gather lettuce,
whether the weather will let us or no.

If the sleeper in a sleeper sleeps,
does the sleeper not in the sleeper on
the sleeper sleep?

Three flee-flow pipes.

A jester
From Leicester
Went to see
Esther,
But as Esther
Was taking her
Siesta,
The jester from
Leicester
Didn't see
Esther.

Even Stephen's even oven's on.

Albert had a habit of eating hot
halibut.

Precocious porcupines plod painfully
through the pickles.

Miranda makes marvellous
marshmallows that melt in the mouth.

Kimbo Kemble kicked his kinsman's
kettle.
Did Kimbo Kemble kick his kinsman's
kettle?
If Kimbo Kemble kicked his
kinsman's kettle,
Where's the kinsman's kettle Kimbo
Kemble kicked?

When you want to wear your woollies
and your wellies wait till winter draws
on.

Quick quiet quarrels.

I love living in Llanfairpwllgwyngyll-
gogerychwyrndrobw-llantysiliogogo-
goch.

The sentinels cast sombre shadows
over the Sahara desert.

Alex from Albany ambled around
Alhambra.

A thousand theatres thunder with
applause.

Rimsky-Korsakov really composed
cracking compositions, of course.

Stop Chop Shops selling Chop Shop
chops!

The swan swims! The swans swam!

Eight ethereal arch-angels each had
heavenly halos.

The owner of the Inside Inn was
outside his Inside Inn,
with his inside outside his Inside Inn.

I do like cheap sea trips, cheap sea
trips on ships.

In July, James Junior just jostled
Julia.

Farmer Fresshitt's fresh farm eggs
fry furiously in Farmer Fresshitt's
frying pan.

Double bubble gum bubbles double!

Crazy cooks cut chunky chips for
cheeky chaps.

He is literally literary.

Angelina oiled the hinges on her oil engine with oil-engine oil.

Great crates create great craters.

If one doctor doctors another doctor, does the doctor who doctors the doctor doctor the doctor the way the doctor he is doctoring doctors? Or does he doctor the doctor the way the doctor who doctors doctors?

Hath Hazel asthma?

A knapsack strap.

Uncle Eric's irksome ulcer.

His hat hit Horace, so Horace hollered
horribly.

Will real wheels really wheel?

I saw a butterfly flutter by
yesterday.

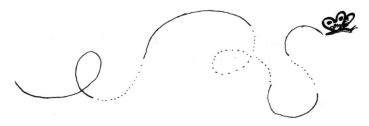

The cheeky Czech choked on
a chunk of chocolate as he
chattered cheerily to Charlie
the chimp.

Palatable prescriptions properly
prescribed please paying patients.

For four far furriers further forward.

Can Kelly catch Clara before she cuts
the chintz curtains up?

Would Willy Watson wander wearily
round Regents Park we wonder?

Daniel Dumont dances daintily with
darling Dilys Dodswell.

Shall Sheila show several sailors
sheets that she has sewn?

Loathsome Lottie laughed less at
Lillie's lilo than at Lulu's loofa.

Midget Michael Merrymore was more
merry than Cherry Bridget Moore.

Simple Simon swallowed several socks
to soak up cider.

Gay Gordon Grassington goes eating
grass on Whitsuntide.

Sister Sarah sang seventy-six songs
several Sundays running.
If sister Sarah sang seventy-six
songs several Sundays running,
What were the seventy-six songs
sister Sarah sang, Susan?

Meek Margaret Mogel mumbled
magic messages.

Jolly Javey jumped
joyously juggling
jellies at the
jubilee.

Will Winnie wander with Will, or will
Will wander with Winnie?
We wonder.

Shakespeare's sonnets show simple
passion.

Pick up the picked plums please Peter.

Valient Valerie vowed vociferously.

Could a clever carpenter chisel cedar
coat racks?

Can clever cooks cook clocks, or should cooks not cook clocks?

Anxious Annie ambled awkwardly up to Averil's oven.

Glorious Gwendoline gave Gloria gladiolis.

Vigorous Vesta voiced voluble verse vociferously.

The prattling prig pranced around the prairie and played his ukelele to the priest.

Fancy Nancy didn't fancy doing fancy
    work.
But Fancy Nancy's fancy aunty did
    fancy
Fancy Nancy doing fancy work!

Three thrushes thrilled them.

Norah needs lock-knit knickers.

The royal lady received the roses
regally at the recent reception.

I thought he fought a thoroughly fair fight.

Cut Caroline's cauliflower and catch crawling crabs, Cynthia.

Don had doubts and didn't dare do anything to endanger the duenna.

The strapping soldiers strived sternly to strengthen the stronghold.

Shy Sam Smith thought Sarah Short so sweet.

Seven Severn salmon swallowing seven Severn shrimps.

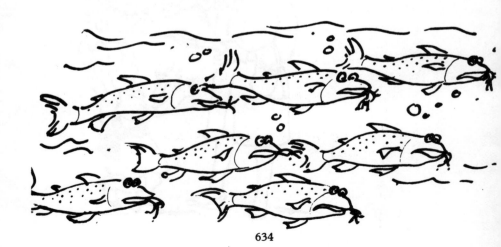

'Sheath thy sword,' the surly Sheriff
said. 'Or surely shall a churlish serf
soon shatter thee.'

Gig-whip, gig-whip, gig-whip.

Cornish clotted
cream cartons.

Send ten tons of
pink tinted toilet
tissue to Tim Timms
of Taunton.

Outrageous Retta ran riot around
Romford roundabouts.

The bleak breeze blights the bright
bloom blossom.

The other mother's smothered in
moss.

Granny's grey goose greedily gobbled golden grain in Graham's gabled granary.

'Sally's solly,' said Silly Sa-si from Siam.

Auntie Annie asked everybody if
  anybody was anti-aunties.
If anybody is anti-aunties, which
  auntie is anybody anti?

A cunning and clever and capricious captain commanded several centurians in Capricorn.

Mozart's music's madly melodious.

'Stick several sellotape strips, not string,' she said.

Prententious Petunia pouted petulantly.

Mrs. Marx marked Mark's mark card with a mark of merit.

Stunning Estella stunned Stanley with astonishment.

Fiona felt fraught at Freddie's
fulsome flattery and frankly thought
it rather foolish.

Sidney Shelley thrust six thick sticks
through sixty-six ricks.

Wood said he would carry the wood
through the wood.
And if Wood said he would
Wood would.

Enlightened Elizabeth eloped in
earnest with Ernest.

Evan Ewan's eaten eighteen eggs.

Moaning Mona moaned
unharmoniously.

Will he? Won't he, Willie?

Miriam at the minaret mused among
the mimosa in the moonlight.

Pink primroses. Primrose pinks.

Fanny fumbled, faltered, then fainted.

Whether the weather be fine
Or whether the weather be not.
Whether the weather be cold
Or whether the weather be hot,
We'll weather the weather
Whatever the weather
Whether we like it or not.

Riotous Ruby runs
rings around
Rubic's cubes.

Lottie licks lollies
lolling in the
lobby.

Milly Muscle suffered measles having
sampled mussells.

A queer quick questioning quiz.

'Pucker, Pearl Potter, please,'
pleaded Pete Perkins politely.

Two boot blacks, a white boot black and a black boot black, stood together doing nothing.

The white boot black proposed that he should black the boots of the black boot black.

The black boot black was perfectly willing to have his boots blacked by the white boot black.

So the white boot black began to black the boots of the black boot black.

But when the white boot black had blacked one boot of the black boot black, he declined to black the other boot of the black boot black, until the black boot black had blacked both boots of the white boot black.

However, the black boot black refused point blank to black the boots of the white boot black, and said he didn't care whether the white boot black blacked the other boot black or not.

He considered that one boot blacked was enough for a black boot black, and that a black boot black with one boot blacked was better than a white boot black with no boots blacked.

Then the white boot black called the black boot black a black blackguard.

Of course, when the white boot black began blacking the character of the black boot black, the black boot black began blacking the face of the white boot black all black with the blacking on the boot the white boot black had blacked, and the white boot black blacked the black boot black back.

When the Society of Black and White Boot Blackers considered the matter, they characterised the conduct of both boot blacks as the blackest affair that had ever blackened the pages of boot-black history.

Snoodles ship snuff for shops.

This is a zither.

The Hebrew blew the bugle
lugubriously.

Villiam Veedom viped his vig and
   vaistcoat.
Did Villiam Veedom vipe his vig and
   vaistcoat?
If Villiam Veedom viped his vig and
   vaistcoat,
Where are the vig and vaistcoat
   Villiam Veedom viped.

Groovy gravy, baby!

Oscar Owl howls hauntingly.

Podgy Paula
Postlethwaite
pockets pies
and pasties.

The chased treasure chest's thrice
chipped.

Clever Clifford clapped conjurer
Clive's clever tricks.

Miserable Manuel marched madly to
meet Mabel Moss.

Peter Piper picked a pack of peppered
    peanuts to pickle.
If Peter Piper pickled a pack of
    peppered peanuts,
Where are the pickled peppered peanuts
    Peter Piper pickled?

She sells seashells on the seashore,
but *she* sells seashells, sherry and
sandshoes on the seashore.

Figs form fine fancy fare.

The crime completed the coward
crawled cautiously coastward.

Sheared sheep shouldn't sleep in
   shacks.
Sheared sheep should sleep in sheds.

A tidy tiger tied a tie tighter to tidy
her tiny tail.

Heavenly bells ring on high.

Ten tiny toddling tots trying to train
their tongues to trill.

I brought the blazer braid I bought to
    bind the blazer blue.
The braid I bought was not too
    bright to bind the blazer blue.

Beryl burned the
brown bread
badly.

Buy Bridges' British breeches!

Suppose Sally shredded suet so
    swiftly that she was sooner done than
        she expected,
How slowly would Sally have to
    shred suet to be done as soon as she
        expected she would be?

A shifty shark selling snake skin
slippers.

It ain't the hunting on the hills that
    hurts the horses' hooves,
It's the hammer, hammer, hammer
    on the hard high road.

Green greengages grow in green
greengage trees.

Something whistled past my head.
'I missed again!' my Mrs said.

What's here was there. That's what
was here.

The first fast master passed faster
than the last just pastor.

Peter Palmer painted a paper peacock,
purple, pink and puce.

Cheryl's chilly cheap chip shop sells
Cheryl's cheap chips.

'The bun is better buttered,' Billy
muttered.

He had him eat his own hot ham, so
his own hot ham he ate.

You sent me your bill, Berry,
Before it was due, Berry.
Your father, the elder Berry,
Had not been such a goose, Berry.

Iced ink.
Iced ink.
Ink iced.
Ink iced.

Flocking shoppers shopping.

The seething sea ceaseth and thus the
seething sea sufficeth us.

'Goodbye, Gertie,' gushed Gussie.
'Goodbye, Gussie,' gushed Gertie.

Francis Fowler's father fried five
floundering flounders for Francis
Fowler's father's father.

Seventy shuddering sailors stood
silent as short sharp shattering
shocks shook the splendid ship.

Pete's Pa, Pete, poked at the pea
patch to pick a peck of peas for the
poor pink pig in the pine hole pig pen.

Clearly the clause in Klaus's contract causes Klaus confusion.

The drain in the train dripped again and again, until the drain in the train dripped dry.

Am I and Amy aiming anaemic anemones on my many enemies?

Thirty thrifty farmers threw a fit.

Viola valued the valley violets in Vera's vase.

The gleaming glass glowed on the grass.

You slipped and I saw you slip on that slip of slide on which you slipped.

Mrs. Lister's sister spoke Spanish, Swedish and Swahili and spent a season in the Sudan where she suffered from sunstroke.

Queasy Quentin quailed and quaked and called for Captain Quequweg.

Nine naughty nanny-goats nibble ninety-nine nice new nasturtiums.

Lester Liversidge the Liverpudlian
loved litigation and learned the legal
rules of the law.

Cynthia couldn't clean the cloisters:
the cloisters were cloying and
claustrophobic.

'Crikey!' cried Chris, 'can't you keep
the gates clear of clutter and keep the
kids quiet?'

A frightened thief from Farnham fought
his way from the floodlit fireworks
factory.

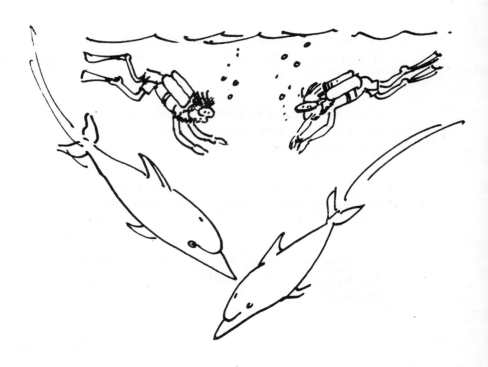

Demented divers drive the dolphins
down to the depths of the sea.

Dodo's dog died of distemper, a
disease which does dogs down.

Maggie Nanning, Maggie Nanning,
Maggie Nanning.

She said she suffered a short sharp
shock, Sean.

Would Wendy wander when it's
windy, Wanda?

When a twiner a twisting will twist
   him a twist,
For the twining his twist he three
   times doth entist,
But if one of the twines of the twist do
   untwist,
The twine that untwisteth, untwisteth
   the twist:
Untwirling the twine that untwisteth
   between,
He twists with his twister the twain in
   a twine;
Then twice having twisted the twains
   in the twine,
He twisteth the twines he had twisted
   in vain.
The twain that, in twisting before in
   the twine,
As twines were entwisted, he now
   doth untwine,
'Twixt the twain intertwisting a twine
   more between,
He, twisting his twister, makes a
   twist of the twine.

Sixty-six shy shepherds serenely
sailing a ship at sea.

Short sweet sausage meat.

In enterprise of martial kind,
When there was any fighting,
He led his regiment from behind —
He found it less exciting.
But when away his regiment ran,
His place was at the fore, O —
    That celebrated,
    Cultivated,
    Underrated
    Nobleman,
    The Duke of Plaza-Toro.
Look at the pug tugging at the rug.

Duke of Plaza-Toro **by W.S. Gilbert**

Eat Esther's early Easter eggs,
Edgar.

Look at the pug tugging at the rug.

Can an actor act at Acton in an action
   packed epic?
If an actor can't act at Acton in an
   action packed epic,
Where can an actor act?

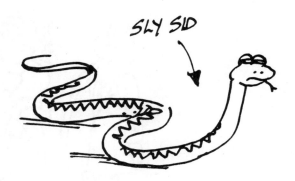

SLY SID

Sly Sid slid
slyly sideways.

Perky Peter Perkins polished paper
plates and plaster plaques for
pleasure.

Miss and Master Mouse gave Mrs.
Mouse mouth-to-mouth resuscitation,
so they were mouse-to-mouse.

Rita Rabbit robbed Retta Rabbit
recently, ruining Retta's warren.

Gracious Glenda gladly glued
Gordon's gumstick.

A canner exceedingly canny,
One day remarked to his granny:
'A canner can can
Anything that he can,
But a canner can't can a can, can he?'

Mr. Hadden had on his new Homburg
hat but Mrs. Hadden hadn't a hat and
after adding her money which was
inadequate she had to adapt her old
hat.

The crazy cockroach crowned the
crooked cricket.

Silly Sammy Stokes spilt some sticky
syrup on the stove.

Who washed Washington's white
woollen underwear when
Washington's washerwoman
went West?

The saucy slippery scoundrel
scampered scurrying by.

Grace's grey-green gloves glided
gracefully to the ground.

Ninny-nanny-nonny-no, say this as
fast as you can go.

A shooting suit that's suitable for
    shooting,
Should be made of a suiting that is
    suitable.
If not made of a suiting that is
    suitable,
Then that shooting suit's
    not suitable for shooting!

Three grey geese crept
into Clitheroe Castle.

Shirley slid the shears
down the slippery
slanting slates.

Blodwin brought back
black bric-à-brac.

The librarian lent his literary list to the Latin master to select eleven lessons.

The man from Middlesborough misappropriated money from the military mess and was remanded for a misdemeanour.

Cheerful Chan the Chinaman sips sister Celia's sherry.

Can Kenneth come crab-catching in Cleethorpes, Chloe?

Mild Madge misjudged Maggie's midget mascot.

Eugene endeavoured to play the euphonium and usually hushed the audience who ushered him from the room.

Jock Jones jumped jerkily on Jimmy
at the juvenile sports last June.

Eight grey geese gazing gaily into
Greece.

An artist went to sea to see what he
could see at sea to draw, but all the
artist saw at sea was what we always
see at sea — sea, see?

The best blowing bugler in the Boston
brass band.

Seventeen slimy slugs in satin
sunbonnets sat singing short sad
songs.

A twister of twists once twisted a
   twist
And the twist that he twisted was a
   three-twisted twist.
Now in twisting this twist, if a twist
   should untwist,
The twist that untwisted would
   untwist the twist.

Rascally ruffians robbed the Regent.

I need not your needles, they're
   needless to me,
For needing needles were needless you
   see.
But did my neat trousers but need to
   be kneed,
I then should have need of your
   needles indeed.

Shy sly Sheila sat
shivering in her
slim, shiny short
silk socks.

Fresh-fried fowl flesh.

Daring Dora dashed dizzily down the
doctors' driveway.

Belinda's beery breath burst the
breathalyser bag.

The gleaming green Glasgow glass
gas-globe Grace gave Greta.

Gaze on the grey gay brigade.

As I was going past Esau's yard, I
saw a man sawing and of all the
sawers I ever saw I never saw a saw
saw like that saw sawed!

Sister Sandy sneezes slightly slicing
succulent shallots.

A rural ruler should be truly rural and
recognise rural raillery.

A plain pinewood police van, privately
packed with protesting prisoners,
plies periodically to Parkhurst prison.

The squirrel squeals with
breathalysing indignation, quiveringly
spluttering complete repudiation of
the impossibly preposterous
allegation of gross intoxication.

Has Hilda heard how Helen hurried
home?

I wish I hadn't washed this wrist
  watch.
I've washed all the wheels and works.
Oh, how it jumps and jerks.
I wish I hadn't washed this watch's
  works!

Do you stock shorts socks with spots
in your shop?

Strikes strangle struggle, squandering
scheduled synthesis.

Three thick black plastic press blocks
as previously supplied.

A clean copper coal scuttle.

I enjoy eggs enormously.

Three fiddling pigs sat in a pit and
    fiddled;
Fiddle, piggy, fiddle, piggy, fiddle
    piggy.

Shall Sarah Silling share her silver shilling?

Lanky Lawrence lost his lass and lobster.

She said she should show the shrewd shrew the same shoe she threw the shrewd shrew.

Two thirsty thatchers thoughtfully thatched a thrush's nest — such a thankless task.

Six Sicilian snakes sibilantly sang six silly serenades to six Serbian serpents.

Four famished Finlanders frying
flying fish.

Slim Sam shaved six slippery chins in
sixty-six seconds.

Can Corky really cook cabbage chips,
Kathy?

Sister Sally sewed silver socks with
silver stitches.

Mr.Knox keeps his socks in a pale
pink chocolate box.
They're orange socks with spots and
clocks.

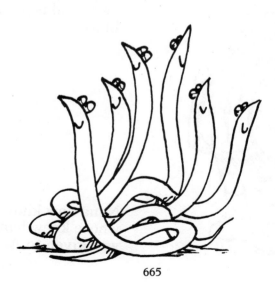

Mr. See owned a saw
    And Mr Soar owned a seesaw.
Now See's saw soared Soar's seesaw
    Before Sore saw See
Which made Soar sore,
    Had Soar seen See's saw
Before See sawed Soar's seesaw
    See's saw would not have sawed
Soar's seesaw.
    So See's saw sawed Soar's seesaw.
But it was a shame to see Soar so sore
    Just because See's saw sawed
Soar's seesaw.

Twenty tiny typewriters
typed in tiny type.

Big Billy has a big
belly and is a big
bully.

Nana now knows
whose knew banana
was given to Anna.

Two toads totally tired trying to trot
to Tidsbury.

Joe joined Jeffrey and Julian in
Jamaica in July not January.

Your Bob owes our Bob a bob, and if
your Bob doesn't give our Bob that
bob your Bob owes our Bob, our Bob
will give your Bob a bob on the nob!

That bloke's back brake-block broke.

Bill Bodger brought Brian a bit of
boiled bacon in a brown bag.

Miss MacIntyre's tiresome tyre on
her tricycle's twisted.

Literally literary literature in lots of
libraries.

Babbling Bert blamed Bess.

A tall eastern girl named Short long
loved a big Mr. Little. But Little,
thinking little of Short, loved a little
lass named Long. To belittle Long,
Short announced she would marry
Little before long. This caused Little
shortly to marry Long. To make a
long story short, did tall Short love
big Little less because Little loved
little Long more?

Charlie chooses cheese and cherries.

Susan shineth shoes and socks,
Socks and shoes shineth Susan,
She ceaseth shining shoes and socks,
For socks and shoes shock Susan.

A snakebite is a serious setback and
some serum should be sought straight
away.

Madcap Michael made mincemeat out
of mustard, marshmallows, and
mulberries.

The dolphin swam dolorously and
dolefully around the dolphinarium.

A white witch watched a woebegone
walrus winding white wool.

Cardinal Crowbridge's cracks creased
the crowded congregation.

Darling Diana danced delightfully
during December's dances.

Thirty thousand Thracians threatened
Thessaly.

Joan joyously joined jaunty John in
jingling jigs.

Our Joe wants to know if your Joe will
lend our Joe your Joe's banjo. If your
Joe won't lend our Joe your Joe's
banjo, our Joe won't lend your Joe our
Joe's banjo when our Joe has a banjo!

Sunshine Susie shone her shoes with
soap and shoe-shine.

She sat in solitude and isolation
sighing and singing sad songs.

Three grey green greedy geese,
Feeding on a weedy piece,
The piece was weedy,
And the geese were greedy,
Three grey green greedy geese.

Cameron came careering round the corner, completing his crazy career by crashing into the crypt.

Susan Schumann shot a solitary chamois and received a sharp salutary shock from such shameless slaughter.

The yearly yield of yarn from Yarmouth is less than the total cocoa crop from Crewe.

Betty Brown blinked and brandished the big broom at the beast.

The flyer furled the flaring flag and
flung it firmly from the fuselage.

The strenuous struggle seemed
superfluous.

Tommy Turner turned away from the
moral turpitude and tried to teach the
two virtues of tolerance and
tranquility to his twins.

The swiftly swirling mill wheel grinds
the gleaming corn.

The sultry siren stood and sulked in
the sand dunes.

Eight hefty hecklers harangued the
orator who had to hurry hastily from
the hall.

Amanda Millicent McGuire amended
a messy manuscript with muddled
emendations.

The rushing river roars rudely round
the regal Roman ruin.

Sly Stevie said sleep walking was
solely the somnambulists concern.

Madame and Mademoiselle Murat
were milliners from Madeleine.

The postman placed the package at
the postern and played peek-a-boo
with Potter's poodle.

If Roland Reynolds rolled a round roll
Round a round room,
Where is the round room in which
Roland Reynolds rolled
A round roll?

Four fat dogs frying fritters and
fiddling ferociously.

The musician made music and moved
multitudes.

Freddie's father is fastidious, fretful
and inflexible.

Hand on heart the hypochondriac
stipulated the hypothesis that
hysterical hyperbole needed anti-
histamines.

A hundredweight of Hopwort will make an awful lot of beer or a lot of awful beer.

Double-O-Seven was dishevelled and disillusioned and determined to discontinue his distorted distractions.

The chief constable concentrated on combing the area around Castlewich where the crooked criminals had committed the crime.

Humphrey Hunchbag had a hundred hungry hedgehogs.

Rory Rumpus rode a rawboned racer.
Did Rory Rumpus ride a rawboned
    racer?
If Rory Rumpus rode a rawboned
    racer,
Where's the rawboned racer Rory
    Rumpus rode?

Sinister silent shapes shock several
soldiers on the seashore.

Weary Willie wheezed woozily the
wrong way round.

The dustman daily does his duty to
dislodge the dirty dust deposited in
disgusting dusty dustbins.

Darren was disposed to disport
himself dressed in dude shirts and
daring dickie-bow ties.

The Mohican was molested by a
mulatto who mistook him for a
Mohawk and mutilated his wigwam.

Evil Edna helped herself to eleven
cups of elevenses.

Six skyscrapers stood snugly side by
side shimmering beside the seaside.

Loopy Lulu looped eleven loops on the
Hoop-la hoop stall.

Shy Sheila shocked sister Suzie as she
shouted shocking sayings.

Were the Waughs at war last year or
are the Waughs at war here?

Cheerful Charles chose cherry
chocolates for Cheri.

Heartless Hannah hung hundreds of
hammers in her house and hit heads
hardly.

Put Percy's presents in the post at
present, Patience.

My mother makes mince-meat mousse
on Monday morning.

A lovely large labrador licked Linda
lovingly.

The cringing crooner couldn't recall
the tune and cried constantly.

Innocent Ian Higgins innocently
insulted Isabel Hartley.

Helen has huge
hats with enormous
hatpins holding
them in her hair.

Shall chef chop chopped meat
chipolatas or chop chipped beef chips
instead?

Did Monty make money madly in
Monte-Carlo, or did Monte-Carlo make
money out of Monty, Mother?

Does Dora adore a door-knob, or does
a door not adore Dora?

The grave games-man groused when
the greyhound growled.

How much caramel can a canny
cannibal cram into a camel, if a canny
cannibal can cram caramel into a
camel?

Once upon a barren moor,
　　There dwealt a bear, also a boar.
The bear could not bear the boar,
　　The boar thought the bear a bore.
At last the bear could bear no more
　　That boar that bored him on the
　　　　moor.
And so one morn he bored the boar —
　　That boar will bore the bear no
　　　　more!

'Help, help,' hurriedly howled the
harrassed Hottentot.

Granny Grumpkins grumbled gravely
as Gavin gobble goose greedily.

Saucy Sally saw silly Sam sewing
sunflower seeds and sobbing
simultaneously.

Malicious Melissa maliciously
maligned Millicent.

Clever Carlton constructed coal carts
out of crates.

Ten thatchers went to thatch ten tiny
thatched cottages, taking ten tight
bundles of thatching straw with them
to thatch with.

Fancy Fanny Franks feeling funny
about Fred Ferraby's fishing flies, for
Fred Ferraby fishes with flies to
flying fishes.

Brenda Blenkiron braised a box of
British bloaters.

Cook cooked a cup of cold creamy
custard.

The interrogator incensed the
interviewee with his incessant
insistence on irrelevancies.

Pretty posies prancing proudly.

Three fluffy feathers fell from feeble
Phoebe's fan.

Should Sarah show Sally some shiny
shoes or silk socks instead?

Four famous fishermen found four
flounders — flippers flapping
furiously — faithfully following four
floppy female flatfish.

One fellow, he felt smart.
Two smart fellows, they felt smart.
Three smart fellows, they all felt
    smart.

Marmalade and melon muesli.

Shirley Bassey shakes big
unsuspecting spenders.

Should Sheila shun sunshine, Celia?

Francis fries fresh fish fillets for
    Frederick.
Frederick fillets four fresh fish for
    Francis' fried fillets.

Six sausages shimmering on a shop
counter.

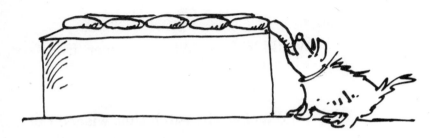

If a top was to sleep in a sleeper,
And the sleeper beneath him went
pop,
It's a logical cert that the top would
get hurt,
For there's no sleeper that sleeps like
a top!

Famous friezes figures fabulously.

Can consuming cold cod cutlets cause
corns?

One violet winkle veering west via
Worthing went wading round
Ventnor.

Soldiers' shoulders shudder when
shrill shells shriek.

Pragmatic politicians pontificate
precociously.

Would William White whisper 'from
whence' and why?

Which is the witch that wished the
wicked wish? I don't know which
witch is which.

The skunk sat on a stump and thunk
   the stump stunk.
But the stump thunk the skunk
   stunk.

A coster carried crates of cabbages
across a crooked court.

If to hoot and to toot a Hottentot tot
was taught by a Hottentot tutor,
should the tutor get hot if the
Hottentot tot hoots and toots at the
Hottentot tutor?

Bandy-legged Borachio Mustachio
Whiskerifusticus, the bald and brave
Bombandino of Baghdad, helped
Abomilique Bluebeard Bashaw of
Babelmandel to beat down an
abominable bumblebee at Balsora!

Big brown bumblebees were buried
beside the bulbs in Bobby Brook's
bulb bowls, basket and boxes.

Gaily gathered the gleaners the glossy
golden grain and garnered it gladly in
Granny's great granary in Godfrey's
green glassy glen.

Wise Wilma while weaving worsted
waistcoats whistled wistfully.

Walter Waddle won a wager. I wonder
which wager Walter Waddle won?

'I can think of thin things, six thin
  things, can you?'
'Yes, I can think of six thin things,
  and of six thick things too.'

The bad lad limps gladly along the
badly-lighted landing.

She saw several swift sloops swing
shorewards before she saw spaceships
soar.

Pink spotted potato puddings.

Many millions must wish Micky and
Minnie Mouse would marry in March.

Theophilus Twistle, less thrifty than
some, thrust three thousand thistles
through the thick of his thumb.

Jumping Jack jeered a jesting juggler.

Diggory Dog dug deep deep dug-outs
down which he dived to dig up bones.

The faun faltered near the
fortifications afraid of the thunder.

Are there any ancient archeologists
abroad agreeable to grant access.

Deirdre was dreadfully downhearted
and depressed when she found she
was deplorably disorientated.

If a chow chews shoes how does he
choose which shoes to chew?

Can you imagine the hindrance when
the Hindu and the Israeli indulged in
inane histrionics on the history of the
hierarchy in India.

The author put his autograph in the
hectograph together with his
photograph and sent a copy with *The
Daily Telegraph* to his grandma in
Arkansas.

Jim-jam, jam-jim.

Many Mau-Mau meandered among
the marshes, looking for missing
missionaries.

Hunting holidays are highly
expensive, Horace.

Carly Coo-Coo cooked cuckoos in cold
custard.

Typing ten-times-tables takes more
time than typing ten-times-two.

The queue in the quadrangle at
question-time was quite quiescent.

If a shipshape ship shop stocks six
shipshape shop-soiled ships,
How many shipshape shop-soiled
ships would six shipshape ship shops
stock?

Cheeky Charlie Ching plays Chinese
Checkers much better than Marjorie
Wong plays mah-jong.

The wild wind whipped Walt from the
wharf.

Fanny Fetter found a fan
A fan found Fanny Fetter,
But Fanny Fetter lost her fan —
And wept till she felt better.

Bold Bob and brave Bea bought a
billion beavers back from Boston.

Crazy Claude catches crawling crabs.

A new snipped sixpence snipped all
round.

At present you can't marry a peasant
however pleasant the peasant may be.

The Aboriginal bush-ranger became a
brigand and battened on the poor
bush beasts.

Did the Dean
drink dandelion wine?

Please prepare Sir Percy for the Prime
Minister's ministerial meeting.

Shall Shadd and Cheri see several
sailing ships on Chautauqua's shores?

Joyful Jeanne jeered jokingly as
Jamie genuinely jogged.

Dorothy dawdled and doodled in a
daydream as she dusted down the
dresser in the drawing room.

Tiptoe Tommy turned a Turk for
twopence.

Forty fat farmers fought over a field
of fine fresh fodder.

Unless the two tots titter, you'll tell
the oft told tale.

'Surely Sylvia swims!' shrieked
Sammy, surprised, 'Somebody should
show Sylvia some strokes so she shall
not sink!'

On the beach I see six small seals.

Some say sweet-scented shaving soap
soothes sore skins.

We had a knocker-up, and our
knocker-up had a knocker-up, and our
knocker-up's knocker-up didn't knock
our knocker-up. So our knocker-up
didn't knock us up, 'cos he's not up!

Sammy sitting singing
Sought Suzie Shaw.
Since Suzie started sobbing,
Sammy's stopped seeking.

Sheila's shetland pony shied, shocked
Sheila's stupified.

Frightened fluffy fowls flying
foolishly through the farmyard.

Round the rugged rocks the ragged
rascal ran.

The desperado designed the desperate
plot to dupe the dreadful dramatist.

Oliver Oglethorpe ogled an owl and an
oyster.

A black spot on the black back of a
black-spotted haddock.

Betty Batter had some butter,
'But,' she said, 'this butter's bitter.
If I bake this bitter butter,
It would make my batter bitter.'

Hull has hosts of huge houses and
heaps of high holidays.

Fiona Fly flew faster than a fine
flying flea.

Handy Hans hands ham sandwiches
with his hands.

Good Goodie Twoshoes took two
shoes to the Goodie Shoeshines
shoe shop.

Betty Bother bathed in bathsuds with
a bathbun sponge.

Twisty twining twirling tendrils
tethering together tightly ten tall
trees.

Wishy-washy wished to win a wager.

Peppercorn pudding and pelican pie.

Timothy took Titus to Tavistock to
teach the tomtits to talk theology to
the Turks that travel through
Tartary.

Mrs. Biggar had a baby, Which was
  the bigger?
The baby we know was a little Biggar,
But what of Mr. Biggar who was a
  father Biggar?
However, Mr. Biggar died. Was the
  baby then bigger than
Mrs. Biggar? No the baby was not
bigger. Why?
Because the baby had become
  fatherless.

Cliff Cross crossed the criss-cross
  crossing.
The criss-cross crossing Cliff Cross
  crossed.
When Cliff Cross crossed the criss-
  cross crossing,
Where's the criss-cross crossing Cliff
  Cross crossed?

Big bugs, bed bugs.

A nice moose married a nice mouse.

If a chicken and a half laid and egg
and a half in a day and a half the
farmer wouldn't half have a fit and a
half.

Big Bill Billiken blew bursting
bubbles by billions.

Sharon shook Aaron's hair on a
Baron's air.

Orange porridge.

Mushy mouthfuls of mushy mash.

Silly Sally's silky shoes and soppy socks.

Bluebottle's bottle's blue.

Ships slip to shore.

Roy's boy's toy truck's stuck.

Nat's black bat's back on the mat.

Lettice's limp lettuces.

Polly Cox ate eight hollyhocks and
now that eight-hollyhocks-eating ox
lies in a great mahogany box. Poor
Polly Cox! Poor ox!

Tom Trapp's tip-top tom-tom.

Slapped slimey slush shivers slightly.

A gleam glimmered in the glen,
glowing ghostly in the gloaming.

Mix Maud more mud Mildred to make
muddier mud pies.

The diplodocus played hocus-pocus
when he couldn't focus on a crocus.

'Lal, lull Lil, will you?'

Barry Broadbread belted out the
'Bartered Bride' ballad bawdily.

Auntie Aggie argued awkwardly in an
august attitude.

Meeny, Miney, Mooney and Mo
Meandered abroad when the wind did
   blow.
They wandered and wondered and
   wanted to know
Whether the weather would turn to
   snow.

A tree toad loved a she-toad
    That lived up in a tree.
She was a three-toed tree toad,
    But a two-toed toad was he.

Margaret and Monica Moore marched
   madly through monsoons,
Meeting many morons and taking
   many moons.

Stop Spot!

The sick sixth Sheik's sixth
sheep's sick.

Moses supposes his toeses are roses
but Moses supposes erroneously;
Because nobody's toeses
Are posies of roses,
As Moses supposes his toeses to be.

Four fat fish fanned flickering
flames.

Six sick city slickers sit.

Bert brought bought bricks.

These thousand tricky tongue
twisters trip thrillingly off the tongue.